TAKING POSSESSION

A VOLUME IN THE SERIES
Public History in Historical Perspective
Edited by Marla R. Miller

TAKING POSSESSION

THE POLITICS OF MEMORY
IN A ST. LOUIS TOWN HOUSE

HEIDI ARONSON KOLK

UNIVERSITY OF MASSACHUSETTS PRESS
Amherst and Boston

ISBN 978-1-62534-415-1 (paper); 414-4 (hardcover)
Designed by Sally Nichols
Set in Verlag and Adobe Garamond
Printed and bound by Maple Press, Inc.

Cover design by Melinda Nan Ok Lee
Cover photo: *Campbell residence and streetscape shot from the northeast corner of Locust and Fifteenth Streets.* From the Campbell House Museum Collection.

Library of Congress Cataloging-in-Publication Data

Names: Kolk, Heidi Aronson, author.
Title: Taking possession : the politics of memory in a St. Louis town house /
Heidi Aronson Kolk.
Description: Amherst : University of Massachusetts Press, [2019] | Series:
Public history in historical perspective | Includes bibliographical
references and index. |
Identifiers: LCCN 2018053114 (print) | LCCN 2018059592 (ebook) | ISBN
9781613766620 (ebook) | ISBN 9781613766637 (ebook) | ISBN 9781625344144
(hardcover) | ISBN 9781625344151 (pbk.)
Subjects: LCSH: Campbell House Museum (Saint Louis, Mo.)—History. | Museums
and community—Missouri—Saint Louis. | Saint Louis (Mo.)—Social life and
customs—History. | Collective memory—Missouri—Saint Louis. | Saint
Louis (Mo.)—History. | Historic buildings—Missouri—Saint Louis. |
Campbell family.
Classification: LCC F474.S257 (ebook) | LCC F474.S257 K65 2019 (print) | DDC
977.8/66—dc23
LC record available at https://lccn.loc.gov/2018053114

British Library Cataloguing-in-Publication Data
A catalog record for this book is available from the British Library.

CONTENTS

ACKNOWLEDGMENTS

Like so many books, *Taking Possession* germinated because the right seed fell upon the right patch of ground—and long before I realized I was cultivating a new plant. The study pursues subjects that originated in a methods seminar I taught for the American Culture Studies (AMCS) program at Washington University in 2004, which involved an extended case study of the remarkable house museum at 1508 Locust Street in St. Louis whose contents represented an exciting but demanding analytical-interpretative opportunity. The students whom I taught in that seminar and those who were involved in subsequent on-site research a collaborative object-mapping project (which I later wrote about in a *Winterthur Portfolio* article) were among my earliest companions on a long journey into the domain of Campbell House cultural heritage. They brought to this activity intellectual energy and curiosity of a sort that I have tried to bring to my own work. While I cannot name all who contributed to the decadelong thought process that began that year, I wish to acknowledge the teaching and research assistants who have left indelible marks on the my teaching and thinking, including Amanda Henry, Danielle Wallis, Hannah Boettcher, Di Wang, Morgan Brooks, Jonathan Karp, and Paige Steinberg.

A good deal of the preparation (and many of the deeper motivations) to write this book began during a long-term residency at Winterthur Museum, Garden & Library, where I was a National Endowment for the Humanities research fellow in 2004. I am grateful to members of the superlative Winterthur staff and to my Foulsham House companions Carl Keyes and Kate Haulman, who gave thoughtful feedback as I began this new work. More recently, a second NEH fellowship supported my participation in a remarkable 2017 Summer Institute at Bard Graduate Center convened by Catherine Whalen and Katherine (Kasey) Grier. The learning I have done with and thanks to them, guest contributors such as Bernard Herman, Joshua Brown, Jack Tchen, and others, and my fellow institute participants informed final stages of my revision process and also motivated new work since.

My dear friend and PhD advisor Wayne Fields offered mentorship at many stages of my development as a scholar of American culture and across the many years of this project, but especially during the early germination phase. From him I learned many of the core values of collaborative research. Other members of the special community I have been part of in AMCS—Deborah Jaegers, Randy Calvert, Nick Miller, Kate Fama, Noah Cohan, Jennifer Gallinat, Terri Behr, Máire Murphy, and Michael R. Allen—have offered all manner of support as well; I am grateful for the many stairwell conversations and all that they represent, and for the companionship and encouragement all of these (and dozens of others) have provided over the years. Among these, I offer warmest thanks to David Kieran, Katherine Mooney, Dave Walsh, Douglas B. Dowd, and Iver Bernstein—my kinfolk and closest collaborators. Their friendship and humor have buoyed me, and their ongoing engagement with this work has deepened it and empowered me to think in new ways. I would be remiss if I did not acknowledge, along these lines, the formative influences of Bonnie Carr O'Neill and Debie Rudder Lohe, whose writing advice still rings true, and Chuck Sweetman, with whom I was fortunate to partner creatively at a key stage in my ongoing exploration of material culture and memory.

The collaborative nature of this project extends also into the Campbell House Museum itself, as I hope the work suggests. I owe an enormous (and ever-growing!) debt to colleagues such as Andy Hahn, Tom Gronski, and the many others—volunteers, docents, interns, members of the board, and other researchers—who have contributed to the body of knowledge that is contained in the museum archive and interpretative materials on which I have drawn. These individuals have also welcomed hundreds of my students and generally helped me find my way, and I have sought in all ways to honor their work in this book. Thanks, also, to those who have assisted with other aspects of this research: Miranda Rectenwald and Sonya Rooney and other members of the Special Collections staff at Washington University Libraries; the staff at the Missouri Historical Society Library and Research Center and the Mercantile Library at the University of Missouri–St. Louis, who have cared for Campbell-related materials over the years; and to Eric Sandweiss, Andrew Hurley, George Lipsitz, Joseph Heathcott, Máire Murphy, Ben Looker, Bob Moore, Adam Arenson, Michael R. Allen, Bob Hansman, and many others who have engaged the material, social, and cultural histories of St. Louis in creative and thoughtful ways, and given me much to think about as I did this work. I am also deeply grateful for the tireless support of Marla Miller, Rachael DeShano, Matt Becker, Maggie Hogan, and others at University of Massachusetts Press who have helped to bring this book to its fullest potentiality.

Finally, I wish to acknowledge my in-house creative team (my three sons), Conrad, Everett, and Dylan Kolk, for their abiding curiosity about my work (and editorial feedback on all aspects of the project!); my parents, Mike and Linda Aronson, and my sisters, Jill Aronson Pfaendtner and Lindsey Blacquiere, who have been lifelong nurturers of my academic and creative work, and also kind encouragers; and the members of my extended friend-family, including John and Kate Early, Noel and Elissa Weichbrodt, Dave and Elizabeth Walsh, Debie Rudder Lohe, Crista Chenoweth-Beracha, Michelle Hand, Tameca Milner, Cindy Clausen, Judy Larson, Rosemary Burrows, and Siobhan Akers, and their families too. These individuals have offered the gift of deep friendship and (countless hours of!) generous listening; they, too, have been my collaborators.

I wish to dedicate *Taking Possession* to my husband, Joe Kolk—the one who knows this work, and all that it represents, best of all; who has walked me through (and out of) hundreds of personal challenges and interpretative cul-de-sacs; and who has been the very best sort of companion—steadfast and loving, intellectually kind, patient—I could have asked for.

TAKING POSSESSION

THE BURGLARY

L ATE ONE SUMMER evening in 2012, a thief broke into a 165-year-old town house just west of downtown St. Louis. The rambling old mansion is a very secure site, with an alarm system, a live-in property manager, and a wrought-iron fence. To get inside, the thief had to jimmy the lock on an enormous pair of solid-mahogany exterior doors and break through an etched-glass window on one of the interior doors. The next morning, a chunk of concrete and several thick shards of glass were discovered in the front hall. No other significant damage was done. The intruder had taken ninety-eight dollars from a cashbox holding receipts from museum tours, showing little apparent interest in artifacts on display throughout the house. But a quick inventory was taken anyhow as this was the second theft at the Campbell House Museum (CHM) in a week's time.[1]

News of the burglary spread quickly on social media, where CHM officials posted a description of the spoiled front doors alongside dramatic black-and-white photos of the damage (fig. 1), pleading for help with what they expected to be expensive repairs. History enthusiasts, museum supporters, and curious bystanders responded promptly, and within a few days' time, more than three thousand dollars flowed in from all over the region and as far away as Alaska. Members of St. Louis's business community were eager to show their support for the historic house museum as well: Commerce Bank executives offered to fund the purchase of a new security system, and owners of a nearby art glass store provided a temporary replacement window. Many expressed solidarity with those cleaning up the "burgled" site in their online posts. One

FIGURE I. Broken front door and shards of glass after the burglary, photograph, Campbell House Museum staff, August 2012. Campbell House Museum, St. Louis, MO.

commenter denounced the thief for breaking a 135-year-old window for a measly ninety-eight dollars: "Some people have no respect for history!" Another counseled museum staff to invest in amped-up security, adding that the whole situation "sickened" him: "I would like to find who did this and string them up!"[2]

Although the thief's identity had not been disclosed, many observers assumed the culprit must be someone with "local knowledge," meaning one of the neighborhood's ubiquitous loiterers, many of them people of color served by the New Life Evangelistic Center (NLEC) across the street, which at the time was the city's last walk-in homeless shelter (the city has since shut the facility down). The presence of the homeless in the area has long been a source of concern for city officials and boosters who see the unhoused as a threat to the city's reputation—particularly among tourists and visitors to the popular restaurants, clubs, and sports venues in the vicinity. While rarely if ever responsible for spikes in crime in the area, the homeless have been easy targets for myriad downtown "clean-up" efforts in recent years, including their forcible removal from nearby Soldier's Memorial Park, and the enclosure and vigorous policing of a smaller park at 14th and Locust Streets that previously had been open to them.

At the time of the burglary, pressures had been mounting for the city to evict the NLEC from the old YWCA building it had occupied since the 1970s. Some claimed the organization had violated local ordinances and were attracting the "wrong kind of people" to the downtown area; others noted that it did not maintain the building or enforce safety procedures. Against such a backdrop, in a city that has lost tens of thousands of residents over the past few decades, the Campbell House burglary took on a kind of moral urgency.[3] For history-minded types, the loss of an original feature from one of the city's few remaining nineteenth-century residences was bound to be distressing, but many others viewed the smashed window as a symbolic desecration. Some who weighed in on social media expressed a sense of violation—not just of an "irreplaceable window" but of a broader ideal of integrity: the CHM's legitimacy as a site of cultural heritage hinged on its material-historical intactness, and the city's confidence in itself depended on the flourishing of the CHM and other sites like it.

The fact that the broken window was a distinctive element of the facade of a beloved museum that has been in operation for more than three-quarters of a century only compounded the sense of violation. Throughout that period, the site has given expression to St. Louis's evolving sense of its own history, including its economic and cultural vitality and "former glory" as a frontier city—the "gateway to the west." In recent decades, the museum's mission has been oriented toward elevated notions of material intactness and continuity, both of which are pinned to the "meticulous five-year restoration" that began in 2005, as the CHM's website notes, and "returned the building to its opulent 1880s appearance . . .

[when it was] one of the centers of St. Louis society."[4] Putting the house "back" into this "opulent" material state has not only legitimized long-standing claims of its historical appeal and significance but implied that elites might yet return to the core of the city, and reclaim it from "less desirable" residents.

This notion of a "return" to intactness—like the view that the burglar's actions were a wanton violation of "private property"—must be understood as a function of the racialization of space in St. Louis, as well as longstanding conflicts over these matters. Online commenters unwittingly acknowledged as much when they expressed outrage at the violation ("some people" and "string them up"), gesturing at the sort of retaliatory violence—and even lynch mobs—that such an incursion might have precipitated in the not-so-distant past.[5] Clearly, the burglary touched on deeper, more amorphous anxieties about the precariousness of social order. In St. Louis, these anxieties, and the politics of urban life more broadly, are almost always matters of race and class.

Assertions of control over public spaces and their meanings past and present—those localized understandings of the cultural landscape that geographers describe, evocatively, as "regimes of place"—have been a feature of urban life in St. Louis for much of its history.[6] But they have increased measurably in recent years, apparently in proportion to growing concerns about the city's reputation as one of the nation's most violent, racially divided, and economically challenged urban areas.[7] In both 2013 and 2015, *Forbes* magazine rated St. Louis second among the nation's ten "most dangerous" cities, and many news outlets followed suit, noting that, while the city's crime rate fell 4 percent in 2014, and is "down 50% from the crack epidemic days of the early 1990s," the city is still "plagued by . . . violent crimes" and ranks fourth in the nation for murders.[8]

The 2014 shooting death of Michael Brown in the north St. Louis suburb of Ferguson only heightened local self-consciousness about these trends, as the national and even international press, and later the Justice Department, scrutinized the city's grotesque socioeconomic disparities and history of police violence. Even those long invested in a kind of willful ignorance about such matters have been forced to reckon with the city's "race problem" and to acknowledge the deep roots of the Ferguson crisis.[9] And the fear of confrontation over such matters continues to dominate public life, as we see in the aggressive policing of protests (for example, those that happened just a few blocks from the CHM following the acquittal of police officer Jason Stockley in September 2017) and in the mayor's preemptive removal of a Confederate monument from Forest Park in June of that same year—before the city could become mired in controversy of the sort that has played out in Baltimore, Charlottesville, and other cities.[10] Both can be seen as efforts to control regimes of place, and to maintain a specific ideal of social order, by managing public spaces.

This abiding preoccupation with local regimes of place extends into all corners of public life—even the domain of sports. Not long after the nonindictment of Officer Darren Wilson for the killing of Michael Brown and subsequent demonstrations, the city experienced another episode of anxiety over reputation—one far less urgent from the standpoint of racial politics, but with serious implications nonetheless: National Football League owner Stan Kroenke announced his intention to relocate the Rams football team to Los Angeles. The real-estate mogul justified his decision with a series of disparaging comments about the city's long-term prospects. Besides seeming ungracious given the economic and prestige advantages he had already extracted from the city, his remarks betrayed condescension toward the Midwest, which he referred to as "flyover country," and a desire to distance his own brand from a city with serious problems.[11]

The backlash against Kroenke was immediate, loud, and full of compensatory bravado of a sort St. Louisans have been perfecting for more than a century—going back at least to 1850, when Missouri senator Thomas Hart Benton extolled the city's virtues as the "gateway to the West" from the floor of the U.S. Senate. Benton hoped to secure coveted railroad contracts, and decades later, boosters were still using some of Benton's arguments to lobby for the relocation of the nation's capital to St. Louis.[12] The Bentonesque view—that St. Louis is perennially underestimated and overlooked on a national scale, and has thus been slighted by history—persists today and comes through in public discourse about the city.

In the Kroenke moment, tellingly, many who rushed to defend St. Louis's good name focused not on geography or economics but heritage and public culture. They pointed instinctively to their city's proven assets—sports arenas, museums, public parks, and restaurants—seeking to reinforce positive associations. Scholars have long observed that such sites are not only vital elements of place and regional identity, fostering a sense of local belonging, but "symbolic [spaces] of meaning that bind" members of the community together.[13] These spots' positive associations fill the storehouses of collective memory, serving as ballast in times of insecurity and hedges against a disordered or alienating sense of place. Thus St. Louisans rhapsodize about their stunning municipal park (*bigger than Central Park!*), their hundred-year-old outdoor municipal opera, their award-winning (*and still totally free!*) zoo, and dozens of other venues, many of which date to the turn of the century, when the city was gearing up to host the 1904 World's Fair and third modern Olympic games. In the time since this high-water moment, furthermore, these sites have been celebrated repeatedly as evidence of the city's socioeconomic and cultural power.

Even landmarks associated primarily with touristic consumption, such as the Cardinals' Busch Stadium, the Anheuser-Busch Brewery, and the Gateway Arch, serve this function, binding together an otherwise fragmented region whose considerable wealth has been dispersed beyond the city. They loom large in the cultural geography of the city, dominating tourist maps and local place memory and anchoring a variety of inordinately sunny place narratives, including those related to St. Louis as a "gateway to the West," an ethnically diverse "city of neighborhoods," a thriving sports town (with the "best fans in the world"), a major stop on Route 66, and an emerging "innovation hub" in the "Silicon Prairie."[14] These sites are loudly celebrated despite darker elements of their material histories, including the extractive tax policies and aggressive urban planning that made them viable.[15]

The historic house museum known as the Campbell House might be linked to any number of these narratives, but given its location and ongoing support by business and cultural elites, it is most strongly associated with the mythos of the endlessly redeveloping, impressive-but-undervalued downtown. This is mainly due to the site's distinctive material history: the house survived many campaigns to transform the city center, including massive slum clearance, the expansion of the central corridor, and countless beautification and rehabilitation schemes that the city has undertaken since the house was first built in 1851.[16] This book focuses mainly on the middle segment of this history, the decades just before and after World War II when these renewal energies were especially intense. During this period, city officials' fears of decay, disinvestment, and the hollowing-out of the urban core—as well as of racial instability—led to an unusually vigorous promotion of the Campbell House site as an unlikely "survivor" of the city's nineteenth-century past. But as this study shows, their investment in the house as a site of memory, like that of today's promoters, turned on other material histories as well.

The Campbell House speaks powerfully of many periods of St. Louis history and of many facets of its historical imagination, including the expansionism and industrial power of the 1880s and 1890s (the period to which the recent restoration is pinned); the slow deterioration and amnesia of the Depression, when the site was documented by the Historic American Building Survey even as the historic fabric of the riverfront and the oldest parts of downtown were destroyed; the era of disinvestment and sprawl, when the city's center of gravity shifted to the suburbs and the CHM was marketed to a white middle-class who had left the city; and more recent efforts to rehabilitate the downtown, which have coincided with new claims of material-historical integrity at the museum.[17] This book engages with all of these, moving back and forth through time to account for the multilayered nature of the site's material history.

While the house has long exuded ideals of continuity, vitality, and heritage, and has been celebrated for its "miraculous survival," it can also be read as a response to—and indeed an unintended symbol of—the opposite of these things: the fragmentation and segregation that have become hallmarks of the city's built environment and social life, the dispossession and loss that many suffered during the period in which a single property was saved, and the many acts of aggression and other dark impulses that have driven much "rehabilitation" of urban St. Louis over the past hundred years. *Taking Possession* considers side by side the material histories of life and death, remembering and forgetting, owning and disowning, that are associated with the site, seeking to understand how positive and negative heritage have come to be woven together there.

We can begin to understand how this has happened by situating the story of "saving" the energetically "preserved 1850s townhouse" (as

Google Maps describes it) within a broader material history of the city. In the mid-1930s, as preservationists began eying the home, which at the time was occupied by the last surviving Campbell heir, for its historic value, the City Planning Commission (CPC) was surveying properties around the city to document social pathology according to common indices, including those of crime, health, and race.[18] When these same preservationists formed the William Clark Society (WCS), a group named for the explorer from the celebrated 1804 expedition and devoted to saving artifacts from what they understood as the city's "pioneer days, and especially the 'golden age' of the 1850s," the CPC's surveys were used to justify reconfiguration, or more properly *disfiguration,* of large swaths of the urban core.[19] As the WCS sought to secure the funds to buy the Campbell residence from those to whom it had been willed, the historic riverfront was cleared to make way for the Jefferson National Expansion Memorial (now just "the Arch"), and working-class neighborhoods south and west of downtown were demolished to create space for low-rise public housing developments—some of the earliest to be built with federal funds from the U.S. Housing Act of 1937.[20]

This pattern continued after the war. While WCS members and museum officials worked to promote the new museum to the white middle-class, planners declared a whole range of structures from the very same period, some just a few blocks away, to be unsalvageable. In 1954, 465 acres were flattened in Mill Creek Valley, a vibrant but physically deteriorating working- and middle-class district west of the Civic Center. That same year, crews started clearing more land in midtown to make way for Pruitt-Igoe, a soon-to-be infamous segregated public housing complex. Pruitt-Igoe would endure less than twenty years, and its traumatic history would never be comfortably absorbed into public memory. The historical particularities (and indeed the whereabouts) of Mill Creek Valley and Pruitt-Igoe have largely been forgotten by many, while their material legacies continue to haunt city and state officials.[21] In particular, the implosion of three Pruitt-Igoe towers, which aired on national television in 1972—an episode of humiliation as powerful as the so-called Ferguson moment—hovers over the city like an amorphous, toxic cloud.[22]

But despite decades of interventionary planning—most recently through means of tax-increment-financed private development—St.

Louis has failed to suture its wounded midsection back together. One project, spearheaded by inveterate suburban developer Paul McKee, has involved the buy-up of hundreds of acres of derelict property across the near north side. Many residents and political opponents see McKee as a bilking and abusive landholder, a "Stan Kroenke in disguise," because he concealed his landholdings for a decade and allowed historic buildings to crumble.[23] But city officials endorsed his "Northside Regeneration" plan, and his most recent acquisition (bought for $1 million in 2016 and promptly cleared to make way for a healthcare facility) was the Pruitt-Igoe site, which he promises will become a "crown jewel" for the city. Another project celebrated by local officials involves redevelopment of a neighboring parcel of land by the National Geospatial-Intelligence Agency (NGA). As with McKee, the NGA has taken advantage of historic patterns of abandonment and neglect, looking to transform a ninety-nine-acre tract into a high-security facility from which the United States' global surveillance technologies can be operated. When the NGA announced that the St. Louis site had been chosen for the project, the jubilance of local officials and many citizens was palpable.[24] Local politicians argued, apparently without irony, that the project would right past wrongs and sweep away the site's, and the city's, negative associations—as if an infusion of $1.6 billion in federal cash and dedication of the site to national security interests could erase this vexed history, not to mention decades of racist urban planning that have only extended its malignancies.[25] The ongoing sagas of these projects show the extent to which vaunted pride and compensatory bravado, rehabilitation and destruction, are bound up together in St. Louis's material history. Both are often at work in the rectification of problematic sites like Pruitt-Igoe but also in the preservation of heritage sites such as the Campbell House.

THE CAMPBELL HOUSE has long functioned as something of a palliative for negative elements of local place memory. For more than a hundred years, eighty of them as a public museum, the site has been the focus of preservation by boosters and cultural elites who sought to maintain the status, wealth, and material cohesiveness of the city's urban core. Successive generations of promoters have held fast to the house as a bolster of place memory—a glorious survivor in a sea of ruins—since the early Depression, when, in the wake of the clearance campaigns and "slum surgeries" described above, the house became one of the last remnants of a disappearing neighborhood known as Lucas Place. Developed as an enclave for wealthy, white St. Louisans in the 1850s and 1860s, by the 1870s Lucas Place was home to "three-fourths of the whole number of millionaires of the city"—a site of concentrated political and economic power.[26] Pioneering deed restrictions allowed residents to exert remarkable control over space in what was essentially the first gated community in St. Louis, a model for even-fancier "private places" to the south and west starting in the 1880s and for inner-ring suburbs built near the turn of the century.[27]

Within a few decades, these early strategies of control and exclusion evolved into the racist housing covenants of the sort made infamous in the St. Louis–based Supreme Court case *Shelley v. Kraemer* (1948). Both the material and the legal control tactics represented experiments in privatization and efforts to rationalize what was seen as an unruly city; with time, they contributed to the profound "spatialization of race" across the whole region, including downtown, the central corridor, Michael Brown's Ferguson, and McKee's north side.[28] Lucas Place involved an imposition of a spatial logic of white control that, with time, would be expanded to produce the sprawling patchwork of segregated municipalities we see in the region today, with ninety-three legally distinct jurisdictions in St. Louis county alone.[29]

While the neighborhood's grandeur and exclusivity could not last, the desire for control certainly did. A whirlwind of speculative activity and civic improvement took hold in Lucas Place and environs in the 1880s, while nearby industrial plants expanded, redefining the city's material as well as its social identity. The city center was increasingly viewed by elites as no longer fit for residence. When the "old Campbell mansion," as it was known, came to be one of the very last private homes in a now thoroughly "mercantile" section of the city, it was also the only property for miles occupied by "millionaire bachelors" who inherited one of the city's great Gilded Age fortunes.[30]

As these bachelor brothers, Hugh and Hazlett Campbell, neared the end of their reclusive lives, St. Louisans viewed their 1850s mansion with growing curiosity, speculating aloud—from the mayor's office and local boardrooms to the editorial pages—about what a house "with no mistress" looked like inside, what untold treasures it contained, and whether it would be spared from the wrecking ball.[31] These last were no idle speculations, for the house's apparently "miraculous survival" entered wider public consciousness just as thousands of residents from nearby rental housing districts were being relocated to Carr Square Village (for blacks only) and a whites-only project on the south side known as Clinton-Peabody.[32] And the house's considerable pathos as the "last of its kind" turned on a growing awareness of the grimmer realities of urban life such as crowding, poverty, and infrastructural decay. While rarely mentioned in the same breath with the house, these realities pressed heavily on many in the region—thanks in part to the CPC's graphic accountings, which ironically came to reinvigorate the very expansionist impulses that had produced Lucas Place in the first place.[33]

Circumstances inside the Campbell residence during this period seemed the direct inverse of all this change, and further enhanced its mystique. Hazlett suffered from severe dementia brought on by mental illness and several strokes, and had been living in the same two rooms of the house for decades. Before he became completely bedridden in the mid-1930s, he could sometimes be seen peering out his window at the traffic-filled street below, while his elegantly dressed older brother, Hugh, was often spotted on neighborhood streets or at the local candy store, where he bought gifts for neighborhood children. Observers sensed the city might have something to learn from these old men, who were hunkered down inside their town house on Locust Street and clung to the material remnants of a passing age, but no one could quite articulate what it was. Mostly, they indulged in the morbid fascination of the sort that often attends the fate of declining aristocrats.[34]

It was in this unstable and opportunistic atmosphere, as the few remaining residences on Locust were sold or condemned and the city continued its never-ending transformation, that preservationists began to conceive of turning the Campbells' house into a public museum.[35] When Hazlett died in 1938 (Hugh having passed away five years prior), a protracted court battle over the estate ensued, and the house and its contents came up for auction. The WCS had gotten their big chance:

rallying hundreds of small donors (and a few key big ones) in the midst of the Depression, they managed to secure the house and its furnishings as symbolic remnants of "the early Middle West." If an 1850s town house crammed with Victorian curios did not exactly suit the sensibilities of those who had been advocating for the city's rapid modernization, it nevertheless had evocative power as a site of cultural origins. The desire to "save" it represented a need not simply to remember these origins but to *recoup* them—and put them to the service of rectifying place memory.

But the Campbell residence would have had little staying power as an emblem of St. Louis heritage if it were not for its meticulous preservation, which had begun decades earlier, in the mid-1880s, when Hugh set about protecting his parents' possessions and keeping the house "exactly as it had been" before their deaths. His efforts were more a matter of honoring Virginia and Robert Campbell's memory and stabilizing his brother's domestic environment than creating a monument to the city's history. Such caretaking required a practice of keeping in a period when many were discarding—of staying put when the city's most powerful citizens, and indeed much of the white middle class, were relocating to precincts west to escape the "growing blight in the city" documented by the CPC.[36] And it could not have been done without the help of household servants.

The curiosity of such a household where "nothing had changed" and "no one threw anything away" might well have motivated a different story than the one chosen by the WCS and its allies in the business community—one of disorder and strangeness, for example, or haunting or hoarding. At the very same moment, New Yorkers had become obsessed with the case of the reclusive Collyers and their massive hoard in an 1850s brownstone in Harlem. That case ended with the elderly brothers' crushing death—and intense public scrutiny of their "pathological" accumulation tendencies.[37] But whereas the New York press viewed the Collyers as aberrant figures who embodied social-material disorder (a chronic disorganization/hoarding syndrome would soon be named after them), the St. Louis public gave the Campbell brothers the benefit of the doubt. As the Collyers' house was being demolished and their collection sold, the WCS advanced a wholly positive narrative of the Campbell residence as a preserve of order, wealth, and social power. They justified its preservation by elevating its links to the city's nineteenth-century frontier history, thus sidelining Hugh and Hazlett and the decline of the Lucas Place neighborhood in the twentieth century.

Today's CHM—known for its capacious, well-curated collection of a single family's possessions—is a product of these early preservation and branding activities. Subsequent rehabilitation efforts stabilized the site and returned objects to the home, but that work obscured as much as it revealed and has had to be reversed by curators in the last two decades. Most of what today's visitors see is "original," meaning elements of the Campbell estate saved by the WCS. Many additional family possessions have been "repatriated" to the house by those who bought them out from under the WCS during the auction. And many objects previously seen as unworthy of display or located elsewhere in the house have been "put back" in place. All of the Campbell possessions can be studied *in situ,* alongside reproduction wallpapers, carpets, and fabrics that reflect the designs, colors, and display aesthetics of the mid-1880s. The museum's display logics have been painstakingly corroborated by forensic and archival evidence, including historic paint fragments, household receipts, business ledgers, personal correspondence, and more. The quality and degree of recontextualization that has been possible at the site is almost unparalleled in the small museum world.

Perhaps the most significant piece of evidence yet recovered is a magisterial leather-bound album of circa 1885 photographs that show the interiors of the Campbell residence. These remarkable images, purportedly rescued from a dumpster in the 1960s, served as the basis for a comprehensive restoration in the early 2000s. They are especially dear to CHM interpreters because they provide such tantalizing glimpses of what the house "looked like when the family lived there." Like the effort to "save" the house and its contents from destruction, "putting the house back" into the state that the photographs document represents one of several defining acts of possession that have occurred since the last heir died. This process of rehabilitation has in turn fostered a new, more vigorous historicism and a disavowal of earlier, now-suspect conceptions of material intactness. Whereas between 1943 and the late 1990s, museum displays flattened multiple periods into a single tableau-like "golden age," today's interiors and interpretations aim to reconstruct one segment of that past in all its material tangibility. This has allowed for a more-nuanced and revelatory conception of "historical context," one less fearful of change and material particularities and more interested too in social and political realities beyond the house.

Still, all these claims to intactness and historicity can seem at best a little precious and at worst openly distorting, given that so little of nineteenth-century St. Louis is visible in today's urban landscape. The reasons private neighborhoods like Lucas Place came to be, and how they were maintained; what they have meant for the city, and how they have shaped public and private life; the ongoing significance—and contestation—of such places in a city beset by race and class divisions; and the broader material politics of domestic and urban space—these and many other elements of "local context" are barely gestured at during the standard tour.

And with good reason: to do more than conjure up a vague sense of "what life was like when the Campbells lived here," docents would need not only to explain but *entirely reconstruct* the material history of the city and the conditions that produced Lucas Place. Visitors, many of them out-of-towners or local suburbanites, would need to engage with this history in a different way than they are inclined to do. So, despite a strong commitment to historicizing its artifacts, the CHM remains a largely self-contained and self-referential site.[38] Most visitors have relatively dim notions of the relevant social context that would lead them to pose questions about how such a house came to exist in a commercial district, why it looks like it fell from the sky, and what it might reveal about the city's material and social history.

Even in 1943, when the CHM first opened to large and eager crowds that included some for whom the Campbell family history was part of living memory, the gap between "then and now" was already too large to be fully accounted for in an hour-long tour. Many early visitors described the experience of stepping from noisy, traffic-filled streets into the tomb-like silence of the house as dislocating and surreal. Again and again, press accounts used "time travel" metaphors to characterize this sensation, often at the same time indulging in sentimental ahistoricism or out-and-out fantasy.[39] While today's visitors are more likely to question their "encounters with the past"—guided by museum practitioners who interrogate the constructedness of "authenticity"—they too are often ill-equipped to move beyond ideas of "St. Louis as it was." The house's unusual intactness stirs them for reasons they cannot articulate yet fosters an amnesic or dissociative style of remembering.[40]

These are common characteristics of what Svetlana Boym terms "restorative nostalgia," that distinctly modern mode of remembrance that revolves around the "transhistorical reconstruction of [a] lost home" and brings with it "a sense of security, and [an] obedient relationship to authority." Boym contrasts restorative nostalgia with more "reflective" modes that are more aware of the past as reconstructed—and that tolerate (or even dwell on) feelings of ambivalence and contingency, the sensibilities of the so-called post-memory age.[41] Both restorative and reflective nostalgia are at work in contemporary American life, and both are often knitted together at historic sites like the CHM. While contemporary preservationists and museum interpreters increasingly privilege reflective modes, they rely heavily on tropes and ideals of restorative nostalgia as a function of their history and methods, and sometimes their politics.[42] The CHM's history has been dominated by the ideals of material integrity and continuity that promise to stabilize a city long defined—and defaced—by private control and development.

As we can see in the reactions to the 2012 burglary at the Campbell House, the concern with material and social instability sometimes comes with latent aggression toward those (such as the homeless) who threaten the ideals of cultural-material integrity. In the weeks following the break-in, CHM supporters offered not only donations but "good internet vibes" and "virtual love" for their favorite local historic site, the kind of moral support that is such a vital currency of museums and nonprofits everywhere. Museum officials thanked these supporters repeatedly like so many pledge-drive loyalists, "generous people like you who see how history can enlighten, inspire and illuminate our modern world, and keep us going."[43] Both groups framed the incident as a matter of principle and culture rather than of politics or economics. Their indignation appeared to have little to do with crime in the neighborhood, much less the conditions that might lead to such a break-in or the changes in the neighborhood (gentrification, efforts to close the NLEC, the pushing of toxic heroin on the area's homeless, and so on). The primary concern was the marring of the dignified face of a local heritage site.

What may be less obvious is why the Campbell House is such a vigorously defended site—particularly given the city's current economic and political climate and penchant for demolition. Admittedly, many St. Louisans have forgotten about the house altogether, if they ever knew of its existence.[44] Yet like the "forgotten" Pruitt-Igoe, it remains a site of heritage many are committed to remembering.[45] In the years since its restoration, the museum has experienced something of a renaissance, drawing interest not only from civic leaders but from professionals and members of the region's growing creative class, those "brave souls" who have moved back into the city, and many more who engage it from a safe distance. And unlike the city's thousands of lost historic structures, the house has long been, and continues to be, an overdetermined site of memory.[46]

This book explains how such a reality came to be—how a property that was nearly swept aside in the name of modernization has served elaborate schemes of rectification and collective memory for almost a century. Through sustained study of the house as the material embodiment of the city's fraught, at times even tortured relationship to its own past, present, and future, I seek to account for the impulses that drove the initial enshrinement of the house as well as the many acts of rehabilitation that have safeguarded it since the disappearance of Lucas Place. These multiple and at times contradictory "operations of memory," as historian Carol Gluck might call them, encompass a wide range of objects, narratives, and practices of remembering (or, as Gluck reminds us, "re-remembering").[47] By attending to multiple operations of memory, and focusing on a site with complex historical, cultural, and political resonances, I aim to show how these operations correspond to trends in planning and historic preservation, as well as to broader patterns of change in American material and cultural life.

I have sought to read creatively the remarkable assemblage of spaces, objects, images, archives, exhibitions, and narratives that constitutes the "Campbell House" as both a place and an idea in order to reconstruct the material history—and logics of cultural meaning—at the site. This interpretative work has been informed by scholarship in urban history, sociology, cultural geography, and literary history, as well as by preservation and museum studies, anthropology, and material culture. My reading begins with a brief history of downtown St. Louis and the Lucas Place neighborhood that attends to its defining characteristic, qualities of space and place that, although not always consciously registered by museumgoers, have contributed to the site's strange allure. This first chapter is the start of a multilayered argument about how the decline of the neighborhood, together with an unusual caretaking regime during the family's tenure, constitute core elements of the site's *memorial unconscious*—that is, the set of painful realities and losses, along with hopes and darker longings, that have been given material expression in the house, contradicting better-known, sunnier place narratives.

Efforts made by the family and their servants to suspend time inside the house—which were intended to forestall psychic as well as material disintegration—presaged more "civic-minded" preservation work that followed. The middle chapters of the book account for the pre- and post–World War II activities of the WCS and their allies, including fundraising and the initial staging of the museum. These activities likewise constituted foundational acts of possession of the site, and they mirrored the work of urban planners already described, suggesting just how intimately related are negative and positive heritage, as well as redevelopment and rectification.

In converting a private house into a shrine to St. Louis's Civil War–era golden age, museum interpreters privileged the history of family patriarchs Robert and Virginia Campbell, pushing to the margins the experiences of their sons and many household servants, as well as the history of the city and Lucas Place itself. The amnesic set of narratives that resulted are explored in two chapters that focus on family possessions that anchored museum interpretation during the 1950s: Virginia handwritten circa 1830s "receipt book" and a pair of buckskin suits that appear to have been given to Robert by Indian trade partners in the early 1840s. Like so many things that were saved at auction and displayed prominently in the museum, these artifacts had real ambiguity as heritage objects. But they were ascribed straightforward symbolic significance by early interpreters and became emblems of frontier heroism, the well-ordered household, and the ideals of private property and possessive individualism—all of which appealed to boosters, planners, and museumgoers.

The book concludes by exploring a more recent act of possession at the site made possible thanks to the discovery of the circa 1885 album of photographs in a dumpster in the 1970s, a time when the board was also dealing with theft, declining neighborhood conditions, and structural deterioration. As board members and museum staff worked to stabilize the house, they thought more deeply about the issue of historical and material integrity, and by the 1980s, officials had developed a new restoration philosophy. Departing from decades of museum practice, they pursued a more fulsome restoration and more time-specific interpretation based on the photographic evidence. It would take better than a decade to complete the work, but the shift was definitive and apparently irreversible; the restoration represents yet another crucial act of possession of the site—one that has reinforced the sense of authentic connection to the past even as it has fostered a fuller awareness that the house is in fact a highly reconstructed site.

Ultimately, the house's survival should be understood as the result not of unlikely "persistence" but of intentional, at times aggressive acts of preservation—and defense—that have been accompanied by the work of negation and forgetting. The work of memory at the site has long been shot through with contradictory, sometimes perverse impulses: in order to *possess* the Campbell House as a "living" historical site, and to safeguard and interpret its local meanings as heritage, its preservers and advocates have had to perform countless acts of *dispossession*, including denial, negation, and plain old forgetting. The site's deeper cultural significance lies in its intactness as an archive of both the former and the latter: acts of possession and dispossession of the sort expressed in the moment of the burglary. Such acts urgently need our understanding now, particularly given the growing racial and economic inequalities in the St. Louis region and across the nation, but also because of Americans' ongoing struggles over the politics of memory and heritage and over the material substance of our historical imagination.

CHAPTER 1

THE NEIGHBORHOOD

Not only can remembering make us feel distant from the past . . .
but being inevitably incomplete, it can also frustrate the desire for
continuity. . . . Vestiges of the past acquire resonance through their
relationship to something forgotten.

—*Elizabeth Hallam and Jenny Hockey,* Death,
Memory and Material Culture

Vestiges of St. Louis Past

WHEN FIRST-TIME VISITORS drive through St. Louis, they soon
discover what everyday commuters know all too well: if you
are not traveling on the highways, there are no easy routes through the
downtown area. Most of the east-west surface streets are one-way, and
the north-south arteries clog frequently with rush-hour and construction traffic. The whole downtown is sprinkled with stoplights timed to
aid those using the highways, and interminable street repairs often slow
cars almost to the speed of pedestrians, who themselves must navigate
crumbling pavement and ever-changing sidewalk configurations. Like
central business districts in many aging industrial cities, St. Louis's has
experienced many seasons of material and economic transformation that
have contributed to its overall spatial incoherence. The landscape of
downtown is a product of some 165 years of building and un-building:
a motley assemblage of glorious, broken and semi-intact parts that are
unlikely to ever be reharmonized. These "vestiges of the past," as Hallam
and Hockey might call them, have powerful resonance given their relationship to "something forgotten," and also, we might say, to a longed-for
whole—that is, a more intact and cohesive city center than St. Louis has
today or indeed has ever enjoyed.[1]

If undeterred by the bewildering traffic and an incoherent landscape, however, visitors can still catch glimpses of the city's former spatial tidiness and economic vitality. Driving west along Locust Street, for example, past the hulking Federal Reserve Building (1925) and the grand second-empire-style U.S. Customs House and Post Office (1884), both testaments to the city's former influence in finance and commerce, one can also find the remains of vibrant dry-goods and banking districts. The area's nineteenth-century buildings—among them Lynch's Slave Pen (as the city's largest slave trading post, owned by Bernard Lynch, was known; it stood at 5th and Myrtle until 1963) and the luxurious Southern Hotel (which stood on Walnut at 4th Street)—were long ago replaced by early high-rises that housed major law, business, and insurance firms. The area has a degree of density that, despite the mixture of old and new and several times refurbished, speaks to its former dynamism as the commercial heart of the city.

This dynamism was already apparent to observers in the mid-nineteenth century, when St. Louis was emerging as a major trade, settlement, and transportation hub, and the steady growth of industry near downtown—especially in shipping, warehousing, meatpacking, and distilling sectors—contributed to the city's cosmopolitanism. For the thousands who streamed through downtown each day—on foot, in carriages, and later in streetcars—the linkages between downtown and the city's manufacturing centers along the river were palpable everyday social and material realities. Shopping, transportation, trade, and entertainment took place in twelve or so square blocks that would soon expand, in fact so quickly that by 1900 St. Louis had become the fourth largest city in the nation in terms of population and productivity.[2] Sectional crisis, compounded by mounting debt and the painful loss of railroad and shipping contracts to Chicago, slowed what could have been even more explosive growth.[3] But the city continued to gain population, and its impending decline would not become fully evident until the mid-twentieth century.

During the Great Depression, St. Louis officials began to fret about losses in manufacturing and corporate tenants, offering a series of proposals to rationalize the unruly city and reindustrialize sections of its core—to clean up the decaying "collar of slums" near the river that was triggering disinvestment. Between 1939 and 1942, city leaders cleared forty blocks of riverfront—aging warehouses and housing—to make way for the Jefferson National Expansion Memorial (or the Gateway Arch as it would come to be known). They proceeded to demolish several other working- and middle-class neighborhoods to free up space for industrial development and later a Memorial Plaza, the highway, and Busch Stadium—most troublingly, Mill Creek Valley, which was home to flourishing community of nearly twenty thousand African Americans, many of whom were recent migrants. The clearance did not slow the snowballing effects of dispersal and decay, however; indeed, it may have catalyzed them, compounding the effects of suburbanization and fragmentation.[4] In the postwar years, the city's mostly white suburbs mushroomed and its downtown shrank: local retail juggernauts Stix, Baer & Fuller and Famous Barr continued to operate their flagship department stores in the hope of a downtown recovery, but they eventually gave up, moving out permanently after consolidation and buyouts.[5]

It has only been in the last twenty years that some of the many empty buildings (the visually and architecturally striking ones) have been repurposed for condominiums, art galleries, server warehouses, and office space. Adventuresome entrepreneurs, emboldened by the success of Citygarden (a popular sculpture park and public garden at Chestnut between 8th and 11th Streets) and Culinaria, a high-end grocery-café at Ninth and Locust, have been increasingly active in the area, and several restaurants, wine bars, catering and specialty shops, and small tech and manufacturing firms have sprung up along sections of Locust Street, as well as Walnut, Olive, and Chestnut. Some larger projects—including the rehab of the Jefferson Arms Hotel at the corner of Locust and Tucker, which reportedly attracted attention from Donald Trump and Marriott International, for example—have been proposed as well. Redevelopment has finally stemmed the tide of abandonment. The Washington Avenue restaurant and club district (one block north of Locust) seems quite stable, and the Historic Garment District and tech corridor in midtown have shown signs of real momentum. These and other projects are predicated on certain faded ideals of a "downtown lifestyle" and an expectation that a more-cohesive urban landscape may yet emerge along Locust.[6]

But as one moves closer to midtown, the redevelopment is rather less vigorous. West of Tucker, a hodgepodge of high- and low-rise, modest and monumental, structures communicates multiple, competing messages about the character of downtown. Between 12th and 16th Streets, grand buildings like Christ Church Cathedral (a Gothic Revival–style sandstone structure built starting in 1867), the Central Public Library (a Beaux Arts–style temple built in 1909–1910),[7] and an art deco high-rise (built in 1926 for the oil company Dutch Shell) are interspersed with empty lots and what geographers would call "weakly classified" structures—those lacking in aesthetic appeal, historical significance, or commercial and cultural vitality of the sort that would contribute to a defined sense of place.[8] The further west one travels, in fact, the less coherent the once-bustling commercial thoroughfare becomes.

Locust's lack of decipherability registers especially strongly at the intersection of 13th and Locust Streets, where the road makes a forty-five-degree turn as it passes by the Central Public Library on the north. Many assume the bend is somehow related to the multi-million-dollar restoration of the library completed in 2010 or more recent improvements to Lucas Park across the street. But it is not: it has been there for more than a century, baffling countless drivers and generations of city planners who have yearned for spatial unity in the civic center extension. The bend in the road looks like a bulging pocket or a half-realized suburban cul-de-sac. St. Louis is positively littered with these "character marks"—dead-ends, inexplicable widenings and narrowings, disappearing sidewalks, and oversized alleys—that impose themselves on locals without warning. A "No Outlet" sign or broken pavement that rises like a strange headstone serve as a "signal that the past has receded" in this place due to a decision no one can quite recall.[9] Locals have come to expect them; people simply alter their mental geography accordingly. Maybe next time they will take a different route.

Such features compound feelings of uncertainty of a sort that geographer Larry R. Ford has described as a product of the overall "dishevelment" of cities whose "uneven, ragged horizons" and material "clutter and chaos" have produced a gradual (or in St. Louis's case, not so gradual) "loosening" of the urban fabric that violates utterly the sense of what a city is supposed to be.[10] The dishevelment becomes more obvious the further west one travels in St. Louis: there are blocks of Locust in what is called midtown where the loosened fabric has come wholly unraveled.

Rundown warehouses and empty lots alternate with 1990s tract homes or crumbling 1880s storefronts and pasture-like green spaces. Some sections have a quasi-rural feel of the sort that St. Louis has not seen near downtown since the mid-nineteenth century. And the bend in the road is the place where this slackening of the street grid begins.

When viewed as part of the long history of the city's making and remaking, this site of the bend at 13th and Locust becomes even more symbolically resonant, pointing to successive efforts to regain material-symbolic control of the city's midsection. Positioned at what was then the outer limit of the city, the bend in the road was initially designed to be the entryway to an upscale neighborhood, the city's first "private place." Built by and named after St. Louis's wealthiest landholding family, Lucas Place was intentionally set off from the established street grid by several hundred feet and closed off entirely on the west end (beyond what is now 18th Street).[11] A cul-de-sac effect, then, was exactly what developers were going for.

As the city grew up around it, this bend became the unofficial boundary between the "eastern and plebeian" and "western and aristocratic" parts of St. Louis, as a *Post-Dispatch* columnist later reminisced, the latter known not only for its beauty but for its visible contrast with the rest of the city:

> For a full three blocks not a shanty rears its head. All the houses are large and handsome, and the shade trees the best the city can show. The street is paved with large blocks of limestone, and is, consequently, very clean. It is an intensely quiet spot, and if children live there, they are kept indoors, and never allowed to make mud pies in the gutter. . . . Locust is not [yet all] a commercial street; indeed, there is hardly a place of business upon it west of Twelfth street, and what is very remarkable for St. Louis, its churches outnumber its saloons. . . . The interference of the park and the general freedom from horse railroads have made it a quiet and untraveled street. As a whole . . . it is a great ornament to the city, and there ought to be more of them.[12]

Besides its "intensely quiet" nature, other elements of the neighborhood— marble sidewalks, grand houses of worship (including Christ Church

Cathedral), and municipal green space boasting neoclassical gardens, fountains, and a picket fence (Missouri Park)—likewise communicated exclusivity.[13] For more than twenty years, Lucas Place was the refuge for elite St. Louis families, embodying certain ideals—privacy, aesthetic harmony, order, cleanliness—of refined urban living during this period.[14] It epitomized what Catherine Cocks has described as the "protected realm of trust and intimacy beyond the reach of the market" that many city dwellers of the period longed for, and served as the model for dozens of other exclusive neighborhoods south and west. In subsequent decades, these mostly white suburbs sprang up just beyond the city limits.[15] Such neighorhoods shared some of the same pretensions and concerns for spatial order, if not the material grandeur, of Lucas Place.

"A Great Ornament to the City"

Lucas Place embodied a bourgeois desire for a well-ordered urban life most foundationally in its remoteness from the grime of the city, but also in its primacy, visibility, and gentility. Platted on farmland that had once been part of the city's large common fields system, the neighborhood had natural appeal both in its elevation and in its relative openness (during the Civil War, some of it would be used as training ground for local militia). The parcel sat outside the incorporated city, beyond the crowding and noise of downtown, where burgeoning industry (meat-packing, metal processing, brickmaking, and other dirty operations) attracted thousands of immigrants and free persons of color at midcentury—so many that the city's population quintupled between 1840 and 1850. An 1849 fire compounded the crowding problem by wiping out fifteen city blocks along the riverfront. And a devastating cholera outbreak that followed shortly thereafter killed some 6 percent of the population, further highlighting the abysmal conditions in the surviving neighborhoods.[16] Lucas Place, by contrast, was greener, cleaner, more spacious, and more peaceful—preternaturally so, to judge by some descriptions. And yet it was not so far from business and transportation centers as to be inconvenient or unfashionable. Residents could get to their downtown offices by coach in ten minutes, and servants could readily access nearby markets and stables. Children could walk to the public high school at 14th and

Locust or to nearby elite preparatory schools without stepping outside the enclave.

Lucas Place residents enjoyed not only more material security but a higher quality of life than most of their fellow citizens. They were the first in the city to have indoor plumbing (Mississippi River water was piped directly into their homes), for example, and a private security detail kept out carriage traffic and beggars as well as riff-raff from nearby saloons. They also benefited from various wholly invisible mechanisms of control, among them deed restrictions that prevented subdivision or commercial development of the neighborhood (the first of their kind in the city) and private assessments for upkeep of streets and walkways, which were notoriously poor elsewhere in the city.[17] By all accounts, visiting Lucas Place in its heyday felt like being transported to a private urban estate: it occupied a position of literal and symbolic elevation, with clear sightlines to the river (fig. 2) that further enhanced the aura of control, a well-ordered and beautiful world unto itself.

FIGURE 2. *View of St. Louis, from Lucas Place,* lithograph, 1865, E. Sachse & Company, Baltimore. Campbell House Museum, St. Louis, MO.

Elite claims on the well-ordered urban life found their fullest materialization in the palatial residences, which grew in scale and lavishness with each passing year. By the early 1860s, the first homes built on Lucas Place, among them Robert and Virginia Campbell's 1851 town house, had been dwarfed by stone and brick mansions two and three times larger, some built right up to the curbs. Many residents, who included influential real-estate investors, military men, and politicians, came to be known by their enormous piles, which were regularly discussed in society columns of the late 1850s and 1860s. The neighborhood came to be seen as the city's "great ornament"—a symbol not only of St. Louis's financial wealth but of its power and influence as "Queen of the West."[18] This identity was bound up in the city's status as an outpost for westward trade and settlement in the 1840s and 1850s, when many of Lucas Place's residents had made their initial fortunes. But it would be most loudly celebrated in the early to mid-1870s, when assertions about St. Louis's "immutable path to preeminence were [at their] shrillest," as Kenneth H. Winn has noted, and "many sensible people began to realize that the coming glory had passed the city by."[19] Indeed, the neighborhood's grandiosity—like that of Robert Campbell's Southern Hotel—was its own kind of boosterism, testifying to the city's material wealth and cultural assets.

Lucas Place's streetscape, like that of St. Louis as a whole, was of mixed heritage. Homes built in the 1860s were Italianate or neoclassical in style—some as large as thirty thousand square feet, with elaborate bay windows and moldings, cupolas and porticos of the sort found in wealthier parts of cities like Atlanta and Baltimore. But others, the Campbells' more staid Greek Revival house among them, drew on older, more understated vocabularies of merchant-class gentility, with interiors that showed a distinctive—one might say Midwestern—blend of high- and middlebrow, southern and northeastern fashions. Many of the homes had been purchased with money from the slave trade and occupied by St. Louisans with business or family ties in the South. Others were owned by Union sympathizers (including General William S. Harney, commander of the U.S. Army's western division at Jefferson Barracks, who lived across from the Campbells), and many prominent residents, the Campbells among them, were known for a more conciliatory style of politics—and social decorum—that allowed them to prosper and maintain influence during and after the war.[20] The neighborhood would become a site of postwar rapprochement.[21]

While St. Louis had been fiercely divided as well as economically depressed during the war, it rebounded within a couple years thanks to continued expansion of the railroads, which helped the city to take advantage of its border zone status in trade and manufacturing.[22] The Nicholas Schaeffer Soap Factory, for example, located just north of Lucas Place and until 1885 the largest candle and grease manufacturer west of the Mississippi, flourished and expanded during the immediate postwar period, as did other nearby factories.[23] The businesses that survived the Panic of 1873 (thanks in part to prudent investments by the likes of Robert Campbell, who stabilized western markets with his personal credit) carried the city's economy into a new stage of growth. In the 1870s, Lucas Place seemed to epitomize local resilience: its stability was a product of wealth accumulated before the war and concentrated political and social power, and its residents—who made up some "three-fourths of the whole number of millionaires of the city," among them two city mayors and one Missouri governor and state senator—would retain their political influence for years to come.[24]

But by the end of the century, the city's center of gravity had shifted away from downtown and its "great ornament" neighborhood. When officials passed a self-governance charter in 1876, the first of its kind in the nation, they sought to manage unchecked expansion at the western edges of the city, where increasingly more of its capital and new development would come to be rooted.[25] In the coming decades, city leaders would see the folly of this charter and be forced to shift their planning focus from strategic expansion to consolidation and infrastructural improvements—somewhat belated reactions to worrisome conditions across the city, including inadequate sewers, aging warehouses, crumbling streets, declining revenues, and pollution of the kind produced by the Schaeffer Soap Factory. During this stage, Lucas Place residents who had not previously been lured to newer, fancier neighborhoods were driven out by unpleasant conditions and increasing commercial development in their vicinity.

Around this time, a new vision of civic improvement began to take hold, one held by a younger generation of business and political elites who wished to energize downtown industry and create a more coherent overall city plan. For these civic leaders, some of whom were involved in planning the 1904 World's Fair and related improvement schemes pursued by the Civic Improvement League (later replaced by the City Plan Commission), commercial development was a major priority. These leaders viewed the grand structures of the nineteenth-century city (including the Federal Reserve and the Old Courthouse) as unsuitable anchors for a rapidly modernizing city, and in coming decades advocated for the construction of a fleet of grand new civic buildings that would express the city's economic and cultural ambitions. Most were in the immediate vicinity of Lucas Place, including the first to be built, the Music and Exposition Hall (1883), which was located right at the bend in the road. The sprawling, 3,500-seat arena spanned the entire six acres of what had been Missouri Park and served as a performance space for the St. Louis Symphony and a stage for the 1888 and 1904 Democratic National Conventions and the 1904 World's Fair.[26] During this same period, Locust served as a major parade route and public gathering place.

These developments intruded forcefully on the privacy and order enjoyed by Lucas Place residents. But such projects were seen by city officials as a major boon, reflecting a broader integrative planning agenda informed by City Beautiful principles such as a concern for monumental architecture and spatial designs that would unify and uplift. This agenda took hold unevenly in St. Louis over several decades, as planners struggled to maintain and organize what Joseph Heathcott has characterized as the city's "teeming, often inchoate" turn-of-the-century streetscape.[27] But slowly, a civic center began to emerge just south of the bend in the road that eventually included a Beaux Arts–style City Hall (1904) and Municipal Courts buildings (1909), the grand Central Public Library (built on the site of the razed Exposition Hall) and neighboring Missouri Park, and two buildings funded by a large bond issue ($87 million) that passed in 1923: the Kiel Auditorium and Opera House (1934) and the Soldier's Memorial (1936). In addition, several substantial commercial buildings were built in the area, including the luxurious Hotel Jefferson at Tucker and Locust (1904); the "fully modernized, fireproof" residential Warwick Hotel at Fifteenth and Locust (1916); and the Shell Corporation high-rise headquarters (1926). All would become landmarks and be high-lighted in city directories, guidebooks, and tourist maps.[28]

During construction of the Music and Exposition Hall, Lucas Place homeowners relented to growing economic pressures and signed a petition allowing commercial development in the neighborhood.[29] Unimproved Lucas Place lots, many now worth ten or even twenty times their original prices, were quickly snatched up, while some of the pala-tial residential properties were converted into storefronts and factories or razed to make way for larger buildings.[30] Startling as all of this rapid change was for locals, the commercial development of the neighborhood had in fact been predicted much earlier: the same *Post-Dispatch* account that celebrated Lucas Place as the city's "great beauty mark," for example, ended with the astonishing claim that before long the neighborhood would be thoroughly commercialized, its remaining residences "aban-doned to keepers of first-class hash houses."[31] A few years later, the *St. Louis Republic* welcomed such changes with the cheerful observation that Locust west of 12th was "destined to become a great manufacturing and business thoroughfare. . . . It is a [already] a good business street today, and . . . getting better all the time."[32] And so it would be: when planners reopened the street to through traffic and changed its name from Lucas Place back to Locust Street shortly thereafter, the neighborhood had been effectively knitted back into the mercantile district that had grown up around it.

Besides the bend in the road, only small traces of old Lucas Place—its distinctive goose-necked lampposts, for example, and fragments of its limestone streets and bricked alleyways—survived into the twentieth century. By the 1920s, just a small handful of its original homes remained, and these had been converted into storefronts and festooned with bill-boards (fig. 3). Locust was fast becoming the predicted thoroughfare. The blocks between 12th and 15th Streets took on the character of a transition zone, a corridor of access between wholesale and dry-goods districts east of Tucker and clothing, shoes, hats, and automobile manufacturers, as well as local print shops, accounting and law firms, employment agen-cies, and secretarial schools further west. Between was the patchwork already described. While it was less crowded than Washington Avenue, where the city's department stores and streetcar lines were located, Locust

FIGURE 3. Locust looking east toward the YWCA and 14th Street, photograph, 1920. Campbell House Museum, St. Louis, MO.

had a decent share of the traffic of businessmen, tradesmen, teachers, YMCA residents, and the many "street urchins" who frequented the area, some of them from "Father Dunne's Newsboys' Home and Protectorate," an orphanage at 2737 Locust.[33]

 With such vibrancy came dirt, noise, and social mixing of the sort former residents had been able to manage—and an indeterminacy of character that no amount of urban planning could resolve. In the decades before World War II, the bend in the road continued to serve as a connector among the city's business, civic, and residential precincts, defining a symbolic "middle space" between downtown and a rapidly evolving central corridor where citizens could assemble for edification and leisure. But the park was relatively unused, and as time wore on the neighborhood continued to show signs of decline of the sort associated with the so-called downtown problem that triggered not only clearance and rehabilitation campaigns but a broader "pandemic of disinvestment" in the years following the war.[34] In this context, the bend in the road was less a supple joint than a weakening ligament—one that could be easily torn.

The Campbell House: "City Living since 1851"

Whether or not they know this history, visitors to the Campbell House are likely to notice the ongoing effects of disinvestment and to register the indeterminate—or as boosters would have it, "transitional"—character of today's Locust Street. The constant presence of the homeless in the area, the bend in the road, the unthinkingly commemorative "Lucas Park" at 14th and Locust (now a well-policed dog park with prominent "no loitering" signs), and the blank-looking intersection at Locust and Fifteen are all evidence of these effects, if not of complete dishevelment. Right in the middle of it all is perhaps the most striking of all material remnants of Lucas Place—the only brick residence for miles and the last single-family home anywhere near downtown. Framed by a concrete slab building, half-filled parking lots, deteriorating alleyways, and an empty homeless shelter, the building often startles people. How on earth, they wonder, can a house such as this be here? And where is the rest of the neighborhood?

A discrete black-and-white sign mounted on the front gate offers a partial answer: the "Campbell House Museum" at "1508 Locus Street" has apparently been in this location a good long while ("since 1851"); it is open for public tours (between 10 a.m. and 4 p.m. Wednesday through Saturday, and 12 p.m. to 4 p.m. Sunday) and, as the Victorian-style cartouche at the bottom suggests, has historic significance. The main slogan—"City Living since 1851"—also appears in much of the museum's print and social media and on its website, inviting visitors to see the house as evidence of former urban vitality, of "city living" as it is commonly understood, and longed for, today.[35] But the sign points to something else as well: the uncomfortable irony of making such a claim given all appearances, and the fact that so many of the city's ongoing economic and political struggles are associated with this very quadrant of downtown.[36] The Campbell House's unlikely material presence in the city, especially here, utterly violates expectations, inviting consideration not only of former vibrancy but loss—not only claims of ownership but acts of abandonment.

Perhaps anticipating these tensions, museum promoters have made the very problem of discontinuity, the ambiguity of the Campbell House as a vestige of the city's history, a premise for celebrating its survival.

The "City Living" slogan effectively names what Elizabeth Hallam and Jenny Hockey observe about "vestiges of the past" in general, as quoted at the beginning of this chapter: that they "acquire resonance through their relationship to something forgotten." At the same time, the slogan asserts claims of material-historical resilience ("since 1851") and former glory—the kind of glory that might yet be regained.

Promotional banners hanging on nearby lampposts go one step further, embodying local ambivalence in a gesture of remembrance, an imaginary encounter between two St. Louisans, one from the past and one ostensibly from the present (fig. 4).[37] "Old St. Louis" is represented by a black-and-white photograph of a barrel-chested man with an expensive looking tuxedo and handlebar mustache (he is in fact Hugh Campbell, the last owner of the Campbell residence), while the modern-day city is represented by a color photo of a much younger man in baggy jeans, a half-untucked (but carefully ironed) light blue dress shirt, and a plain black baseball cap turned backward. The latter is reaching across the vertical "frame" of time (and around the lamppost, as it were) to put his hand on the elder man's shoulder. He seems to have taken literally the museum's invitation to come "meet some folks from Old St. Louis," and he is posing as one might for a photograph with a statue of a famous personage such as Chuck Berry, Dred Scott, or Stan Musial (three famous St. Louisans recently commemorated with public statuary).

The design is meant to be lightheartedly ironic, turning on the forced bodily juxtaposition of two figures who represent divergent conceptions of "city living." The older man's gentlemanly appearance and aristocratic reserve contrast comically with the white, middle-class insouciance of the younger, whose posture suggests he is perhaps less constrained by social codes but also less at ease in the (no longer white) neighborhood than his new friend. His gesture of familiarity and backward-facing cap cannot conceal—in fact may heighten—the awkwardness of their encounter, which has been achieved through unapologetic Photoshop editing. "Reaching back in time," as he does quite literally, the young man expresses the tentativeness of a first-time encounter with the city's past. Clearly, he is not a typical museumgoer nor a downtown resident: he looks like he would be more at home in a sports bar than a Victorian parlor, a PR firm's conception of a tourist or a baseball fan, perhaps, or a suburbanite discovering downtown St. Louis for the first time.

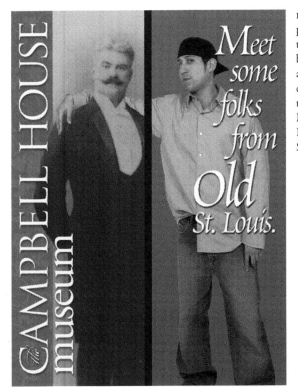

FIGURE 4. Design prototype for promotional "Old Folks" banners developed and installed during the 2000s by the Campbell House Museum. Campbell House Museum, St. Louis, MO.

The young man's encounter with a would-be ancestor seems to have been shaped by an overweening sense of indecipherability, dishevelment, and decline. "Old St. Louis," locals and visitors know all too well, is long gone, and with it the material, economic, and social realities that once made downtown a desirable place to live for many white, middle-class residents. But it is forever being gestured at by those who promote the city's heritage sites with pride. Perhaps that is why the banners continue to be displayed all these years after they were made: promoters have hit on a core truth about the city's fraught historical consciousness—one that still resonates today and indeed has intensified as the city has faced new humiliations of the sort described in the introduction to this book.

Efforts to save and promote this lone survivor of Lucas Place have always turned on such ambivalence. Indeed, even before it opened as the Campbell House Museum in 1943, the house was understood as a vestige of a lost golden age, when "city living" had a wholly different character.

The young man embodies the multilayered nostalgia of a city that has struggled with forgetting. His gesture is profoundly ambivalent, suggesting not only a longing to remember and recuperate Old St. Louis but also an awareness of the impossibility of doing so. His nostalgia manifests as both a feeling of kinship with urban life and a sense of entitlement to the past and its meanings—what anthropologist Nelson H. H. Graburn characterizes as the "ever-unsatisfied yearning to be able to return to a past time—to live and be engaged in that past time rather than to inherit it as 'the received truth.'"[38] The young man's grasp undoubtedly expresses a sense of pride (the kind that museum promoters themselves feel and presume visitors will soon share), but also the swagger of would-be ownership and familiarity, of the ability to grasp the meanings of the site and the city's history. The need to assert such a grasp, however, is an acknowledgment of the social, economic, and political forces that work against a sense of kinship with the city, including decades of disinvestment by whites in general and ownership classes more particularly.

Such claims of possession over the domains of public space, local memory, and cultural heritage have been recapitulated many times by white urban elites in the years since 1851. The many preservationists, boosters, museumgoers, and patrons who have found the Campbell House compelling as symbols of their city's history have often sought to reclaim pieces of that history without fully engaging its origins and meanings, and certainly without acknowledging the relationship between acts of preservation and ongoing disinvestment in the city. The distinct material and cultural history of Locust Street, for example, and what the city's first private neighborhood—and its evolving relationship to the city—tell us about the political economies of development, planning, and heritage are not foregrounded elements of this celebrated past. Yet they constitute some of the primary reasons for the house's survival and may indeed be unconsciously reclaimed through such symbolic acts of kinship with Old St. Louis.

The choice to use a photograph of Hugh Campbell to represent Old St. Louis is likewise an ambivalent one. While it shows the last homeowner of the last house on Lucas Place in hearty middle age, in a posture that exudes the social-economic power long enjoyed by neighborhood residents (and later planning elites), it also points to the inevitable passing of time and the problems of discontinuity that hinder true understanding of the past. And even as it communicates optimism about the Campbell House as a site of heritage, this photograph, like the bend in the road, represents something forgotten, or at least not wholly decipherable to modern viewers. In fact, the photo was taken during a period when the family experienced debilitating loss and estrangement from community; it became familiar to St. Louisans when it was printed with a front-page announcement of Campbell's death in 1931.

While most visitors to the site do not know this, they may well sense these darker associations, particularly once they learn the story of the family and their reasons for remaining in their Lucas Place when everyone else was abandoning the city. As we see in the next chapter, Hugh Campbell's caretaking efforts during the first three decades of the twentieth century, a period of intense private grief in the household, ensured that the family's home and its contents would survive and be claimed as objects of heritage and indeed as symbols of a kind of household order that was consoling to St. Louisans who no longer felt a sense of control over their city. At the same time, his caretaking imprinted on them other less positive associations, including the fragility of ownership and control, and the inevitability of death and suffering—associations that might appropriately be linked to the state of dishevelment of the contemporary city.

CHAPTER 2

CARETAKING

A Retreat from Life

I T WAS A curious coincidence—one of those convergences of private and public life that takes on a certain dark poeticism in hindsight. But as it turned out, the fate of the town house at 15th and Locust Streets bore an uncanny resemblance to that of Lucas Place itself at the end of the nineteenth century. Just as deed restrictions in the private neighborhood were set to expire and local developers began their speculative maneuvering, one of its best-known residents, Robert Campbell, passed away at the age of seventy-five in 1879. He was followed in death by his wife, Virginia Kyle Campbell, three years later, leaving a large inheritance to their three surviving sons—a fact noted in the press with more than idle curiosity. Like the Campbell residence, the family fortune—acquired in the fur trade and multiplied through successful investment in banking, real estate, and trade—grew in concert with the frontier city itself. Together they might be said to have expressed the city's sense of its own economic and political might during the last quarter of the century.

But the passing of the Campbell patriarchs also signaled the end of an era. While their millions would sustain the next generation of the family for years to come, the money could not prevent the withering of Lucas Place, whose transformation reflected larger economic and social changes that would only speed up in the coming decades. One high-profile property in the mercantile district to the east, owned by Robert Campbell, was especially emblematic of such transformation. The Southern Hotel, which occupied an entire city block between Walnut and 4th and Elm and 5th Streets, was a posh, six-story structure, the first of its kind west of the Mississippi. At the time of its opening in 1865, it was celebrated as the "finest hotel in the world," and it quickly became a hub of local trade and business dealings, particularly by those in the Campbells' circle.[1] The Southern signified a new public culture of trade and a new style of urban sociability which St. Louisans were proud to claim as part of their national brand.

The hotel quickly became nationally famous, its regulars including illustrious locals such as Ulysses S. Grant; James B. Eads, the distinguished engineer-architect behind Civil War gunboats and St. Louis's most famous bridge; Samuel L. Clemens (Mark Twain); and the intrepid booster Logan Reavis, who made his argument that the capital should be moved to St. Louis at the hotel in 1869. Its success and glamor seemed to prove that the city had officially arrived and would maintain its prominence for years to come.[2] But the hotel burned nearly to the ground after a decade of operation, killing more than a dozen people—a disaster that shocked the city and hit Campbell hard. He would not live to see the hotel reopen in 1881 nor the dramatic changes in his own backyard that followed. Neither would his sons carry on hotel ownership; while it was rebuilt, its material destruction represented the end of the family's visibility and economic influence on the city.

There would be many other such correspondences—between material and symbolic domains of life, between public and private losses—for the Campbells in the coming decades. While workers were breaking ground on the gargantuan Music and Exposition Hall just a block east of the family's residence in 1883, a project that greatly increased noise and traffic in the vicinity and ushered in the era of commercialization described in the previous chapter, Virginia's mother, Lucy Ann Kyle, died. She had lived in the house for more than thirty years during which time she buried several grandchildren and witnessed the steady outmigration of most of the family's social peers. The changes that followed would be more devastating still: the last wave of departures by Lucas Place residents and the death of another Campbell, James Alexander, in 1890. James, the youngest of Virginia and Robert's three surviving sons, succumbed to influenza in Paris at thirty years of age. He had been the apparent picture of health and urban gentility, having recently completed a Yale law degree and moved to Place Vendôme, but he was in fact the eleventh of thirteen Campbell children to die young. He and his brothers Hugh and Hazlett had all been the second in the family to be christened with those names, and James's death, coming so close on the heels of losses not yet fully mourned, was especially devastating.[3] As Lucas Place disintegrated, the house fell silent, frozen in a grimace of misery few outsiders could have fathomed.

This misery took many forms and had long-lasting material effects. Hazlett, who was in his twenties when James died, suffered from depression and paranoia, and his condition deteriorated dramatically around this time, to such an extent that he seems to have descended into what Hugh politely referred to as a "mental retreat from life." Specialists were consulted—the best in the United States and Europe—but no effective treatments for his depression and delusions, a complex referred to as *dementia praecox* (which today might be diagnosed as schizoaffective or bipolar disorder, or schizophrenia), could be discovered.[4] By the turn of the century, he could not leave the house. Hugh refused to have Hazlett committed to an asylum, which would have been the common destination for many of lesser means, instead cocooning him inside the their childhood home. Live-in servants provided for their every need, and the family physician made daily house calls, all of which continued for the better part of four decades during which Hazlett was dosed with substances (including laudanum and cocaine) that must have further diminished his capacities. He watched from his window overlooking Locust Street as the world fell apart.

Hugh, Hazlett's protector and only source of contact with the outside world, passed away in 1933, at which time Hazlett's mental state became the subject of intense public scrutiny. During months of court hearings, the family's physician and attorneys, as well as relatives and household servants, were called to testify about his health. They confirmed that Hazlett had become a "demented" man with a "blank mind" who had to be "waited upon by five servants, carried about [the house], dressed and undressed and fed as if . . . a baby."[5] This was a stunning portrait of pain and isolation—one made all the more dramatic because it was playing out in a shuttered old mansion sitting on some of the city's most valuable property. Before long, the "last resident of Lucas Place"—both the man and the house—had merged into a single object of pity. As with the Collyer brothers, whose hoarding of family possessions and mounds of trash inside a packed Harlem brownstone had been eagerly documented by the New York press throughout the early 1930s, Hazlett's sorrowful case—including his mental incapacities, reclusive habits, and untold fortune—became something of a public spectacle.[6]

His condition must have been a source of embarrassment, especially for Hugh, who had once been a gregarious socialite, known for hosting lavish parties. But the family's descent into antisocial behavior, hastened by the succession of deaths, called new attention to the squandered Campbell legacy in both social and financial senses. Their father's exploits in the fur trade had already become the stuff of legend, and his work as a merchant, bank president, military leader, and diplomat (including service on the nation's Indian Commission) were remembered as heroic achievements well into the twentieth century. At the time of Robert's death, his was still a household name, and Hugh seen as his presumed successor in business—well-educated, having studied law at Washington University, and socially poised. Like many in his position, however, Hugh lacked a formal career, or much of an obligation to find one, and spent his twenties touring Europe and hosting lavish high-society soirees.[7] He might have permanently joined James in Paris if he had not been called to manage the family estate and serve as de facto parent to Hazlett, roles he settled into during his forties.

At midlife, when it became clear he would not follow in his father's footsteps, Hugh did what many of means would have done: he became a philanthropist, a kind of St. Louis "Daddy Warbucks," instead.[8] In the 1890s, he entertained not only some of the city's richest and most-influential citizens but some of its poorest, including local "street children" and orphans who routinely spent time in his parlor. The photograph of Hugh used in Campbell House Museum promotional materials and discussed in the previous chapter shows him at this stage of life, when he was still known as one of the "gayest, most charming young men in St. Louis . . . extremely eligible and sought after," and known for his generosity.[9] He spent thousands annually on gifts for employees of the Southern Hotel, where he spent much of his time, and the neighborhood poor as well as orphans from Father Dunne's Newsboys' Home. In 1907, he donated money for construction of Dunne's orphanage a few blocks northeast of the Campbell home, on Washington Avenue.[10]

When times were tight for neighborhood families, many of them immigrants, Campbell gave them money, food, streetcar fare, clothes, and even school fees. For several decades, he was the "secret benefactor" who provided annual Thanksgiving and Christmas dinners at Father Dunne's—generosity that went largely unknown to St. Louisans until after his death.[11]

Still, as the "secret benefactor" role suggests, Hugh became increasingly reclusive in his later years, when his caretaking energies came to be centered at home. The three "bachelor sons" (as they were called by the press) had all formed strong attachments to their parents' possessions when they became joint owners of the estate, at which time each one claimed a suite of rooms in the Locust Street town house for sleeping, study, and entertainment. While James was still alive, the brothers made a few changes that reflected their evolving lifestyles, the most significant being the enclosure of a porch between the existing formal parlor and dining room, which yielded space for an informal parlor, now called "the morning room" by museum interpreters. The brothers had the informal parlor decorated with expensive art nouveau furnishings, including a sofa framed in walnut (unlike the rest of the house, which was filled with 1850s teak, rosewood, and oak), Chinese import goods (likely purchased overseas), and William Morris–inspired stained glass and fabrics. They also upgraded plumbing and electrical systems, adding the home's first flushing toilet.[12] But the material evolution of the household slowed considerably after James's death and eventually stopped. Around the turn of the century developers began to call, and the brothers' attorney started to ask why they did not move someplace more suitable for those with resources. But Hugh had promised his parents that he would care for Hazlett, who could not withstand the shock of relocation: material and psychic order must be preserved at all costs.[13] So they stayed put.

And the costs were indeed significant. While the family had shrunken considerably, and their social footprint was miniscule, several live-in servants had to work tirelessly to care for Hazlett and the aging house, which had only been partially modernized. The servants were instructed to keep Robert and Virginia's furnishings—now fifty years out of date—exactly as they were, to keep Hazlett literally and figuratively "grounded," and to maintain meticulous order throughout the house. When the circa

1880s photographs discussed in the introduction were taken, possibly by Hugh himself, the house's interiors were appointed in this well-ordered, outmoded style: the images show tranquil, light-filled rooms filled with plants, curios, paintings, piles of books, and hundreds of other items positioned just so, according to a system whose logic we can only partially decipher.[14]

This logic seems to have evolved with time, as more and more of the Campbell possessions were subjected to elaborate caretaking rituals. Once a year, for example, servants brought out textiles, including Virginia's silk gowns and works of embroidery and the family linens—quilts, sheets, Irish lace, and more—from their assigned places in the attic or cupboards, and spread them out on the grass to air in the sunshine before being carefully repacked. By this means, Hugh sought to prevent damage from moths, mold, and dust and to keep them intact for future viewing; few if any items were sold or given away, and the elaborate sequestration technique was extended to many other objects in the house. Extended family who visited later recalled that by the early 1910s, the house had already become something of a shrine, with much of the furniture covered in sheets. Hugh still played the parlor piano and cranked the music box for Hazlett (who listened from his room) or "his boys" in the neighborhood, and Hugh insisted that a place be set for his brother at the dining room table (although his brother never came down). But true social events were few and far between: only a handful of outsiders came into the house for the occasional wedding (Hugh hosted receptions for several members of the household staff) or Christmas dinner.[15]

The public knew little about what went on inside the so-called mystery house during this period. There were rumors, of course: some said Hugh had "closed up" the house after an especially humiliating episode in which Hazlett came downstairs and greeted guests in an agitated mental state, raving aloud, perhaps without his clothes on. If something of the sort did happen, it did not find its way into official family lore. Servants described Hazlett's strange reclusiveness as if it had always been a factor of daily life in the house that had grown steadily worse with time, explaining how they sought to foster an atmosphere of tranquility for a man with a disordered mind.[16] With time, they pared down the furnishings in Hazlett's rooms, removing area rugs, side chairs, plants, occasional tables, and a settee his mother had used every day, perhaps to give him room to pace, which he was said to do constantly. Servants also replaced floral Persian rugs with a neutral carpet, heavy drapes with lace curtains, and the elaborate chandelier with a simpler fixture, and at some point stripped the patterned wallpaper as well, painting the walls light grey. The result of these changes, as we can see in 1930s photos, was a lighter, airier-feeling room with far less visual clutter and a palpable sense of quiet (fig. 5). The contrast with the outside world could not have been starker.

Suspended Animation

The changes made to the house represented an effort to control the rhythms of daily life and a means of keeping the conditions of that life private. In the work of preservation too Hugh seems to have discovered a way to manage the chaos within, as well as to hold onto a semblance of the past, albeit one that, like life lived inside a bubble, lacked the joy of spontaneity and bore little relationship to the world beyond. What such an enclosed universe meant to its few inhabitants, including the servants who spent most of their time tending vestiges of a bygone world, can only be partially glimpsed in household records. The logic and significance of this household order has been partially captured in the family archive, but much of the surviving evidence is ambiguous. What should we make of the fact that Hugh and Hazlett, who in the 1880s upgraded their plumbing and heating systems—long before the rest of the city— were at the end of their lives likely still using 1850s porcelain pitchers and bowls in their rooms to wash every day? Why did they never install modern sinks or upgrade to marble tubs? And why, when he enjoyed up to date medical care, did Hazlett sleep on a horsehair mattress in his mother's mahogany bedstead for most of his life? A hospital bed was brought in only when he suffered a paralytic stroke in 1936, and he seems to have resisted sleeping in it.[17] One thing *is* clear: all the tending and keeping had little to do with frugality or keeping up with appearances. Hazlett and Hugh enjoyed comforts most could hardly fathom, paying more for each of their hand-stitched linen nightshirts in the 1920s, for example, than most Depression-era laborers earned in two weeks. But

FIGURE 5. Front bedroom of the master suite, photograph, ca. 1935. Campbell House Museum, St. Louis, MO.

such comforts were enjoyed in sorrowful isolation. In an inversion of the usual relationships, the elder Campbells' status objects came to serve the purpose of their sons' private consolation.

Through these means, the Campbells maintained a modicum of privacy and peace during a time when economic, material, and social instability dominated St. Louis. Given the agenda of expansionism in the city, for example, and ongoing efforts to "rehabilitate" the downtown and central corridor, safeguarding the Campbell home required vigorous protection measures that would have made little sense to their peers, who in some cases abandoned all their furnishings when they moved out of the neighborhood. In their proto-preservation activities, Hugh and his household staff laid the groundwork for the William Clark Society (WCS), which, just a few years after Hugh's death, set out to save this "unlikely survivor" of Lucas Place as a potential heritage site. Although the group's conception of continuity was different from Hugh's, it was influenced by the idiosyncratic conception of intactness that he had imposed on the house. Indeed, all the lovingly kept possessions seemed like evidence of St. Louis's "golden age"—one defined by gentility, material splendor, and social order.[18]

Hugh's preservation efforts had little to do with an interest in the history of the frontier city, but they did have the character of memory work—with public as well as private expressions. In the early 1880s, he made two sizeable donations to the Mount Vernon Ladies' Association (MVLA), the storied grassroots preservation group that had been so energetic in its tending of George Washington's estate and other similar properties in the decades following the Civil War, in his mother's honor.[19] The first, a gift of three thousand dollars, paid for the restoration of the first president's "Deer Park," which overlooked the Potomac River. During the first president's life, it had been stocked with white-tailed deer, but in the mid-nineteenth century the space had degraded to the point where much of the hillside and fencing had collapsed. A sign affixed to the new fence acknowledged the Campbell sons' donation in honor of their mother, who had served as Missouri's MVLA vice regent for three years before her passing.[20] A second gift funded the purchase and restoration of a pair of Chippendale candle-stands made of carved mahogany that purportedly had belonged to Martha and George Washington and were given by the first family as a wedding gift. Today, the candle-stands are prominently displayed in the Washingtons' newly restored dining room without attribution to the Campbells.[21]

In both cases, Hugh's commemorative gestures provided for the preservation—and more specifically, the material *stabilization*—of objects with strong sentimental value not only for his family, but for cultural elites and citizens across the country. In this respect, the gifts corresponded to other kinds of preservation work of the period aimed to protect family heirlooms and historic sites that had perceived national heritage significance. But they seem to have served private needs as well. When Hugh assembled a multivolume album of hundreds of images collected during the brothers' travels in Europe in the Middle East, for example, he included photographs of the candle-stands and Deer Park dedication plaque, other Lucas Place residences, the interiors of James's rooms at Yale University, and the family monument at Bellefontaine Cemetery, along with a card reproduction of E. F. Andrews's 1878 portrait of Martha Washington.[22] In this context, material objects were assigned meaning as anchors of memory (public and private) during a period when the family's social lives had effectively come to an end.

Such efforts to find material expression of family memory and honor seem to have had other dark significance as well, coinciding as they did with Hugh's growing preoccupation with the physical remains of his dwindling family. When James passed away, Hugh's first action was to arrange for his brother's body to be sent back home.[23] This involved exorbitant cost and complication: the body had to be stabilized for overseas travel and interment, a feat not easily accomplished given that embalming was not yet readily available in France, and overseas passage took months (James died in July and was not buried until November).[24] But Hugh was intent on James's being buried at Bellefontaine Cemetery, just as he was determined to have his brother's personal belongings returned, including books and furnishings from his Paris apartment and an enormous portrait of James that was completed posthumously by French portraitist Jules LeFebvre (see fig. 6). The portrait was hung in one of the large bay windows in the parlor, where it could be viewed alongside other family portraits, and the rest was returned to the upstairs bedrooms, where some of the items are still on display today.

Once these tasks were complete, Hugh set about altering his will, adding a provision that stipulated that the portrait and the Campbell mansion be donated to Yale University when he and Hazlett died. The painting was to be hung in a campus building that would be named for James. The bequest drew on the idea of a donor memorial that many elites of the period pursued. As Carol Duncan explains, these memorials, whether in the form of art collections, period rooms, or wings in public museums, were often intended to embody the collector him- or herself but also to foster "ritual reenactment of a visit" to see the (deceased) donor.[25] For Hugh Campbell, as for Henry Clay Frick, J. P. Morgan, and other industrialists-turned-collectors who created public memorials, symbolic rematerialization and elevation of the family name were key: if Hugh could not bring James home alive nor pull Hazlett back into his right mind nor prevent the dissolution of the neighborhood, he *could* reconstitute his own family's domestic universe and enshrine it—along with their possessions—as a site of public commemoration.

FIGURE 6. Jules Lefebvre, *James A. Campbell,* oil on canvas, 1895. Campbell House Museum, St. Louis, MO.

Hugh's safeguarding of family memory was expressed not only in acts of caretaking and tribute but in some of the memorial objects themselves. The portrait of his brother, which eventually did find its way to Yale (where, ironically, it languished in storage), served to reembody a lost family member. Like many such commissioned works, the painting depicts its subject at the height of social power and public achievement, while highlighting his humanity (his affection for his dogs and his interest in fine art) and details of his appearance (the tailored suit and gloves, the air of casual refinement, the patient expression on his face). All these elements are meant to express qualities of James's character; they must have taken on special poignancy for those who knew him best, sanctifying elements of his personhood that physical interment could not.[26] Hanging in the parlor, the portrait could have been seen by visitors, but it served a private function too, like the photos of the restored Deer Park and candle-stands Hugh placed in his albums.

A set of stuffed birds that Hugh acquired around the same time took on a similar resonance—and like the portrait, had a tangible, bodily presence that gave them special potency as memory objects. The Campbells kept many pets throughout the years, including the spaniels shown in James's portrait, with whom he traveled (and whose photographs were displayed throughout the house). At least two of their beloved dogs were eventually buried at Bellefontaine Cemetery. But Hazlett's favorites were birds, and one of these, a yellow canary named Beauty, who lived in a walk-in cage Hugh had installed in one of James's rooms after his death, was especially dear. Beauty joined the household in 1892, as Hazlett's mental condition was worsening, and seems to have been his constant companion until she died in 1902. Shortly thereafter, she came back to the house under a glass dome, in a display of dried grasses and silk leaves painted in autumn shades (fig. 7), where she achieved her own version of suspended animation on a bureau in Hazlett's room.

Beauty's was the sort of self-contained world found in many Victorian parlors, when, as Celeste Olalquiaga observes, domestic interiors were thickly layered with objects intended to "form private realms of safety, refuges of stillness which were highly conducive to personal reflection and remembrance."[27] These objects took many forms: terraria and "Wardian cabinets" (aquaria); fossil and "natural history" collections

that included shells, snake skins, and stuffed birds and rodents; glass
paperweights; skeletons encased in amber; and mourning art and other
funerary artifacts made of hair, dried flowers, and ribbons. They prolifer-
ated throughout the United States and England during the nineteenth
century, and were understood to evoke a world of private associations
and practices, from grief and nostalgic reflection to curiosity and ethnographic study. Virginia Campbell owned one that incorporated locks of
hair (likely from some of her family members) that she may have woven
herself into a bouquet of flowers.[28] Like the stuffed birds, the hair collage
was mounted under glass for protective purposes but also visual impact,
so that its intricate details might be contemplated for their beauty and
association with certain characteristics of the dearly departed. In the
Victorian period, such objects served as symbols of refinement of taste
and feeling, though by the turn of the twentieth century, they would have
seemed old-fashioned.[29]

Hugh purchased several other stuffed birds during this period, all
mounted in a similar style, possibly by the same taxidermist, including

a pair of plumed birds of paradise from New Guinea, one displayed by itself, the other grouped with smaller tropical birds, as well as a second canary. It is unclear which of these was acquired first and whether they had a primarily decorative or memorial function (or even if the distinction would have made sense to their owners). They spent the next several decades in the informal parlor and brothers' bedrooms, where they remained until the family's butler, Gus Meyers, showed "Mr. Hazlett's birds" to WCS members on their first walk-through of the house in 1941.[30] When they came up for auction with the rest of the Campbell estate in 1943, the public marveled at the "American Victorian Taxidermy Specimens (under glass)" for rather different reasons, as quaint reminders of an age gone by or as antiques—objects that, as Jean Baudrillard notes, are often sanctified anew as symbolic "ancestors."[31]

A More Complete "Refuge of Stillness"

WCS preservationists viewed the stuffed birds as part of the household decor and decided to buy them for the museum. But it seems unlikely this was their main function during the period in which Hugh and Hazlett owned them. In the context of Hugh's caretaking, they served as sources of comfort and tribute or memorial objects.[32] The latter meaning is confirmed by oral histories given by servants and by a card that has been kept with the stuffed Beauty all these years on which someone—Hugh or Hazlett or maybe Gus—wrote the bird's birth and death dates. The notation signals a feeling of familial attachment and maybe also an effort to claim her life as part of family history, as when one inscribes new names and dates on a cemetery monument. When preserved (and displayed) alongside the bird, furthermore, it reveals the intention to remember by means of ritual contact with mortal remains, as with mourning jewelry made from the deceased's hair.

Like other objects that Hugh acquired during periods of mourning (including the portrait of James), furthermore, the birds gave expression to a desire for continuity and kinship with the past—two defining elements of the antique's "mythological character," as Baudrillard conceives it. In the modern household, he explains, the antique "no longer has any practical application, its role being merely to signify. . . . Yet [the antique] is not afunctional, not purely 'decorative,' for it has a very specific function within the system, namely the signifying of time." The antique becomes a "family portrait" by "immemorialization, in the concrete form of an object, of a former being—a procedure equivalent, in the register of the imaginary, to a suppression of time."[33] In stabilizing animals' bodies, the taxidermist (like the photographer or the embalmer) does all of these things: he suppresses time, objectifies living things (making an object of Beauty), and turns them into symbols. Mounted in "lifelike" poses, their beaks open as if they were singing or perched lightly on a branch, they embody "former being" and a desire for continuity, and in this case, paradoxically, tether the owner to the here and now.[34]

In the end, it was Hugh's fastidious caretaking regime and sense of material order, as much as Hazlett's mental state, that came to be imprinted on the Campbell house. The stuffed birds were Hugh's purchase, just as the bird motifs found throughout the house were his selections—made with Hazlett in mind, certainly, but during a period of intense sorrow that he suffered in relative isolation, confronted by the limitations of his own power. The art glass windows he commissioned for the informal parlor and the flocked wallpaper he selected for the stair hall—two places Hazlett rarely if ever spent time—also featured songbirds in idealized woodland scenes; they had striking similarities to their stuffed counterparts, suggesting they were part of the same system of symbolic association. At the very least, they were core components of the preternaturally "intact" domestic universe that Hugh, Gus, and the other servants curated over several decades.

The circa 1885 photos are powerful evidence of this curatorial work: they show the results of Hugh's selecting and arranging of his family's material remains, and also his efforts to document those remains. As cultural theorists André Bazin and Hugh Gray noted many years ago, photographs serve to "embalm" time, "rescuing it simply from its proper corruption," and in so doing highlight the psychology of preservation, which is rooted in self-protection.[35] Hugh's photographs "rescue" the house from decay but also from more amorphous threats such as the impairment of the mind and the deterioration of social bonds. What he enshrined in the photos, and throughout the house, was not precisely his parents' world "as it was" in the 1850s, nor the "golden age" many St. Louisans conjured up in the decades that followed, but a set of carefully chosen material vestiges—ancestral portraits—whose private significance could not be fully fathomed by those who carried on his work decades later.

Hugh's curatorial efforts must be understood as foundational elements of the material history of the Campbell House—and not just because the house would not have survived the Depression without his interventions. Applying a logic of private control, he sought to slow time at a moment when it seemed to have sped up, and to preserve a nineteenth-century home when city officials were declaring many others worthless, offensive, or "obsolete." And because he had resources that most did not, he was able forestall the harms wrought by planning and industrialization (including clearance) elsewhere in the city, just as an earlier generation of homeowners had kept Lucas Place pristine while the rest of St. Louis faced the harsh realities of deteriorating streets and sewers, disease and fire. Inside the "mystery house" at 15th and Locust, he transformed the stuff of human suffering and grief into private as well as public memorials.

For all the human pathos and dignity of these efforts, there was a perversity in Hugh's caretaking as well. While he protected more than personal property—and even extended the boundaries of "family" to include those without property, neighbors in need, and members of his staff—creating a "refuge of stillness" involved fetishizing his family's possessions. Such an act depended on material-symbolic aggression, sublimated of course and wrapped in the mantle of "restorative nostalgia," a fantasy of past wholeness.[36] Restorative nostalgia manifests not only in the memorializer's desire for continuity but in the planner's ideals of unity and social-material order, and the preservationist's commitment to intactness. All three are at work in this case, and others perhaps as well, suggesting that the convergence of private and public life at the Campbell House is not a coincidence but a set of complexly intertwined actions whereby individual and collective losses, and efforts to compensate for them, have been materialized. The house that "survived" thanks to Hugh's caretaking, like a taxidermied specimen under glass, was as much an expression of what had been *lost*—or propped up and pinned in place—as of what had been studiously saved. Yet that specimen embodied a past, an idealized golden age, that had little to do with Hugh and Hazlett, which St. Louisans longed for and would set out to keep.

CHAPTER 3

THE AUCTION

Cabinet of Wonders Opened

ON A CHILLY Saturday in February 1941, several hundred St. Louisans descended on a warehouse at 4100 Olive Street known as Ben J. Selkirk & Sons' auction and consignment house.[1] They arrived early and stood on the sidewalk, many dressed as if for a funeral, in dark suits and dresses, wool coats and Sunday hats, and even some fur and feather stoles. The air of anticipation grew as more and more people assembled, some having come from the outskirts of the city. Gambling on a big turnout, Selkirk's had taken the "unprecedented step" of printing 1,500 copies of the *Dispersal Resumé,* a 131-page illustrated catalogue containing descriptions of everything to be sold. Idle looking was discouraged: only those who purchased the catalogue (priced at one dollar) would be admitted. But many who had never stepped foot in an auction house (and had little more than a dollar to spend) came to be part of the spectacle.[2]

Upon entering, auction-goers discovered a remarkable scene: two enormous showrooms filled to overflowing with carpets, lamps, mirrors, wooden chests, statuary, paintings, "marble-topped washstands, mahogany beds," and row after row of porcelain, glassware, and silver—all that had before "reposed in the mansion at Fifteenth and Locust."[3] As the catalogue explained, these were the bulk of the worldly possessions of the "intrepid explorer and fearless Indian fighter" who had "figured prominently in the dawning days of St. Louis' great Western trade," Robert Campbell, and his wife, Virginia (though she received only a small nod).[4] Intrepid though Robert had been, the Campbells' estate could not be defended against the depredations of time and the work of lawyers. Heirs to the family fortune had demanded total liquidation, and every last candlestick would be sold. The frontispiece of Selkirk's *Dispersal Resumé* shows a photograph of the Campbells' "Prominent Civil War Residence," the "sole survivor of . . . St. Louis's distinguished and exclusive 'Lucas Place,'" suggesting that the house too would soon be lost—converted to a storefront or razed for a parking lot. Covered in a light snow and framed by barren trees and high-rises, the mansion looked venerable but antiquated, and now that it was empty, not long for the world. The situation was a grim reminder of the warning not to lay up treasures on earth, "where moth and rust doth corrupt, and where thieves break in and steal."[5] Perhaps this *was* a kind of funeral.[6]

But most who came to Selkirk's that day were not there to mourn. They came to revel in the anticipation of new life—the moment when the musty old things that long had "reposed" in the Campbells' town house found the joyful light of rediscovery. Audible ripples of delight passed through Selkirk's galleries as observers made their way through the aisles. Two women stood in a corner studying a set of "Victorian costumes" displayed on mannequins—Virginia's stunning taffeta, silk, and velvet gowns, most dating to the Civil War period, and all in near-pristine condition. Fingering the fine brocades and laces, they noticed the marks of past ownership, such as monograms, hand-stitched collars, waistcoats altered to fit just so, and even the faint impress of the body. Still, everything looked remarkably "fresh and ready to wear," as one woman later commented.[7] The temperature began to rise inside the galleries.

Another gaggle of auction-goers stood at the top of a stairwell eyeing their catalogues. Where to begin? Some exchanged impressions in hushed tones, wandering through the aisles and studying the Campbell crystal and silver, each grouping lovelier than the last.[8] The auction house regulars moved more swiftly, jotting notes as they went. Dealers recognized one another, nodding politely as they eyed the cases with studied disinterest. Some of St. Louis's well-known art collectors gathered along the back wall, where several mid-nineteenth-century paintings and drawings—mainly portraits, hunting scenes, western landscapes, and a handful of etchings—had been hung. A few, including a genre painting by George Caleb Bingham (*The County Election*, 1854), were familiar but most were not the kind of period paintings that appealed to collectors at this time.

A throng had gathered, and it became difficult to walk in some corners of the showroom. Many were choosing items on which they planned to bid at the auction the following day; others were simply fantasizing or trying to picture what all these things had looked like inside the same house.

The Campbell estate was the most distinctive collection Selkirk's had exhibited in decades, if not in the firm's entire history. Besides fancy things—expensive mahogany and oak furniture suites, hand-painted china and Baccarat crystal, imported lamps and linens, and hundreds of decorative objects—there were some true marvels: stuffed exotic birds, samurai swords, tin washtubs dating to the 1850s, a hand-carved, gilded alabaster model of the Taj Mahal, a pair of "Chinese Gold Thread and Velvet Mandarin Hats," two matching fringed buckskin suits (one adult- and one child-sized), a bearskin rug, and a first edition copy of Hall and McKenney's *History of the Indian Tribes of North America* (with a complete set of hand-tinted lithographic plates). To bring such a large and motley collection to order, Selkirk's officials had sorted not by room or period but by category: "Traditional Americana," "English Furniture," "Objets d'Art," textiles, porcelain and china, Persian and Oriental rugs, and more. The trade terminology was typical, and it advantaged big-ticket customers, the dealers and high-end collectors who knew what they were looking for. But this was no average estate sale. As the richly illustrated *Dispersal Resumé* suggested, Selkirk's expected an unusually broad audience, many of whom remembered the Campbells or had followed the court proceedings related to their large estate with fascination.

Some objects announced their own value and significance. A gleaming mahogany music box, for example—the sort that plays old-fashioned waltzes and ballads on punched-metal discs, a relic of the pre-radio age and an exceedingly expensive item even when it was new in the early 1890s—captured a lot of attention. A man in a derby hat stood by transfixed, considering whether to make a bid when his wife observed that it would not fit in their living room. Other things seemed more generic, the sort of upmarket antiques one could find in New York or Chicago galleries, albeit in larger quantities and more complete assemblages than those in attendance had ever seen in one place. It was a lot to take in. A *Post-Dispatch* columnist observed that women in the galleries "fairly swooned when their eyes lit upon the glories that once belonged to the Campbells." They just could not help themselves; there was so much to admire, and they "so dearly longed" to have a couple Campbell "chairs for their bedroom, or a 'what-not' for the front hall." And a "silver soup tureen would look handsome in their dining room if it didn't cost too much. Or perhaps the silver oyster plates—they'd impress the guests," he added condescendingly.[9]

Signs and wonders, truly, like relics of a lost civilization or a Depression-era dreamscape. The collection as a whole was the finest displayed in St. Louis since the city had hosted the 1904 World's Fair, and the previews turned out to be the most heavily trafficked in Selkirk's history, triggering waves of speculation and excitement as a four-day bidding extravaganza ensued. On Monday afternoon, more than a thousand turned out for the first round of the auction, many of whom were "forced to stand" as "spirited bidding" played out for several hours.[10] Some 1,500 showed up for round two that same evening, and Selkirk's ran out of catalogues before it began. Photographs of the event show a densely packed showroom, attendees craning their necks to watch the auctioneer or see what porters had hoisted into place on the velvet-lined platform. A "nerve-tingling atmosphere" took hold in the room as "hundreds of eager bidders" raised their hands. At several tense moments, all eyes seemed glued to a mustachioed man in horn-rimmed glasses in the second row who fiddled with his sheaf of notes and made rapid-fire bids.[11]

Those who had been following the saga of the Campbell probate case in preceding months knew the players. The man with the glasses was Harlow Donovan, a seasoned art dealer bidding on behalf of the William Clark Society (WCS), which in recent months had been working frantically to raise money for a museum devoted to antebellum St. Louis, a time when it had been "one of the most cosmopolitan [cities] in the world."[12] He worked in tandem with "experts" in the WCS, whose members included local businessmen, architects, and engineers (many of them amateur collectors) to place bids on Campbell possessions deemed to have historical or aesthetic significance. But the large crowds complicated the group's plan: Selkirk's decision to open the auction to the public meant the WCS would lose key objects to private bidders with more staying power, and that many of the large sets would be sold piecemeal.[13]

Staking a Public Claim

During the WCS's eleventh-hour campaign to "Save the Campbell House," the idea that the Campbell estate embodied a golden age in St. Louis history had gone from a vague inkling to a publicly articulated rationale in just a couple of months. Internal discussions began in preservation circles but soon moved out to those of city leadership, including the mayor's office. These initial efforts to rally support were unabashedly promoted by the press—to such an extent that, at a time when they might have been overshadowed by stock market instability, mounting war casualties, and a growing footprint of destruction across Europe, everyone in the region seemed to know something about the Campbell estate. Local newspapers reported on fundraising progress on an almost-daily basis, each update more fretful than the last. "Unless last-minute attempts to preserve the home as a museum are successful," the *Globe-Democrat* intoned a week before the auction, "these are probably the last photos to be taken of the mansion and its surrounds intact."[14] The statement came in the middle of a photo-studded article documenting the opening of the Campbell mansion to the first outsiders to enter the house in decades: the WCS and Selkirk's staff. The discoveries they had made on their initial walk-through inspired a flurry of donations. The WCS collected nearly $5,000 in just a week, an impressive sum for a city struggling to sustain social services and pay city employees' salaries.[15] Evidently, the "golden age" ideal had captured the public's imagination; many in the crowd were first-time auction-goers, there mainly to see what all the fuss was about.

Others had less-benign interests. The fate of the Campbell estate had been a subject of dispute—not to mention a concern for historically minded citizens—since Hugh Campbell's passing in 1933. Recent events, including lengthy probate proceedings following Hazlett's 1938 death, as well as city-planning discussions, had increased awareness of the "mystery house" at Fifteenth and Locust. As noted in previous chapters, redevelopment efforts in the vicinity of the Campbell family residence had been uneven but transformative. Locust was now a commercial corridor, its last remaining structures, excepting the Campbell residence, having been torn down in the late 1930s. As the court was hearing testimony from hundreds of would-be Campbell heirs, some from as far away as Ireland,

city officials were discussing the fate of other historic neighborhoods—
the so-called collar of slums that framed downtown, which city leaders viewed as economic liabilities. At the same time, the City Planning
Commission (CPC), armed with millions in New Deal funds, was also
embarking on the largest land-use survey in the city's history, which
authorized the wide-scale clearance described in early chapters.[16]

Thus, interspersed between daily updates on the Campbell estate
hearings and WCS fundraising came notices about progress on the clearance of forty square blocks along the riverfront for a national monument
(the Jefferson National Expansion Memorial) and the opening of housing projects Carr Square Village and Clinton-Peabody in former "slums."
The Jefferson Memorial, a historic district established under the National
Historic Sites Act of 1935, would not be completed for more than twenty
years because of the war.[17] But the housing projects, the first to be funded
through the Federal Housing Act of 1934, represented an impressively
quick response to critical housing shortages and spurred talk of clearance
elsewhere in the city.[18] Such activity would have continued, in fact, were
it not for the United States' entry into the war. That same year, Harland
Bartholomew, the city's chief engineer and a national celebrity in urban
planning, published *St. Louis after World War II,* a report that called for
"massive reconstruction of the built environment."[19] Thus, the physical dismantling of the Campbell estate—*casser maison,* as the divestment
process has been poetically named in Quebec—began while St. Louisans
were watching the dismantlement of several historic neighborhoods
across the city and being urged to consider the effects of "creeping blight"
and "obsolescence" in "tax-gobbling slum districts" near downtown, as
well as unchecked growth at the outer edges.[20]

Needless to say, salvaging an 1850s town house filled with Victorian
furnishings would have no measurable impact on the city's overall civic
and development agenda. Neither would it advance historic preservation
as a principle of planning. Bartholomew often lamented the deterioration of older neighborhoods and spoke of saving historic fabric (generally, the kind located in wealthier districts of the sort modeled on Lucas
Place). But his renewal priorities, which would find their fullest expression in a comprehensive city plan published shortly after the war (1947),
privileged clearance, consolidation, and new construction. Nonetheless,
the WCS's rationale for preserving the Campbell House resonated with

Bartholomew's claims about the need to assert control over the increasingly unruly city, with its aging housing stock, unregulated growth and fragmentation. Between 1930 and 1940, the city of St. Louis had experienced a net decline in population (1%) while St. Louis County saw a staggering 30 percent increase, impacting projects reliant on tax revenues and causing growing concern about the vitality of the city's downtown.[21] Many businesses, and even some venerable old churches (including two that had been anchors of Lucas Place), had relocated to precincts west or were planning to do so, which compounded the disinvestment Bartholomew so desperately sought to address. Those in city government and in fields such as advertising, building, and planning (all well represented on the WCS) were likewise concerned and came to see the Campbells' house as an endangered cultural resource with symbolic significance for the city—an island of stability in the middle of a turgid sea of uncertainty and material change.

Certainly, the house had sentimental appeal, given its distinctive history. But there were other reasons that the WCS chose to save it. Such a preservation project met the need for a unifying social cause during a period of economic, social, and political unease, and lent coherence to amorphous civic longings. And the house itself represented a potential heritage destination that might add to the appeal of downtown. With relatively modest upfront investment, a museum would be established that could be maintained with the funds collected from a low entry fee. In an age when few could afford to travel (once the war started, rationing would prevent it outright), a new historic site that was also reachable by streetcar would, the WCS felt certain, have strong regional appeal. Saving a single half-acre site with its contents "intact," furthermore, seemed more feasible than the elaborate rehabilitation schemes that some in the CPC had been proposing and that had been rejected for the historic riverfront.[22] But it would still be an uphill battle.

Open Bidding

Even with strong public support from the local press, who depicted the campaign as a struggle between civic-minded cultural stewards (Jesse P. Henry, the WCS's mild-mannered spokesman and local "saver of landmarks," for example) and callous developers, it was not at all clear that the WCS could win the battle to "save the Campbell House" and its contents.[23] The market for antiques in a war-taxed economy was unpredictable, as were the behaviors of collectors and local enthusiasts who now had a chance to claim a piece of the much-vaunted "fur-trade fortune." Early bidding was swift: in the first two rounds, every one of the WCS's appraisal estimates was surpassed. On the afternoon of the second day, Henry grumbled about private bidders driving up prices, citing the example of an elaborately carved rosewood piano "worth just $20" that had sold for a hundred dollars thanks to bids motivated by sentiment or self-interest rather than historical attachment. Noble intentions would not be enough to save such pieces from oblivious housewives and buccaneering collectors, he told reporters. Would the citizens of St. Louis see fit to allow the WCS to stake a claim for local heritage and national significance?[24]

By Tuesday evening, it appeared that they would. Despite repeated reminders from the auctioneer that Selkirk's was selling the Campbell goods "purely on a commercial basis," many auction-goers "displayed an obvious reluctance to bid against the [WCS] committee," as the *Globe-Democrat* reported, and fewer than "a score of auction lots upon which the [WCS] bid were purchased [by] outsiders."[25] A columnist for the more-sensationalist *Star-Times* observed that while portions of the Campbell estate "continued to be sold under the decisive thumping of the auctioneer's hammer," when "Ben J. Selkirk had chanted his last price of [Tuesday] evening," the committee had obtained "the bulk of the pieces it desires to retain in the house which it expects to refurbish and turn into a museum in about six months."[26] Still, the press's triumphant tone could not fully conceal the undercurrent of anxiety shared by WCS members and their allies. For crowds continued to assemble, among them not only the expected "society matrons" and dealers but innumerable curious onlookers, amateur collectors and treasure-hunters, local descendants, and even some of the family's household staff.[27] The only group not evidently in attendance were the Campbell heirs, who stood to collect thousands from this most dramatic *casser maison*.

These were crowds the WCS had built through public campaigning but now could not control, and the group was forced to adjust its strategy midway through the auction. On Tuesday, Jesse Henry paid emergency visits to see the Advertising Club (an influential group of marketing executives and local commerce promoters whose membership overlapped with the WCS) and other corporate backers to petition for additional funds that would allow the WCS to fulfill its promises to the public. Thanks to his efforts, the club ultimately donated $1,500, but Henry later confessed that this was an especially "dark" moment—one in which the auction committee had confronted the strong possibility of failure.[28] The WCS's purchases later that day—a calfskin rug, a mahogany tilt-table, a fine enamel tea and coffee service, a pair of imported gilt candelabra, and other items—made the front pages, and many declared the mostly completed auction a coup for its campaign. But by then, the group had already lost—or, as its members preferred to say, "let go"—dozens, perhaps hundreds, of objects that once graced the Campbell home, including plate-glass mirrors, rosewood chairs, oak and mahogany tables, a walnut high chest, bed linens, draperies, men's jewelry and clothing, and a bearskin rug stitched with Robert Campbell's initials.[29]

Harlow Donovan and Jesse Henry made no bids whatsoever on the Persian rugs and Chinese teak- and lacquerware, imported textiles and tapestries the family had collected during its travels abroad. And they stood by resignedly as the family's silver, crystal, glassware, and decorative arts collections were divided into lots.[30] Items purchased as ensembles and displayed on the same mantel or tea table for decades were sold piecemeal, their household relationships permanently lost. The committee secured only half the hand-painted French porcelain supposedly purchased for a famous Ulysses S. Grant dinner, for example; the rest, including several showy serving pieces, would be sold to dealers. But the group celebrated its acquisition anyhow, noting the set's "historic significance" and hefty price tag ($750 for 161 pieces)—the largest paid for any "single offering at the auction," and to its great relief, less than the members would have paid on the "open market."[31] It was a distressing situation, a bit like watching the breakup of a family.[32]

Enough?

At the end of each new round, the WCS auction committee's members again reassured reporters—and, it would seem, themselves—that they had secured "enough the of the Campbell home furnishings to create an authentic museum of St. Louis civil war and pre-civil war days."[33] Their conception of "enough" had evolved considerably since the start of the museum campaign and even since their tour of the house the week before, when there was still talk of making an offer on the entire estate as a single lot. Such an opportunity to preserve the whole thing intact never came to pass, and by the time of their walk-through, the household had already been "partially dismantled." During their cataloguing, Selkirk's representatives had taken down artwork, unloaded bureaus, bookshelves, and closets, and hauled smaller furnishings to their showroom. When the WCS's auction committee entered the Campbell home for the first time it discovered that while most of the bigger items were still onsite, they had been moved around and small items, including "clothes, books, [and] all manner of [personal belongings,] were in confusion on the deep-pile carpets," much of it the result of Selkirk's rifling.[34]

This rifling had a significant impact on the WCS members' first impressions of what they began calling the "collection" but also, crucially, on their sense of the Campbells' symbolic and domestic ecologies—the underlying material-spatial-social logics that defined the glorious old Victorian home.[35] If such logics revealed the values and uses of a specific period in time—and this was the premise on which the WCS's claims that the house was a specimen "artifact of its time" were made—they were no longer intact or available for study. Put simply, the domestic world that was "opened" to them was *not* intact; it had already been jostled, broken apart, and resorted according to a logic of commoditization the WCS never acknowledged. When its auction committee emerged from the Campbell residence declaring the "unanimous verdict" that "some means should be found for preserving the house and its furnishings as a public museum," the members characterized it as a marvel of "untouched mid-nineteenth-century magnificence" without apparent irony or ambivalence.[36]

Yet those involved in the appraisal brought distinctly different frameworks for understanding this sort of "magnificence." Some, including Perry Rathbone, the director of the City Art Museum (today's St. Louis Art Museum) and Marjorie Douglas, a member of the staff of the Missouri Historical Society, had curatorial sensibilities and tended to think in terms of craft and aesthetic appeal; they focused mainly on high-end furniture and art. The more historically minded, among them Arthur C. Hoskins, advertising executive and chairman of the Historic Sites Committee of the local Chamber of Commerce; Charles Nagel, architect and representative of the local Architects' Committee on Preservation of Historic Buildings; and Ned J. Burns, the chief of the Museums Division of the National Park Service, emphasized "period" look, advocating for acquisition of all of the oldest furnishings in the collection (mid-1850s or earlier) and anything associated with the fur trade. Political and business leaders, the city's newly installed mayor, Joseph Darst, foremost among them, were, however, more concerned with showpieces—those whose heavy ornamentation signified "Victorian extravagance" (although that quality might well have been attributed to most of the house's contents).[37]

The idea of material intactness—the supposed "untouched" condition of the Campbell possessions—was likewise an unstable concept. To some it apparently meant some combination of "mint condition" and "beautiful," while to others it signified subtler qualities of age and stood for objects that both looked and felt "old," that had a "patina" or aura of antiqueness. For individuals from local cultural institutions like Rathbone, who likely had the Metropolitan Museum of Art's period-room schematic in mind (several such rooms having been recently installed in St. Louis's City Art Museum), the term meant a more specific ideal of historical, stylistic, and visual integrity. The fact that the house's decor was actually an eclectic mix (a few inherited late federalist pieces; a large quantity of mid-1850s rococo and neoclassical Philadelphia furniture; and some 1890s Beaux Arts wallpapers, carpets, and objects imported from various locations worldwide) seems not to have fully registered.[38] The WCS committee indulged a certain willful naiveté in claiming that the contents of the Campbell House made it representative of "the most-fashionable residential section [in the city] during the post–Civil War period," and that this status was proven by the presence of the "finest collection of art and furniture a man of taste and means could assemble."[39] No one questioned these tautologies nor asked why a fiction of historical-material integrity had to be spun at all.

Anyhow, time was a-wasting: the group's ballpark estimate of the value of choice objects would have to be acted on immediately. The WCS settled on a vague mid-nineteenth century—the period of the house's origin—as its target timeframe and set a fundraising minimum of $5,000.[40] Henry made a point of stressing more than once that the committee would make no bids whatsoever if it were unable to reach this threshold. It was a matter of principle: if the group could not secure "enough" to make a "representative showing," it would return every dime to its donors.[41] Committee members understood that some of the target objects were not especially prized among modern collectors but asserted that, as a group, these items had "tremendous value as a record of life in St. Louis in the 1850s."[42] By Sunday afternoon—less than twelve hours before the first auction began—they had managed to secure the required sum, much of it coming in small increments: a few cents each given by hundreds of enthusiastic schoolchildren, a dollar or two sent in by retirees, a series of donations from working St. Louisans, and of course several larger amounts from wealthy friends.[43] In the weeks to come, these donations would repeatedly be referenced as evidence of broad public support for the cause.

Next came a final round of list-making, which might well have simply restated the decisions made during the onsite appraisal process. But the WCS found itself constrained by the auction house's categorization schema, which would complicate efforts to bid selectively. In a philosophical sense, choosing from among items in any given category, or indeed choosing any subset of the Campbell estate, was at odds with the group's stated intention. As Henry and his colleagues frequently noted, the truly remarkable thing about the family's possessions—the quality that made them unique and museum-worthy—was their degree of intactness: "Probably nowhere in America, possibly nowhere else, is such an integral and intact display of the elaborate and ornate furnishings of the middle-Victorian period to be found."[44] As they finished their tour of the house, WCS members claimed to have discovered a domestic universe seemingly unaltered by time:

> Still against the walls were the great gilded mirrors, with their French rococo frames, canopying clear across the drawing room. Still on the walls were family portraits and painted copies of masterpieces, ranging from a detail of Murillo's Assumption to Guido Reni's Aurora. Statues of no particular distinction, yet interesting in that setting, stood below

the great ornate chandeliers. A curious music stand held a Strauss waltz published in St. Louis in 1875 by Weber & Balmer. There was a square, mahogany piano. Great mid-Victorian pieces of mahogany with marble tops stood vacant. . . . A steel engraving of the U.S. Senate—way back—was on a stairwell wall. All was of a piece. A period piece! It was a section of St. Louis from the golden age of steamboatin', from the days when this city was the gateway to the west, when there still flowed into the city the riches of the fur trade and gold from western mines.[45]

Such a parlor could be said to symbolize not only historical continuity but a kind of material-moral-cultural integrity—an aura of permanence—of the sort WCS wished to claim.

Still, the actual choosing represented a practical challenge. To judge by surviving invoices and annotated copies of the *Dispersal Resumé* and numerous press accounts, the WCS's official game plan was to bid on major furniture items (the dining room, parlor, and bedroom suites; the piano; and other conspicuous pieces such as a large étagère); art objects with regional appeal (the Bingham painting) or biographical significance (family portraits, the buckskin coats); and decorative items that would contribute atmospherically (mirrors, lamps, valances, etc.). The members paid no attention to items found on the third floor, including Hugh's and Hazlett's personal belongings, much less the "old beds and bureaus . . . in the 'help's' quarters," which they believed were lacking in "age and value."[46] Anything that was not both "Victorian" and a "museum piece," nor conspicuously associated with the original owners, was expendable.[47] Anticipating future period-room-style exhibitions, they also sought items that bore a clear relationship to a given display logic, for example pairs of lamps, side-tables, and chairs.

From this set of decisions emerged an ideal of high-society antebellum St. Louis, a world defined by order, grace, and material integrity and untouched by the messiness of daily life in the city, much less of Hazlett's mental illness or a court-ordered dispersal. The WCS privileged the period "before"—when the Campbells' marriage and household were new, when the nation had not yet gone to war, when the rich controlled most of the city, and when St. Louis was the most economically powerful urban center in the West. Like the Locust Street mansion in which the group planned to display these glorious things, the newly curated collection was a kind of glittering gem plucked from the unruly heap of the modern city—or so it had come to be seen by those who believed they were intervening in a crisis situation.[48]

"It's *Mine* Now!": Private Claims on Local Heritage

American Victorian Taxidermy Specimens (under glass)
Sumptuous bird of paradise on a naturalistic perch.
Regina Mahogany-Case Mechanical Disc Music Box
Mechanism and twelve playing discs enclosed within glass-paneled case.
Table-type understructure with shelf.
 —*Two of the Campbells' possessions as represented
in the* Dispersal Resumé

The biggest challenge to securing this newly conceived collection was bidding by private individuals, which drove up prices and chipped away at such principles of integrity. The presence of such competition created considerable apprehension for WCS members on the auction house floor, where a "spectacle of valuation" played out—the kind of dramatic encounter between competing interests, ideals of ownership, and claims of significance that is so common at estate auctions, but was relatively new to many in attendance.[49] In the early modern period, as Cynthia Wall has argued, this drama corresponded with broader processes of wealth redistribution, as when estates owned by England's landed gentry came to be "dismantled" and acquired by the bourgeoisie. Playing to the interests of the newly wealthy, celebrity auctioneers such as Christie's and Sotheby's staged auctions as pageants of acquisition drenched in social-symbolic meaning. By treating sales not only as contexts for claiming ownership but ceremonies of legitimation, they could maximize their profits.[50] The auctioneer and his experts would assess value and authenticity before bidding began, and—not surprisingly—their assessments were typically reinforced by the public. Such ceremonies of legitimation reflected the broader dynamics of the growing capitalist market economy and informed pricing and fashions in other cultural sectors, as they still do today. But for the wealthy at least, they also forestalled the most troubling effects of *casser maison* by allowing for the reconstellation of esteemed old collections in new households.

During the Depression in the United States, these dynamics shifted significantly, and not just because of economic crisis. As American cities continued to industrialize and spread out geographically, many gained in population even as their status and property values underwent dramatic downward shifts. As we have seen, this set of changes was especially noticeable in St. Louis, where once-massive industrial and land wealth held by families like the Campbells eroded and capital investment, as well as the location of the richest households, shifted to regions outside the city limits.[51] The impacts of such material dispersal were evident in neighborhoods where the poorest and most transient populations lived, as city planners certainly registered, but even some of the brownstone mansions built by the city's railroad, beer, and real-estate tycoons were starting to show signs of neglect and declining property values by the late 1930s. Not unlike the case of vast country estates once controlled by Britain's nobility, the decline and eventual dispersal of these properties signaled the arrival of a new ownership class along with efforts to manage the value of these former elites' possessions. If St. Louisans had previously lacked full awareness of such changes, the saga of the Campbell estate provided a quick tutorial. Even middle- and working-class St. Louisans seem to have registered the symbolic significance of the "dispersal" of the Campbell's property, and some made bids on the family's possessions with these things in mind.

But what were all these bidders after? And why would anyone purchase a music box that plays old waltzes or indeed a pair of "Victorian Taxidermy Specimens (under glass)" in a depression economy? Neither of these items was particularly fashionable anymore, and both were garish and expensive—hardly classifiable as token souvenirs. One obvious explanation is their status as former luxury items: both were "sumptuous" not only in appearance but in association with the very rich. Like many Campbell objects that found buyers at Selkirk's that week, furthermore, both had the appeal of decipherable provenance—a history of ownership and point of origin that, as Jean Baudrillard has argued, gives antiques their special status, especially for collectors who wish to claim some relationship to aristocratic legacies.[52] While provenance is often confirmed by evidence such as receipts, affidavits of ownership, or marks of age and use (often termed "patina"), collectors are also drawn to more amorphous qualities of association and character that cannot be proven—the "numinosity" of a given historic object.[53]

Patina and numinosity can, however, be affirmed through rituals of valuation. In this case, much of it happened offstage before bidding began. Selkirk's catalogue provided a shorthand for those qualities that buyers could verify with up-close observation at the previews. And the auction house's staging techniques—gloved handling, fawning verbal descriptions, velvet-lined pedestals—further heightened the sense of preciousness and value. All the items in the auction had beforehand been ascribed a degree of ancestral significance, association with an esteemed family that gives material goods a sense of lineage, significance, and even moral grandeur. Baudrillard explains that the quality of "inward transcendence" many antiques seem to possess is rooted in a fantasy of origins.[54] These objects seem to represent a symbolic point of (familial or cultural) origin and a chain of connection "back" to that point. The catalogue notes, for example, that items for sale had been part of the "home established by ROBERT CAMPBELL, father of the late HUGH CAMPBELL, who upon his death in 1931 bequeathed the [estate] . . . to Yale University," and press accounts reiterated these details.[55] And some Campbell possessions announced their own ancestral significance—for example, the silver tea service engraved with Virginia's initials or the stuffed birds, which (subconsciously at least) could be interpreted as memory objects or even relics.

But even as the auction confirmed certain elements of ancestral association, it stripped away or downplayed others, among them private meanings and idiosyncratic histories that did not align with official narratives about the city's glorious past. Most obviously, the objects' recent history and significance for the younger generation of Campbells were never acknowledged, despite the fact that they had been their final owners and that Hugh was the caretaker responsible for the house's revered intactness. Selkirk's in fact showed little interest in the biographies of *any* of the owners, attending mainly to aesthetics, age of manufacture, and style. The woman who wrote the *Dispersal Resumé* had been guided through the house by the Campbells' longtime servant Augustus Myers, who cared for Hugh and Hazlett in their old age, but the author made not a single reference to "inside" knowledge about the family and their possessions that Myers is known to have shared. Occasionally, a tidbit would surface in press accounts, but such facts played no part in the emergent narrative of the house as a historic site and museum collection. Nor did it impact the valuation process. Bidders interested in historical significance or stories of ownership such as those featured on *Antiques Roadshow* had to use their own imagination.[56]

There did, however, seem to be a few bidders of this type: an unnamed "Clayton resident," for example, paid seventy dollars for a silver tray engraved with the Campbell crest for the museum out of a sense of commitment to history. The matching pieces of the silver garniture set were purchased shortly thereafter by a "distant relative" of the Campbells who could not bear to see them sold to collectors, and a local businessman bid on a "favorite painting" of the "pioneer fur trader and founder of the Campbell fortune," which he believed "belonged with the house."[57] Made by citizens who wished to support the WCS, many of these purchases also involved aesthetic valuation. The mahogany music box, which sold for $52.50 and caught the attention of the press, had a strong Campbell association but was described mainly in terms of its beauty and expense. And the music box's purchaser was not a member of the local elite; he was a tradesman named Theodore Harris with a touching backstory. "Crippled since childhood from infantile paralysis," he had once lived in Father Dunne's Newsboys' Home, the orphanage in which Hugh Campbell had been so "intensely interested," and was later hired by Hugh to install the music box in 1915—a job he fondly recalled for a reporter all these decades later. A front-page article on the subject included a photograph of the dressed-up Harris smiling triumphantly over his purchase, his weathered face seeming to confirm the reporter's hypothesis that although he was "only 39 years old, he had lived a hard life."[58]

Harris cut a modest figure compared to the well-dressed citizens who had gathered at Selkirk's, and his story had a *Ragged Dick* quality about it: the poor laborer who must suffer humiliations to attend the auction (he reportedly struggled to get up the stairs on his crutches) suddenly finds himself in possession of a remarkable heritage object. Through steadfastness, he has earned not only a material but a moral victory. "I've got it! It's mine now!" he reportedly shouted upon hearing that he had won the bidding, nearly falling off his crutches as he waved his arms from where he stood in the audience. If the *Post-Dispatch*'s supercilious account suggested something less than full tolerance of Harris's working-class manners, the newspaper nonetheless treated him as a sympathetic victim of circumstances. On some level, he represented the collective indignities of economic decline; his right to ownership was based not on nobility or inheritance but on efforts to overcome adversity and rehabilitative labors. Readers learned that Harris intended to fix up the music box and "keep it to brighten [his] old age," and that "if his luck held," he might buy another that was slated for auction later in the week.[59] The fact that he needed a small loan from "an old friend" to make the purchase seemed to underscore his legitimacy; there was poetic justice in his purchase that all those "swooning women," with their status obsession and empty sentimentality, could never achieve.

St. Louis needed this story of rightful repossession; it dignified the whole enterprise of saving the Campbell House as a site of public memory. While the WCS could not preserve everything the house once contained, it could pursue symbolic reclamation on behalf of "the people." And while the loss of the music box and other such items was regrettable from the standpoint of the integrity of the site, it anticipated future arguments about the need to save other objects that had no such claimants. Like the small donations sent in by newsboys and other working-class St. Louisans, furthermore, Harris's purchase confirmed what the WCS would characterize as a "whole-hearted response" to its call for public support of the campaign.[60] The *Post-Dispatch* profile of him ended with an approving note about the WCS's efforts to "preserve the house and its most important contents intact as a public museum," quoting Jesse Henry's declaration that "victory seems in sight!"[61] Harris's investment in the music box exemplified the group's own civic-minded stewardship, at least as the members understood it—a kind of everyman's desire to preserve that had the added virtue of sincerity. Letting the music box fall into Harris's hands not only seemed humane but pragmatic. Perhaps they even imagined he would someday give the music box back, his efforts to keep it in working condition serving the integrity agenda in the end.

The purchases of another, far better endowed supporter of the campaign also made headlines that week, though they signified a very different style of stewardship. The same day Harris acquired the music box, renowned dress designer Grace Ashley (a.k.a. "Mrs. Harry Papin of the Central West End" neighborhood, a bastion of moneyed elites) went after the most revered—and, as it turned out, the priciest—of the parlor furnishings. Ashley was something of a media darling whose ready-to-wear "shirtwaist" dress designs had brought her a windfall in the previous decade. She was also known for her philanthropy, and her involvement in the campaign to save the Campbell House automatically raised its profile. Before the auction began, she announced that she would bid on a whole room of Campbell furniture for the museum, and she wound up spending a lot more, at least $1,830.[62] Ashley reported to "surprising even herself" when she bid on many other objects—vintage textiles, a pair of Cantonese vases, two carved wooden easels, and other small furnishings—apparently intended for her private collection. She explained to a reporter that she thought "someone ought to donate a complete room . . . [but no] one else offered, so under the combined lure of the auction and the furnishings, I succumbed."[63] While she had more than a museum in mind, the press painted Ashley as an altruist, the *Star-Times* devoting a front-page spread to her "saving" of the parlor furnishings, the "Victorian costumes," and more than a dozen "other items," including "the bulk of the pieces" the WCS "desire[d]" on day three of the auction.[64] Thus, both public and private, modest and extravagant, acquisitions served to legitimize the work of the WCS during the auction. Taken together, they seemed to prove that St. Louisans had indeed done "enough," and that they had done it together.

It's *Ours* Now: The WCS Takes Possession

Buoyancy of tone notwithstanding, the likelihood that all these purchases would lead to the establishment of a public museum rather than the enrichment of private collections was still something of a question. The aforementioned *Star-Times* article carried a headline—"Who Would Own the Campbell House as Museum Unsettled"—that literally hung in the space between the profiles of Harris and Ashley, implicitly asking whose interests would actually carry the day. And many bidders, little guys and elites alike, had mixed motives. Several WCS members purchased lots they would then divide into "keep" and "donate" piles, and they often had personal reasons for purchasing items they later gave to the museum. When Ashley bid on Virginia Campbell's dresses, she was building up a private collection that several years later would be installed in a semi-permanent "Costume Room" museum exhibit named in her honor and paid for by the St. Louis Fashion Creators, a garment industry guild she had founded. In many respects, the textiles collection symbolized her life's work, much as did Harris's small collection of music boxes. Different as the two bidders appear on the surface, both suggest the degree to which claims of ancestral significance could be bound up in private interests and needs.[65]

Selkirk's officials too had mixed intentions. While they emphasized the priority of "open bidding," they quietly authorized the WCS's idiosyncratic preservation agenda, at times actively colluding with the group. Henry and Donovan got just about everything they deemed significant, and other WCS members secured items they desired as well. Their patterned style of bidding suggests advance conversations had taken place and may even have informed the chosen process of dispersal that week. At the end of the last auction session, when Selkirk and Henry took the stage together, the former spoke first, thanking "the people for the interest they had taken and the consideration they had shown in refraining from bidding against Henry," which, at least one local paper acknowledged, amounted to "thanking them for a course of action which had been hurtful to his business."[66] Then Henry made a little speech acknowledging Selkirk's for its expert management of the unusually large event, and the citizens of St. Louis for their support of the campaign. In the days to come, Selkirk's allowed the WCS to negotiate for unsold items for modest prices instead of rolling them into future auctions, and the auction house waived its usual restrictions on long-term storage—a form of behind-the-scenes support and "discretion" for which the firm became known. Not long after, it was named the official appraiser for the U.S. District Court for Eastern Missouri, a tremendously influential position that it held for decades.[67]

In the final assessment, the auction was a coup for the WCS and its supporters in the business community. For while the group lost its grip on some of the Campbell possessions, it gained control over the social-symbolic meanings of items it did acquire and asserted a persuasive argument for the idea that the would-be collection was all "of a piece" and thus worth saving as a museum. The spectacle of valuation confirmed the WCS members' role as cultural stewards of this collection, and while bidders from many walks of life showed enthusiasm for the Campbell possessions, in the end most deferred to the WCS as self-declared agents of local heritage.

Despite all the background noise of the competing of opportunists, treasure-seekers, and "swooning women," furthermore, the WCS dominated the stage, using the auction to legitimize its claims on the "Prominent Civil War Residence" as a site of public memory. The auction became a valuable platform from which to exhort St. Louisans for support. Even at the end of the dispersal process, Henry pleaded with those who had purchased Campbell possessions to return them to the museum and asked for additional donations.[68] At the same time, the auction gave the objects that the WCS had secured a kind of social visibility and moral grandeur—an aura of authenticity—that trailed behind them, and the larger museum collection, like the tail on a comet. The group's sense of what mattered about these items became the basis for subsequent claims of the collection's cultural-historical significance, informing press accounts, museum interpretation, and public perception for years to come.

Yet the auction revealed a subtler aura that hung about the possessions of the former fur trader and his family—one of unfulfilled longings, quiet ambivalences, a sense of loss or even shame. Given all the threats to the city's well-being, its physical and social intactness, there was a futility in trying to control the material-symbolic resources of the city, as WCS members were coming to understand. These feelings comprised a darker subtext—what I have called the memorial unconscious—at work in the "Save the Campbell House" campaign and indeed in historic preservation more generally. At key moments, the auction revealed the public's uncertainty about the changing face of their city and a willingness to aggressively, if at times opportunistically, resist that change. The threat of dispersal of the high-profile estate represented many things, not all of them articulable: material losses St. Louis had already felt and would continue to inflict upon itself; the growing problem of disinvestment from the city's urban core, and the accompanying dispersal of political power, already well underway; and a growing distance from its own nineteenth-century history. Put more simply, the drama at Selkirk's was for many St. Louisans—the WCS among them—a spectacle of valuation in the deepest sense. It involved the renegotiation of the very claims of significance and shared identity that had given the city its existing sense of integrity and would inform future acts of possession of its material assets.

CHAPTER 4

THE OPENING

"The War Has Stopped Our Effort"

A S THE TENSE week of the Campbell estate auction came to an end
in February 1941, members of the William Clark Society (WCS)
and their allies had reason to celebrate. With the endorsement of politicians, business elites, and the local media, they had raised $15,000 in
donations from a cash-strapped city, including $8,000 in "popular sub-
scriptions" from citizens who wished to see the town house at 15th and
Locust saved as "an enduring monument to the American way."[1] And, in
spite of competition from private bidders, they had secured "enough" of
the Campbell family possessions to justify ongoing solicitation of funds
in support of the creation of "a truly representative Victorian period
museum."[2] The *St. Louis Post-Dispatch* declared their work a triumph,
adopting the war rhetoric that had crept into so much daily speech:
"Victory has been won in the first phase of the campaign to create a
museum reminiscent of the days when westward-bound wagon trains
rumbled romantically through the unpaved streets of a bawdy, booming
St. Louis!" They urged St. Louisans to "take satisfaction" in this victory,
adding that it would "be an empty triumph unless the next phase is
negotiated with equal success."[3] The WCS likewise voiced optimism, for
while the Campbell mansion sat on a highly desirable piece of property,
officials from Yale University had expressed a willingness to "cooperate
fully" with the city in its sale.[4]

But St. Louisans were distracted. Like Americans across the nation,
they were preoccupied by housing shortages, labor strikes, and the

economic pressures caused by war-related spending freezes. And it would be difficult to get their attention as an air of instability set in due to the nation's anticipated entry into the war. Only a few hundred dollars trickled into WCS coffers during March and April despite active campaigning in the business community. But Jesse Henry, Grace Ashley, and their colleagues in the newly established Campbell House Foundation (CHF) pressed on, launching a new $15,000 campaign in early May that began with a tickets-only luncheon at the luxurious Hotel Chase. While an orchestra played "old-fashioned waltzes," local debutantes wearing Virginia Campbell's gowns and "period accessories" (those Ashley had purchased at auction) promenaded across a stage set with choice furnishings from the Campbell parlor. Later in the day, the general public was treated to a pageant by the local Boy Scouts (some wearing Robert's buckskin suits) and rides in the family's 1860s horse-drawn carriage. CHF members participated in a live radio broadcast touting the heritage value of the would-be museum, and the press enthused loudly about the tantalizing objects in the collection.[5]

But the funds raised to date would not be enough to acquire—much less restore—the Campbell residence, and by late May newspaper accounts of CHF activity (advanced by core members of the WCS, many of whom served as CHF board members) were once again tinged with worry.[6] Henry expressed perplexity as the *Post-Dispatch* reversed its earlier claims, predicting the campaign would have to be abandoned.[7] The city's newly installed mayor, William Dee Becker, voiced strong support of the campaign, imploring citizens to dig deep to save a local landmark.[8] One local citizen urged schoolchildren to donate their pennies and nickels (Henry had made a similar plea before the St. Louis Board of Education months earlier), and another opined that if St. Louis did not have "*many* persons ready and glad to join in the acquisition and preservation of the last survivor of Old Lucas place and its nineteenth century magnificence, it is poor indeed." Writing from Hannibal, Missouri, the chairman of the Municipal Board charged with maintaining Mark Twain's historic home, which had opened as a museum in 1912, urged St. Louisans to acknowledge what a remarkable asset it had in the Campbell House, a site that, unlike the Twain house, could be preserved intact with the very "furniture used by a man who helped to make St. Louis the great trading point it is today."[9]

The CHF certainly agreed; they had been making the same arguments for years, much as their counterparts in other cities were doing with historic structures that had fallen on hard times during the Depression.[10] In spite of real concerns about how it looked to be petitioning a public so "distracted by war news and high taxes," the group pressed ahead, running weekly advertisements soliciting donations.[11] But it appeared the war had stalled the campaign. Later that fall, alongside reports of decisive Nazi victories in the Soviet Union and the strong expectation that the United States was going to enter the war, St. Louisans learned that the interminable Campbell probate case was finally coming to a close: modest payments from the sale of the "city's most famed trust estate" would be distributed to 161 "collateral heirs" from Central Iowa, Kansas City, New York City, and County Tyrone, Ireland.[12] Reports about an eleventh-hour appeal of this ruling heard by the Missouri Supreme Court were eclipsed by news of the bombing of Pearl Harbor and, apart from a long-planned event hosted by the Women's Advertising Club—a subdued "Gay Nineties" Skating Party featuring more debutantes in period costumes—the CHF was forced to cease public fundraising.[13]

Many presumed the Locust Street mansion, along with other parcels of Campbell-owned property that had been deeded to Yale, would be sold to private developers.[14] Henry traveled to New Haven to relay distress about this likelihood to the university's president; to everyone's surprise, he returned with a ninety-day option to buy the house for the "bargain price" of $10,000.[15] But the foundation still had to raise half that sum, so once again, he and his colleagues pleaded with a public preoccupied with war rationing and scrap metal collection to claim their "share in preserving this historic landmark for future generations."[16]

Hedging its bets, the CHF also cast about in search of some other "Victorian-type residence" in the city that might be a suitable location for display of the Campbell possessions, suggesting there was considerable leeway in their principle of "integral and intact display."[17] The Board of Trustees of the Missouri Botanical Gardens turned down the CHF's request to use Henry Shaw's 1849 Italianate "country house" in Tower Grove (designed by well-known architect George I. Barnett) in this fashion, and no other viable options seemed in evidence.[18] The CHF had run out of ideas—and friends with deep pockets.

"Please Accept as Our Gift the Campbell House"

But then, right as the ninety days were running out, a corporate donor stepped forward. The exciting news item was wedged in among daily war reports in September 1942. The "historic landmark" would be saved thanks to a gift from owners of the St. Louis–based Stix, Baer & Fuller (SBF), a high-end retailer founded in 1892 whose enormous flagship department store occupied a whole block of Washington Avenue less than a mile from the Campbell house.[19] Yale had been on the verge of selling to a developer when SBF made an offer "on behalf of the city" to buy the property for $10,000, which the university turned over to the CHF for "safekeeping." Store executives kept the plan quiet for weeks, apparently so that the news would break during a well-choreographed (and suitably modest) fiftieth anniversary celebration.[20]

SBF's "gift to the city" was not a disinterested act. It sought to tap into the well of public enthusiasm for a site associated with the city's glory days, when (as they chose to describe it) "the unpaved streets of a bawdy, booming St. Louis were lined with [such] mansions." The day the story broke, the company ran a full-page ad in the *Globe-Democrat* announcing its "anniversary wish to enrich . . . the great city that has given us the confidence by which we have grown," adding that, while "no single gift can repay that debt," saving the Campbell residence as "a shrine for St. Louisans of today and the tomorrows that are ahead to visit and enjoy" was a good start.[21]

Company executives had been paying attention during all those months of talk about the "one civic asset in which all St. Louisans may take pride." They saw in the house a way to boost public morale while improving the reputation of neighborhoods near downtown. Despite some war-related growth, the area continued to experience overall decline, high unemployment among its poorer residents (especially black workers, who had largely been kept from jobs in war industries), increasing disinvestment by whites (which was already impacting tax revenues), crime, and pollution. While saving the house could do little to slow these trends, investing in cultural heritage served as a symbolic counter to negative press, especially the sort related to strikes and civil rights protests in the city, among them the "Double Victory" demonstrations against white-owned businesses staged by organizers of the March on

Washington Movement. At one such rally, held at the Civic Opera House (three blocks south of the Campbells' house), activist gave speeches arguing that saving democracy at home—meaning granting full citizenship for all African Americans—would ensure victory for democracy abroad. Several incidents of white-on-black violence followed, raising concerns about a possible "race war" in the city and compounding anxieties about the city's "decline."[22]

In a political moment such as this, Campbell House "heritage" took on new connotations. Conceived as a museum devoted to a nineteenth-century "spot of growth" associated with elite (white) control of the city, it would come to be perceived as a symbol of all that such control had once meant, and might still mean, for the city. SBF wagered that its reputation among the most powerful St. Louisans would be strengthened by association with the "sole survivor" of the city's first exclusive private suburb.[23] And in the months that followed, its promotions department worked vigorously to establish material and symbolic links among the house, SBF's corporate persona, and the city's ethos of private control.

SBF would promote the house as an appealing wartime destination and a source of civic pride, drawing inspiration—and even some Campbell family possessions—from the new museum collection for its campaigns. An exhibit of Virginia's antebellum-era gowns and some of the "furnishings that once graced the Campbell parlour," for example, were exhibited in SBF's downtown store windows while the house was being fixed up for its grand opening.[24] Later, the company unveiled a "Lucas Place 1944 Victorian Wonderland" display inspired by the "magnificent homes" of the old neighborhood on the sixth floor of the same building. Designed to evoke the feeling of "walking into a dream—a dream of a lush, Victorian setting," the exhibit included period objects said to be "salvaged from attics and obscure shops" and refurbished so that their "gracious beauty" was "greatly enhanced."[25] Both of these exhibits adopted the logics of display that the CHF would use for the new museum.

Had SBF not emphasized "gracious beauty" over extravagance, and salvaged goods over fine antiques, such a display might have seemed distasteful to wartime consumers. And the company's self-restraint did not last after the war: within a few years, marketing aimed at middle- and upper-class white women would brazenly celebrate this same "Victorian past" in its most lavish permutations, explicitly linking the Campbell House with upper-middle-class fantasies of the "good life" that dominated postwar consumer culture. One memorable advertisement from 1946 presented the museum as a scene of conspicuous leisure: a pair of young mothers and their children—"Proud St. Louisans . . . show[ing] off" at the house—are shown standing before a pier mirror in the Campbell House Museum (CHM) parlor, admiring themselves as much as their surroundings. The "young sprouts" sport knickers and a pinafore dress from SBF's "Young St. Louisan" collection (prices and descriptions included at the bottom of the ad), and ad makers have playfully swapped out the stuffed bird usually displayed inside a bell jar for a bobby sock, a pair of "Tucker detachable collars," and a flowered hairpin all sold by SBF. "Bring your history-maker in tomorrow" for "the cream of the crop in fabrics, designers, and tailors," mothers were advised.[26]

Not long after the ad ran, SBF staged an all-day event that likewise linked bourgeois consumption with the Campbell House. After a tour of the museum, women who were in town with their husbands for an advertising conference hosted by the Ad Club were treated to "demonstration[s] of gracious living today," a fashion show, an interior decorating presentation, and a luncheon at the Missouri Room, SBF's swanky in-house restaurant.[27] In these and other postwar promotions, SBF drew explicit associations between the lifestyles of elites past and present. It also sought to recoup the "prestige factor" of its earlier charitable act, as had many other corporations during wartime.[28]

Saving the Campbell House not only represented SBF's legacy of corporate largesse but served as an opportunity to craft new narratives about its role in a rapidly changing city. The aforementioned advertisement announcing its 1942 "gift" to the city included visual elements comprising a distinct brand identity that they would use in promotional material for years to come. Perhaps drawn by the same artist who later produced the "young sprouts" image, the ad shows a pint-size Campbell House nestled in a woman's outstretched palm (fig. 8). She is holding up—and protecting—the property while also presenting it to the city as a token of appreciation, as a "memorial to an unforgettable epoch," as the copy reads. Floating nearby are other hand-drawn symbols of "Old St. Louis": a horse-drawn carriage, an album containing a portrait of a woman in a

Victorian gown, and an hourglass framed by a flow of bunting draped between two gold rings, a common fiftieth anniversary symbol. SBF used a similar insignia on its packaging that year; every new dress shirt or hat purchased at the store went home in a box with gold rings on it, and other promotional material used the motif as well.

By positioning one ring next to the company's logo and the other near the house, designers evidently meant to suggest SBF's sense of devotion, sacralizing the bond between city and corporation as a marriage rooted in a love of local history. More subtly, the ad associated local history with claims of private ownership and "gracious living," evoking new forms of domestic consumption as a means of tapping that legacy. But the image had other valences as well. Depicting the miniature Campbell House as a kind of landmark on a tourist map, or a piece on a Monopoly board, the ad suggested that SBF and its proxies now controlled the site and its meanings. In later advertising the motif served as a stand-in for the company's actual logo, reminding readers that SBF had "saved" the property and claimed the building as its own, part of its corporate portfolio, even if the property actually "belonged to the public." While less aggressive an act of self-promotion than emblazoning its name across the top of the house itself (like "Anheuser-Busch" on St. Louis's baseball stadium), SBF nevertheless marked the Campbell House as branded property. The woman's gesture could be read not just as an act of *giving* but of *taking*, or at least of *taking credit*, her upturned hand showing SBF taking possession of the house in both material and symbolic ways.

Even if we read the act as one of benign saving—of "giving the house back to the city"— or ceremonial consecration, we can see in the gesture a latent aggression toward those who might claim the house for another purpose or tell its history in some other way. No doubt, the company chose a woman's hand because it softened and domesticated the message— and appropriately so, given that preservation of the home and collective memory had historically been the domain of women. These ideals found expression in countless wartime images showing women in postures of "homeland defense," from vacuuming to welding to "remembering our boys on the front" (images the promotion emulated stylistically).[29]

Representing SBF's commitment to cultural heritage in this manner allowed it to downplay its own economic and political interests while

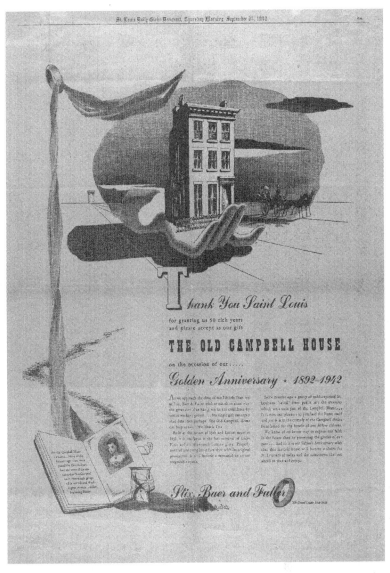

FIGURE 8. Stix, Baer & Fuller advertisement, *St. Louis Globe-Democrat*, September 24, 1942. The copy reads, "Thank You, St. Louis for granting us 50 rich years and please accept as our gift THE OLD CAMPBELL HOUSE on the occasion of our . . . *Golden Anniversary* ★ 1892–1942." Campbell House Museum, St. Louis, MO.

affirming would-be shoppers who were likely to be invested in ideals of "gracious living" past and present. The woman's outstretched palm, which looks waxen, almost like a store mannequin's, casts a dark shadow against a background that reads almost like a segment of the urban landscape. The vignette may be meant to represent Locust Street proper, but it looks like empty stage on which SBF performs as symbolic caretaker, or an abstract plane of time in the background of which is a door like that of the Campbell House, a portal between past and present. In this imaginary space resides the generous hand of the corporation who, like the city planner, is an agent of "improvement."

As suggested in previous chapters, this sense of control over the city and its place narratives found expression in earlier claims on the Campbell residence, including those associated with the establishment of the Lucas Place neighborhood itself, which epitomized what George Lipsitz has called the "spatial imaginary of whiteness." Lipsitz traces the history of this spatial imaginary from the nineteenth century, noting that in the later stages of westward expansion, which arguably continued well into the twentieth century in many cities, it became "more difficult for Americans to believe" in a pure, redemptive landscape in which "the properly-ordered and prosperous domestic dwelling [served as] the nation's key symbol of freedom, harmony, and virtue."[30] But it was exactly this ideal of private ownership that Lucas Place developers sought to project, and that in turn SBF longed to "save"—or more precisely *recoup*—for St. Louisans of the 1940s. "Saving" the house reinforced broader agendas of progress and privatization by solidifying the mythos of a "properly-ordered and prosperous domestic dwelling" as *the* defining element of the urban landscape, one in which the corporation could insinuate itself and private citizens could stake a claim.

Unshuttering the "Mystery House"

It did not take long to ready the "mystery house," as the press had nicknamed it, for its ceremonial "unshuttering."[31] After all, it had been a "properly-ordered and prosperous domestic dwelling" long before the WCS had acquired it, meticulously maintained by household servants for some eighty-five years. But the CHF had been busy all those months, not only speaking to the press and writing promotional copy but choosing a strategy for refurbishment of the house. Primarily, they were concerned with staging the house to reflect life "as it was lived in St. Louis" during "a time of early wealth, pleasant social life, and important cultural beginnings," as they described it in many press documents.[32] They rushed to open the house to the public.

The "Robert Campbell House Museum" (as it was initially called—the "Robert" would soon be dropped) opened to yet another round of fanfare in February 1943. For a small fee (twenty-five cents for adults, ten cents for children), museumgoers could take a tour of six rooms and wander the garden in search of the evidence of "Mid-Nineteenth-Century St. Louis in One of Its Most Glamorous Moods," as a typical press account put it.[33] Hundreds turned out on opening day, many of whom had to be turned away to accommodate the scores of political and corporate dignitaries who were already assembled. In the weeks following, thousands more made pilgrimages to 1508 Locust Street, some of them driving in from neighboring states. By May 1943, an estimated seventy thousand had taken the CHM tour.[34]

From the front, the house was admittedly an understated affair, its "pre–Civil War style inspired by an ancient Greek design" and wrought-iron fencing comprising what preservationists liked to describe as a "genteel, well-maintained look" that persisted "despite the surrounding smoke and commercialism" (fig. 9).[35] Its most striking aspect was its out-of-placeness. The rest of Lucas Place had entirely disappeared from view—now only "a phantom" in public memory—and the house stood out dramatically among the sleek ten- and twelve-story buildings lining the street. Indeed, it looked like something fallen from the sky, or perhaps lifted from the currents of time and placed on a pedestal marked "lone survivor."[36]

Many St. Louisans must have felt they "knew" the house already, having seen it, and the large Campbell family fortune, invoked so frequently by the press over the previous decade. The *Globe-Democrat* played to their sense of anticipation in reports, promising those who long wondered "what was behind those closed doors" that they would "find even greater magnificence than their imagination conceived . . . [of] the Victorian age in the splendid gracious days . . . when the city's foundations were

FIGURE 9. Facade of the Campbell House, photograph, ca. 1935. Campbell House Museum, St. Louis, MO.

being firmly established."[37] The *Post-Dispatch*, which had been the unofficial voice of the WCS during the campaign, was similarly invested in savoring the long-awaited threshold-crossing. One columnist likened the experience of entering the house to time travel, characterizing the CHM as a treasure palace from another age (a metaphor also used during the auction).[38] Official publicity, such as a pamphlet distributed during tours entitled *The Campbell House: A Romantic Survival of Early St. Louis,* likewise nurtured feelings of reverie, inviting visitors to "feel an analgesic release from the present in contemplation of this reminder of the past."[39]

If the front hall represented the threshold between the smog-filled city of the present and a gloriously "analgesic" past, the enormous double parlor was the site of actual crossing over. High-ceilinged, exaggeratedly symmetrical, and lined with reflective surfaces, the room had a magical quality everyone felt the need to describe. Tour guides encouraged feelings of wonderment, calling attention to the most dazzling and expensive items in the room (most of them featured in the pamphlet): imported marble mantels, gilded mirrors and cornices, French chandeliers, carved rosewood furnishings including two "particularly fine" Belter chairs and an "unusually elaborate" square piano, of which it was claimed that "no finer example of wood-carving exists in St. Louis."[40] Docents similarly praised artifacts elsewhere the house, translating the rhetoric of "refinement" that dominated the Victorian age—in which tasteful, orderly homes were understood to express the ideals and habits of a cultivated bourgeoisie—into a modern public relations vernacular.[41] This was no surprise given that many on the CHF board had once been advertising executives, and most of the museum's promotional copy was tried out on Ad Club members before it was introduced to the general public.

Like SBF advertisers, early museum promoters had to frame this dazzling encounter with Victorian finery for wartime visitors who still vividly recalled the deprivations of the 1930s. In his speech at the opening, Jesse Henry felt the need to say that the Campbells' considerable wealth had been "acquired in the American way of opportunity." He emphasized the "simple dignity" and "functional beauty" of their furnishings, as well as the family's resourcefulness and civility.[42] These were not the Rockefellers or the Hearsts; their furnishings should inspire not suspicion or jealousy but admiration and a "mood of remembrance of the things that were too fragile to endure."[43] The newspapers also sought to capture the CHM wonders with tasteful restraint. A few weeks after the opening, the *Post-Dispatch* published "The Color Camera at the Campbell House," a spread containing some of the first color photos taken of the house's interiors (fig. 10). The accompanying narrative focused mainly on intactness, emphasizing the authenticity of the "appearance and the character of the house."[44]

FIGURE 10. Campbell House parlor, photograph, ca. 1943. The photograph shows the room as it appeared at the time of the museum opening, with a new color scheme and display logic. Campbell House Museum, St. Louis, MO.

Early museumgoers were repeatedly told the objects in the collection were the very ones the Campbells had cherished and kept for so many years, now fully restored and displayed as they had always been. These were knowing distortions, for preservationists never intended to save everything in the house; they had carefully culled objects that evoked "untouched mid-nineteenth-century magnificence"—those readily seen as trappings of high-society cultivation.[45] Furthermore, restoring the house involved considerable disturbance of all that untouched magnificence; integrity was not some "original state" to which the house and its contents had been "returned" but a result of intervention and stagecraft, the kind that heightens the aura of historicity and ancestral significance which had been imbued during the auction.[46] During the opening ceremonies, advertising executive and CHF president Arthur Hoskins asserted that these qualities of intactness and magnificence were nothing less than the museum's raison d'être: "Some houses lose their story through the years; few retain the furniture and contents of their hey-day. But in this last home of Lucas Place are still its early household things, ornate Victorian pieces, integral and intact," all of which bespoke St. Louis's "golden age."[47]

Rehabilitation

What CHM officials called a "complete restoration" was in fact a highly selective refurbishment aimed at transforming certain rooms in the house into tableaux of the Victorian age.[48] This transformation took just a few months start to finish, requiring little of the research that dominates historic preservation work today. When members of the WCS had visited the house after Hazlett's death, what they found, besides all that "nineteenth-century magnificence," was a complete mess—what some might today call a "hoard": piles of books, mementos, personal correspondence, clothing, linens, and even cooking implements that had been "strewn about," parts of it the result of rifling by Selkirk's officials, but much of it the sediment of the brothers' reclusive life.[49] The auctioneers and WCS might have seized on this moment for a bit of urban archaeology, or at least to make notes about where the brothers had placed their furniture. But the scene itself was unsettling, as all the nervous joking about "bachelor brothers" who never had to submit to the "domesticating influence of women" suggests. Within hours they had imposed order, sorting possessions into "keep" and "sell" piles with an eye toward building a "museum-worthy" collection.[50]

As the previous chapter shows, the emerging museum collection gained legitimacy by means of public spectacle of valuation and through the WCS's interpretative control before and after the auction. It had determined which objects were the "finest furniture and art a gentleman of taste could assemble," declaring the household "the center of St. Louis wealth and fashion," and now that the house had been secured, its members (modern-day "gentlemen of taste") would reassemble the house's contents.[51] This involved further consolidation and rearrangement but also wholesale redecorating.

Many of the most dramatic interventions happened in the parlor, where the group imposed a new color-scheme: muted grey paint on the walls, uniform pale blue and red silk upholstery on the furniture, and all white ceilings and trim (contractors apparently being asked to paint over ceiling decoration and faux-grained woodwork throughout the house). The members replaced the existing woven rug with brand-new wall-to-wall crimson carpeting (supplied at cost by SBF), which gave the room a saturated, uniform base-color it never had before. Similarly, they removed heavy floral wallpapers, not only in the parlor but throughout the house, replacing them with paint or simple appliques such as a floral-swag motif in the master bedroom. These tactics were analogous to practices popularized in magazines like *Good Housekeeping* and *House Beautiful* during the 1930s and 1940s, in which home decor experts offered advice for "sprucing up" Victorian homes: removing "oppressive" fabrics and patterned wallpapers and replacing them with more "modern touches," painting woodwork or old furniture white, or adding "simple but elegant" surface decoration.[52] Such approaches were also commonly shown in department store displays and advertising.

CHM officials made over six rooms in total, choosing two dozen or so objects (vases, silk floral arrangements, lamps, candelabra) for exhibit—only a small portion of what had been purchased at auction and an even smaller fraction of what had been on display in the house in the mid-1880s. These pieces were not placed where they had been found (neither were many of the larger objects); they were instead positioned to highlight their elaborately decorated surfaces or play up the room's architectural symmetries (placing identical figurines on matching parlor mantels, for example). Tour guides sometimes offered tidbits of "Campbell history" related to these objects as they moved through the house. Visitors learned, for example, that the "bog oak" furniture on display in the dining room had been brought over from Robert's "native Ireland," and that the rose-colored Limoges porcelain service had been "purchased for the occasion of the visit of President Grant" (and that Virginia had "had a dress made to match").[53] Neither claim was true, but such stories reinforced elements of a new museum narrative in which Anglo-Saxon heritage and hospitality dominated.

In this "restoration" work, museum officials also drew on techniques used in public museums across the country, including St. Louis's City Art Museum (whose director, Perry Rathbone, was a founding member of the CHF) and the American wing of the Metropolitan Museum of Art, which opened in 1924 and featured a number of period rooms.[54] Objects in these tableaux-like assemblages were usually from the same region and sometimes the same household of origin (usually a prestigious personage), or else reflected the same broad style and period, for instance, "Victorian" or "Colonial Revival." Achieving the desired "period look" involved elaborate sleight of hand: designers fit elements together like puzzles, relying heavily on a stagecraft metonymy—the part-whole logic that unites disparate objects through theatrical arrangement—to make them fit. Museum curators were concerned with "typicality" and "representative context" as well as affective association. A pair of eyeglasses and a letter-opener placed alongside a copy of Benjamin Franklin's *Autobiography* on a writing desk in an "Early Federalist" room, for example, might represent literacy or rituals of letter-writing in the period, while indicating the class status of the fictitious owner. Certainly, it was also meant to stimulate feelings of pride of Franklin himself as a "founding father." Objects were made to "speak," not of a specific household or its owner's biography but of a sense of the period. This is what CHF members understood when they spoke of mid-nineteenth-century magnificence: visual manifestations of social milieu, in this case, that of the ownership class in the frontier city during the "golden age" of expansion.[55]

While CHF members gave preference to showy and expensive objects of the kind regularly featured in art museum period rooms, however, they showed little interest in matters of regional style and manufacture, points of origin, or craft histories (which institutions like the Metropolitan Museum of Art often privileged). The fact that many of the Campbell possessions had been imported from Philadelphia, New York, and Paris, if it registered at all, was understood to reveal "expensive tastes and cosmopolitanism" and perhaps more generally a generic Midwestern heritage.[56] But this interest did not yet extend to that associated with everyday world of nineteenth-century St. Louis. Visitors might have learned from their museum guide that the porcelain tea service in the parlor belonged to the family, but the particulars of the Campbells' social world, what serving tea involved and who served it, who might have called at the house and why, were not discussed. Nor was material evidence of the family's daily life that had survived in the house (which included kettles, tea towels, and other such items) displayed. "Victorian whimsies" such as silk lambrequins, porcelain miniatures, perfume bottles, carved wooden boxes, works of needlepoint, and myriad knick-knacks once densely layered throughout the house were thinned out to suit modern tastes. Nonetheless, visitors often singled out such idiosyncratic objects for comment, longing, it would seem, for some human presence in the house. One early visitor, a prominent architectural historian and preservationist associated with the WCS, even claimed that the house had a "lived-in look," arguing that its interiors were superior to those in more "academic display" (period rooms) because of their comparative realism.[57]

However these exhibits were experienced by early museumgoers, it is clear that the CHF's conception of untouched magnificence was in fact highly retouched. Their invasive curatorial work aligned more closely with what urban renewal advocates called "rehabilitation" than what today's preservationists understand by the term "restoration."[58] This process involved selective safeguarding of hand-selected properties (often from the "best" neighborhoods) and period-oriented reconstruction, both with the end-goal of visual and material order. Rehabilitation on a regional scale amounted to a principle of managed growth, in which the integrity of the existing urban fabric was maintained while signs of blight were addressed through clearance and redevelopment. Rehabilitation of a single neighborhood involved trimming away structures of negligible aesthetic or historic value and vigorous curation of specimen properties like the Campbell House.

St. Louis planners had been preoccupied with both rehabilitation and blight for years.[59] But in the months following Pearl Harbor, they became more aggressive in their messaging about "decadence" (a term that implied both material-economic and moral decline) in the city. In 1942, they published a report that conjured postwar St. Louis as a rapidly expanding slum filled with "unattractive and unsatisfactory places of residence" (neighborhoods beyond rehabilitation) and ravaged by a "succession of difficulties and evils—higher taxes, tax delinquency, and foreclosures." Pull-out maps showing "Obsolete and Blighted Districts" across the city illustrated how patterns of "unbalanced" growth had produced a city whose outer edges featured attractive housing but whose inner core suffered "a deep-seated malady" whose "portent" could not be ignored.[60] Even as it prioritized rehabilitation, the report's loudest message—that the city had failed to act at critical moments past, and now should pursue wide-scale redevelopment to salvage its remaining historic treasures—advanced the case for the opposite.[61] Such arguments would be persuasive for business leaders who had taken up wartime mantras of progress and industrial development as well as those who fretted more quietly about changes in the city center. Some from both categories (and many workaday St. Louisans) had supported the Save the Campbell House campaign.[62]

In a very real sense, the ideals of rehabilitation and material progress crystallized together inside the Campbell House during this period. Both could be seen in the CHF's selective improvement of defining features (showpieces signifying a "Victorian golden age") and its imposition of overall material order, and both saturated press accounts of the museum's opening. The paradoxes of such curatorial work were many, just as had been those defining Hugh Campbell's zealous caretaking regime. The CHF pursued a scheme of restoration that "forgot" entirely what Hugh had set about preserving, even as it benefited from his efforts, and that mystified the very history it meant to enshrine. Whether conscious or not (no doubt some would have objected to the idea), the group's work obscured the effects by which "untouched magnificence" had been preserved, and excluded much of what was "originally there" in material and historical senses. Just as city planners seeking to "save" venerable old St. Louis properties cleared historic neighborhoods seen as deleterious and unkempt, the CHF sought to stabilize the "best features" of the Campbell property while making changes that were definitive and difficult to reverse.

Perhaps to manage these paradoxes, the story of the Campbell House that the CHF delivered during the dedication ceremonies emphasized the cooperation and self-sacrifice that had made the property's saving and restoration possible. In a radio address recorded on opening day, Henry celebrated the fact that "ten cents from a newsboy" to as much as "$10,000 given by Stix, Baer & Fuller" had saved the project from "the threat of collapse—due entirely to the burdens of a total war," adding that their efforts, and thus the house itself, symbolized nothing less than the "Spirit of American Democracy." Using language that was to become boilerplate promotional copy in years to come, Henry characterized the museum as "a monument to the opportunity America afforded an Irish immigrant lad who came to St. Louis in ill health, [and also] to the democratic pride of St. Louis in the great part this City has played in making the West American." Building on themes of expansion and national greatness, he extolled St. Louis's role as a "gateway" city, working to "transform the West from a desert to a fruitful land—from exploited colonies to a free and democratic civilization."[63] After years of experimental messaging, the CHF had settled on a mythos of material integrity that served claims of the city's might and significance and supported broader ideals of American culture and democratic civilization. These values would exert a strong pull on the wartime imagination.

"How America Lived"

The sense of "victory" in this moment would probably have been enough for the CHF and their many supporters, who had been laboring for years to save the house and were now gratified to see that St. Louisans loved the museum. But there was a surprise ahead that would change how they understood their work. Editors from *Life* magazine had gotten wind of the campaign to preserve a St. Louis landmark, and within a couple months, they had sent a photographer to shoot the house for an article they had planned featuring historic homes representing "200 years of American cultural beginnings." Among the properties chosen for the feature (including two seventeenth-century Massachusetts homesteads, Andrew Jackson's Hermitage, and an 1830s New York City mansion), the Campbell House was not only the youngest but the only one west of the Mississippi—a "picturesque architectural relic" of the Midwest, as it would be described for readers. Apparently, *Life* editors bought into the intactness and "Spirit of American Democracy" arguments made by the WCS and CHF, each of which was compatible with the themes of *Life*'s own publication and especially the "Americana" series in which the photo essay, "How America Lived," would appear. The piece eventually ran in the VE Day issue of the magazine, the cover of which showed three sober-faced Germans who had just climbed out of a foxhole and, as the caption notes, knew "firsthand the bitterness of defeat" but had "not yet confronted the barbaric violence committed in their name."[64] The rest of the magazine chronicles this barbaric violence and early attempts at political reconciliation in Europe.

"How America Lived" featured vignettes comprising photos showing the light-filled historic interiors and furnishings of each home and brief descriptions of the period it was meant to represent. The images must have soothed the eyes and minds of readers as they moved between the war-torn villages and concentration camps—some of the earliest evidence of Nazi barbarity to be viewed by American civilians—that filled the magazine. But the juxtapositions were strange: wistful-looking women in period costumes appeared to be tending immaculate rooms while traumatized civilians picked through the rubble of their homes. Readers could study southern plantation scenes through nineteenth-century window glass and French farmland riddled with landmines and abandoned tanks. As the war dead were buried across Europe, rituals of remembrance and reunion on the other side of the ocean seemed still to be unfolding anew.[65]

The article made little sense in an issue devoted to war reporting. Its inclusion seemed almost like an editing mistake or a poorly conceived notion of "filler." What had a seventeenth-century scullery to do with the "German People" and their terrible war? How could one savor a beautifully restored Victorian parlor when confronted with the ruins of an historic church—or indeed an entire people group? Even in a magazine known for sentimental, jingoistic copy and sensationalizing images—not to mention pandering to white audiences with images of American national unity—the juxtapositions must have seemed bizarre or even distasteful.[66]

But there appears to have been *some* logic: the caption on the scullery photograph, which shows a young woman in period costume calmly scrubbing a pile of rustic-looking cookware, points out that the ceramic jugs, butter churn, "hand-hewn" corn-grinder, and sandstone sink that appear in the scene served as "ballast in one of first ships to bring settlers."[67] These were evidently "meaning-heavy domestic relics" of the sort that featured prominently in house museums of the period, as Patricia West has argued—"relics" in the sense that they were taken as tangible evidence of "simpler times" and of visitors' ancestors' frugality, resource-fulness, and moral uprightness.[68] *Life* editors seem to have intuited that visions of "how America lived" in the past would bolster the American spirit. They saved the article for a moment when "victory" in Europe had brought with it unsettling evidence of the opposite of these ideals: nation-alism as brutality and the attempted annihilation of whole cultures.

Whatever readers made of the juxtaposition, whether or not they asso-ciated scenes of the American past with the events unfolding in Europe, *Life* chose to portray the nation's historic homes as places of escape and consolation. The accompanying article offered visions of domestic tranquility and material-moral integrity, framing them as elements of a national past that strongly resembled the one the CHF had been working to solidify, one in which, as the first paragraph of the article noted, "even the most prosperous people lived in small frame houses with one big all-purpose room and a few small bedrooms" and "slept on beds with leather thongs and mattresses of feathers and straw."[69] Editors did not rely on meaning-heavy relics alone to conjure this sense of integrity. They also staged scenes in which costumed actors acknowledged the material and moral dimensions of domestic tranquility, thus claiming a knowledge and appreciation of the material past rooted in historic preservation.[70] Like the woman in the SBF advertisement, these reenactors performed ceremonial acts of protection, claiming moral authority over the material past, and by extension, over the domains of civic-minded remembrance and wartime nationalism.

In the vignette featuring Andrew Jackson's slave plantation, these acts involved material as well as moral rehabilitation of the (historical) home front. A hoop-skirted woman stands on a spiral staircase, appar-ently awaiting the return of a master who will never come back from the Civil War: she is a literal and a symbolic caretaker, dressed like Sarah Yorke Jackson, Jackson's daughter-in-law, who inherited the plantation and became its first preservationist after the war (it may also be her dress in the photo).[71] A second image shows the same costumed actor with two others standing in a tight circle on the covered porch, surveying the green fields beyond like characters from the wildly popular film version of the novel *Gone with the Wind* (1939). The scene is shot through glass that distorts our view of "how America lived" and reinforces our sense of the distance between past and present. The women look regretful as they gaze out at the yard. Like Scarlett O'Hara, they long to lay claim to what remains of their heritage even as the world presents them with haunting images of loss and violence.

The modern images of war found throughout the magazine are echoes of earlier losses and violence that the article suppresses—those inherent in the plantation economy and the "southern way of life," for example, which is conflated with a generalized national past. Serving up this way of life as national heritage required mystification of the sort that is embodied in material rehabilitation. The Greek Revival–style manor house shown in the photos was the successor to Andrew and Rachel Jackson's modest log farmhouse, which in the early nineteenth century became the nucleus of a slave plantation of some two hundred acres. The Jacksons struggled to make the plantation viable, and by the 1850s had subdivided the property to pay family debts. Thanks to efforts by Sarah Jackson to keep the estate intact, however, both the manor and the farmhouse survived the war and various redevelopment schemes, including proposals to convert the property into an asylum for wounded Confederate soldiers (which the Ladies Hermitage Association opposed vigorously) and a branch of the U.S. Military Academy at West Point.[72] In spite of the fact that the estate had never been a successful plantation and no longer included much of the original plantation property, the Hermitage took on the status of "miraculous survivor" just as had the Campbell House.

The moral and material rehabilitation of the property can be glimpsed in the panoramic wallpaper that dominates the photograph of the woman in the stairwell of the manor. Imported from France in the early nineteenth century and replaced at least once during the Jacksons' lifetimes, the wallpaper's distinctive design features fountains, classical temples, and mythological figures meant to represent Telemachus's adventures on the island of Calypso. They seem to fill the entire room and then merge with the shady front yard, which viewers can glimpse through an open door.[73] Shot in this fashion, the *Life* photo heightens the *trompe l'oeil* effect of the wallpaper and extends the allegory into the realm of the "real world" plantation, with the shadow of slavery airbrushed away. "With servants plentiful," readers are told in one caption focused on the recently restored stairwell, "it was no problem to keep the poplar floor and mahogany rail polished." The stair has been made into a relic, a gleaming symbol of dutiful household service (rather than slave labor) and, implicitly, of the loving (white) stewardship of the Jackson shrine.

This otherworldly "innocence" of the Hermitage-as-idyll must have registered powerfully for readers as they paged through a magazine filled with horrors, including the now-infamous photos of emaciated concentration camp survivors peering out from their crude bunks, the mounds of shoes that constituted evidence of Nazi "barbarism," the scenes showing men at the very lowest "point of human degradation."[74] Perhaps readers even detected a consonance between the reenactment and war scenes: in each, material objects give expression to loss as well as consolation, and to a longing for survival. French citizens rummaging through "the debris left by armies," among them repurposed "wheels, canteens, blankets, mess kits, [and] even dead men's shoes," show human resilience not unlike that embodied in butter churns and corn grinders. Callous as the comparison may seem, both images assert metaphorical kinship between past and present, between one nation's history and another's; both suggest national innocence.

There may also have been a perverse pleasure in contemplating scenes of war side by side with those of restored domestic tranquility and material intactness. In a 1941 fundraising document, Jesse Henry made a plea for donations in which he conjured such trauma as a motive for saving the Campbell House: "War with its terrible destruction is wiping out the landmarks of Europe! We are powerless to stop this, but we can help preserve the historic points of interest in Saint Louis."[75] Preservation could no more restore victims of genocide than it could bring back recently leveled working-class neighborhoods (in St. Louis or in Europe). But it could offer a vision of the past brought back to life and also a seeming national innocence in the face of sweeping guilt and violence. Ultimately, the unifying theme of the whole VE Day issue of *Life* was rehabilitation, and "How America Lived" expressed victory for "survivors"—triumph over death and loss and the humiliations of war—in another register. The essay expressed a sense of vicarious suffering and survival Americans could indulge when otherwise there would have been no words to account for the "atrocities they were now forced to see."[76]

It would be difficult to overstate the impact of the *Life* photo essay on the fledgling St. Louis museum and its promoters. Having been included in the inventory of national treasures confirmed ongoing claims about the house's historical significance and strengthened the house's aura of moral and historical grandeur. *Life*'s endorsement—and its photograph of the Campbell House—could be touted for any number of purposes. When *Life* refused to grant permission to reprint the image for promotional purposes, the CHF launched a letter-writing campaign to secure hard copies of the article from around the nation, which were in short supply given the rationing of paper and oil.[77] And the group would use the original copies in publicity of all kinds for years to come. As late as 1948, the St. Louis Convention and Publicity Bureau was still using them in displays at its registration desks, for example, where out-of-towners sought information about the city. The museum used the tagline "as seen in *Life* magazine" in their publications much longer than that. In short, the *Life* moment signaled national visibility for the city, of having been *seen*.

The Campbell House, too, had been seen—and seen in a special new light, as a "fully restored historic site" with claims to national heritage status. *Life*'s treatment of the Campbell parlor magnified the effects of the new museum's period-room-style exhibits. The photograph the magazine chose features two women in period dress in that room—the same debutantes who had worn Virginia Campbell's gowns at the 1941 fundraiser—one seated on a Belter sofa, the other standing, gazing out of a north-facing window (or is it at her own reflection in the pier glass?). The women are not the primary focus, however; the image invites us to admire the room's "ornate Victorian pieces," and especially a gilt-porcelain tea service on an occasional table, as meaning-laden objects.

To create these effects, a telescopic lens was chosen that imposed extra distance between foreground (the tea service and marble table) and background (the women ruminating over unnamed losses). The room looks enormous, and thanks to mounted spot-lighting of a sort the *Post-Dispatch* probably did not use, has an exaggerated tangibility. The women's clothing and the tea set fairly shimmer. By comparison with the glorious "Victorian Double Parlor . . . resplendent with gold leaf, rosewood and brocades . . . admirably suited to the pretentious entertaining of the Mid-Victorian era," as a caption describes it, the flesh-and-blood humans in the photo look almost ghostly.[78] The Campbell House had been so completely fetishized that the material remains of the past seemed more real than those who survived to enjoy them. These effects, and the broader mythos of intactness that it underscored, would be put to many new purposes in the decades that followed.

CHAPTER 5

THE RECEIPT BOOK

Threshold-Crossing

O N MAY 13, 1943, the day that Axis forces surrendered in Tunisia and news of their anticipated invasion of Italy reached the United States, a society columnist writing under the penname "Boo" took a private tour of the new museum.[1] Boo had been a vocal supporter of the "Save the Campbell House" campaign, and she was now conducting research for her weekly column in the *St. Louis Censor,* where she planned to report on the new museum—a significant departure from her usual fare of debutante balls and society weddings. Upon entering the "beautifully quiet" parlor, Boo breathlessly told her readers the following day, several "gracious, witty ghosts" greeted her with bows and curtsies—a welcoming committee that included "the beautiful and vivacious . . . mistress of the mansion," Virginia; the "two bachelor brothers who lived on and on in the house for 61 years after its mistress died" (Hugh and Hazlett); and several celebrity dinner guests, among them President Ulysses Grant, General William Sherman, and James Eads, architect of the city's iconic railway bridge. No longer a mere "sightseer," Boo was now a guest at some gathering in "the golden decade of the 50s." As she wandered the house, she encountered hospitable ghosts and "fine old rosewood and walnut, gas chandeliers, china washing bowls, [and] marble-topped washstands" that constituted the previous occupants' social universe. The "scent of old lavender and lace" enveloped her, and for a time, she took leave of her senses.[2]

Boo did not explain this little reverie. Readers were given to understand only that she had been "transported" by what she saw in the museum and that it was a (mostly) pleasant experience. Was she indulging a flight of fancy or reporting an actual ghost encounter? Perhaps she meant to satirize the swooning accounts of so many museum visitors. Given how much she joked around in her columns, it is hard to judge. What is clear is that she soon stepped out of the "shadowy, courtly world" of the Campbell House past—a world that, as she put it in an uncharacteristically sober sentence, stood "in bold, sharp relief against the present war-mad, shell-screaming year." By the end of the column, the sense of dismay is unmistakable.³

Maybe the specter of war that haunted preservationists and lurked at the edges of the *Life* spread on "How America Lived" had gotten to her. Or maybe she was acknowledging what cultural geographer Tim Edensor describes as the "ghostly" elements of public sites—the fragments of the material past that are "ineffable and mysterious" and resist "representational fixing" through official museum narratives.⁴ Such elements proliferate in the postindustrial cities in the United Kingdom that Edensor studies, but 1940s St. Louis also had its share, and the early Campbell House Museum (CHM), despite all the rehabilitation that had been done, was one such site. As we see in early accounts that fixated on the moment of crossing the threshold of the new museum, engaging the "last survivor of Lucas Place" produced cognitive dissonance. Indeed, "stepping back" into an "intact and integral" Gilded Age parlor could trigger not only disorientation but feelings of profound ambivalence, even for a society columnist. Boo had to will herself to the task at hand, namely reporting on all that rosewood and marble, objects meant to be read as "social hieroglyphics."⁵

When she discovered the museum's guest register in the kitchen, Boo was at last back in her element: she reported that she had "the time of her life peeking . . . at the names of prominent people who have visited the house since it has been restored." Here, she discovered a row of call-bells used by the Campbells to summon their servants, who would "dash upstairs when a particular bell 'tuned'" to tend to their every need. This "charming vestige of a vanishing age" was hardly fathomable to those in the current "servantless" one, and it led her to ruminate on the reduced circumstances in which she and her readers found themselves. She ended the column with an anecdote about an estate auction she once attended in which "a heavenly grandfather clock that [once had] stood in the grand hall" of the Whitney mansion sold for only seventy-five dollars.⁶

The Campbell possessions narrowly missed such dispersal, and she was pleased to see they had been mostly returned home.

But something was still off: while the gloriously intact world of the Campbells had been reconstituted and was ready for visitors to enjoy, the noise of the "war-mad world" was roaring in her ears. Other visitors from the early period in the CHM's operation experienced this same bewildering disorientation of being caught between two worlds. They only "came out of the fog," as Boo put it, at the end of their tours, when hieroglyphic objects could be seen in the cold light of day. The official tour sequence encouraged this coming-down feeling, starting as it did with the glorious "double parlor" and ending with the kitchen, the plainest room in the house. As guests moved through—from parlor to dining room ("indicative of the hospitality of the Campbell household") to library (an "intimate place where an elderly bachelor . . . could entertain his men friends and smoke to his heart's content") to the "unusually large" master bedroom suite filled with Brussels lace, mahogany bedsteads, and marble-topped walnut bureaus—they could certainly lose themselves in the glories of life "as it was." But descending a narrow, creaky servants' stair and entering a kitchen with grey linoleum, yellow-ochre-painted wood cabinets, and a circa 1880 cast-iron stove, they were wrenched back into the here and now.[7]

An Unlikely Favorite

On the north wall of the kitchen, just below the servant call-bells, sat a glass case, the only one in the entire museum at the time. Inside was displayed one of the most unassuming objects in the collection, a small manuscript measuring just 7.5 x 9.75 inches, covered in marbleized pasteboard, and identified by a label as "Virginia Campbell's Receipt Book." Inside were family recipes Virginia had copied by hand when she was a teenager and consulted throughout five decades as mistress of the house. As an object, the book was utterly unremarkable—the kind of mass-produced copybook used as a journal or record of expenses throughout the nineteenth century. Indeed, it was the antithesis of all the rosewood, lace, and marble, and already in a fragile state by the time of the museum's opening. Nothing about it encouraged aesthetic or interpretative privileging. Nor had the receipt book been on the William Clark Society's (WCS) priority list years earlier; it had survived by good fortune.[8]

But around the time of the museum's opening, someone placed it inside the case, where it remained for decades—an unlikely choice for such special treatment, as the display made it hard for early visitors to make out Virginia's spidery handwriting. Certainly, many other of her possessions would have been more alluring evidence of her accomplishments as St. Louis's "busiest and most gracious of hostesses."[9] Yet the public's reverence for the receipt book was striking: within a few weeks, it became the most talked about object in the whole museum collection. Boo found it so "perfectly fascinating" that she devoted an entire second column to it the week after her visit.[10] And many other early visitors felt the urge to mention the book in their accounts of the museum—even those who otherwise showed little interest in personal possessions. Gaile Dugas, a correspondent from *South* magazine, described the sensation of moving from the "soft golden half-light" of the parlor, where "it was not hard to think someone with quick, light steps has just crossed the hall, an intangible body, moving with a faint swish of crinolines" (she, too, flirts with the idea of ghosts), to the "pleasant, sunny kitchen" where "Virginia Campbell and her servants worked over the recipes collected in her own cookbook."[11]

For Dugas, the receipt book made the kitchen a familiar, reassuring place, offering a sense of continuity between past and present that was not felt elsewhere in the house. It confirmed her desire to see Virginia first and foremost as a wife and keeper of household order—not only a lady of wealth and leisure. A *Post-Dispatch* columnist who toured the house in its first week as a public museum likewise noted that, on entering the starkly utilitarian space of the kitchen after immersion in rooms where "one can almost visualize the elaborately gowned ladies and the courtly gentlemen who were once entertained there," she was charmed to discover "the inner workings of a home of that period."[12] Again, the reassurance of coming back to earth is clear.

Positioning the receipt book in the kitchen reminded visitors that the room had been used for everyday household activity, an aspect of Campbell history that had been actively disregarded by the WCS but took on new meaning in wartime. It also put Virginia, known heretofore mainly by her reputation as a hostess and socialite, at the center of that activity. Even the taciturn author of *Historic Midwest Houses* (1947), a compendium of landmark buildings in the Midwest primarily concerned with architecture and period furnishings, turned to the receipt book at the end of his entry on the Campbell House. Indeed, his memory of the charming object motivated his culminating gesture in the essay, where he compared Virginia to "that most renowned colonial hostess, Martha Washington."[13]

The first lady reference suggests that visitors' fascination with the book was part of the general craze for "homespun"—meaning not just homemade clothing or yarn (the term first used in the United States to reference textiles spun at home by colonials boycotting English-made goods) but the ideas, manners, and even values of "simpler times," of a Martha Washington–style graciousness. The images from the 1943 *Life* magazine article, as we have seen, were full of "hand-hewn" things— butter-churns, water jugs, wooden plates, and utensils that were meant to inspire viewers with their elegant simplicity and association with simpler times. The fascination with homespun went beyond the generic nostalgia we might associate with the antiques market, fueling curiosity about mundane objects in the Campbell House that the WCS had never given a moment's thought. The copper-lined sink and painted-wood cupboards in the kitchen, for example, were particularly noteworthy, as were a handful of other strategically placed, "meaning laden" objects, including a set of tin bathtubs that received increasing emphasis on the official tour starting in the mid-1940s.[14] These objects reminded visitors of the labors that lay behind the family's "gracious living."

The receipt book was a perfect compromise between gracious living and wartime frugality, gesturing at once to high-society cultivation and middle-class resourcefulness. Many visitors were drawn to Virginia's "flowing" handwriting, which was taken as evidence of her cultivation and charm, or to the "fine art of living of the Southern aristocracy," as it was described in *Historic Missouri Houses*.[15] But museumgoers were even more taken with her recipes, which evoked middle-class domesticity. Boo reproduced one of them, a recipe in verse for a stove-top apple custard known as "Eve's Pudding," in its entirety, reveling in its folksiness. The recipe had been a staple of early American cookbooks and a vehicle for "female instruction" of the kind Virginia would have experienced in finishing school, as Boo seemed to realize. She chose to interpret it as evidence of quaint Victorian notions about women and their "place."[16]

Curiosity about Virginia's receipt book might have been linked, initially at least, to the Campbell sons' veneration of their mother, which was a minor motif in early tour narratives. While the extent of Hugh's caretaking of the house was never acknowledged, the fact that her things survived—and that he was "very devoted" to his parents—sometimes made it into tours. As we have seen, he sought to honor Virginia's memory publicly, such as in donations to the Mount Vernon Ladies' Association and the prominent display of her portrait. But unlike these heirloom objects, no references to the receipt book were discovered in family records. Neither was the book included in early museum inventories or public accounts of the museum campaign. Members of the CHF such as Grace Ashley latched onto more conventional heirloom specimens, such as Virginia's gowns and fine jewelry, and saw to it that they were regularly featured in fundraisers and promotional material.

These objects became "celebrity" possessions many heard about before visiting the museum, including in early fundraisers as well as estate-related notices. In November 1943, for example, the Famous-Barr Company (another of St. Louis's well-known department stores) offered a grouping of Virginia's most "sumptuous" jewels at an estate sale in their downtown location, including an Italian coral pendant necklace and earrings and a thirty-seven-carat diamond cross estimated to be worth $20,000.[17] Descriptions of the jewelry appeared alongside drawings of the pieces and a woman in a Victorian gown who might have been taken to be Virginia. And museumgoers could view some of her other finery on mannequins that were positioned throughout the house. Furthermore, socialites continued to wear Virginia's gowns for heritage celebrations such as garden parties and teas until 1948, when CHF members prohibited the wearing of clothing from the collection to prevent further damage.[18]

But while the visibility of the gowns in official interpretation only increased (as with the opening of the Costume Room in 1948), the attention paid to the receipt book outstripped that given to any of Virginia's other possessions. Virtually every promotional document produced in the first decade of the museum's history made special mention of it, and during the war, feature articles dotingly described its contents, many of them imagining the everyday uses to which the recipes had been put. Reinforcing this fascination, the CHF continued to display the book to every visitor. Perhaps the same reasoning that led them to build an enclosure for items displayed in the Costume Room, a desire to keep Virginia's gowns safe "from dust and inquisitive fingers," guided their decision to put the book under glass.[19] Security was certainly a factor during the first few months of operation, when several hundred visitors toured the museum each day and small objects sometimes went missing.[20]

The glass case represented a major departure from the interpretative agenda of a museum otherwise devoted to "realistic portraits of life as it was lived in St. Louis almost a hundred years ago."[21] And, as early visitors' accounts suggest, this mode of display encouraged a different kind of fascination than did period-room-style curation. To stand before the "very cookbook" used by Virginia, written in her "own hand," was for some a pleasure akin to viewing a relic like George Washington's wooden teeth (which, while not in fact made of wood, were displayed under glass and treated with gravest respect for more than a century).[22] The "intangible or invisible quality of . . . significance" that infuses such "numinous" objects also contributes to the overall magical quality or aura of grandeur that Boo and many others came to the house to experience.[23]

If close contemplation was key to ritual veneration, engagement with a reproduction was a close second. The museum's only major merchandising effort in the early years involved a facsimile edition of the receipt book billed as a souvenir collection of Virginia's "favorite recipes," which the CHM sold for twenty-five cents starting about a month after the opening. Besides dozens of her recipes, which museum officials updated for the "modern cook," they included a portrait of a middle-aged Virginia in a silk gown and a photograph of the Campbell House dining room as it might have looked when "set for a coming dinner party."[24] The booklet was promptly reviewed by the press, who hailed it as an "attractive and flavorsome . . . addition to St. Louisiana" and an appealing memento of a tour of the museum.[25] Reviewers also appreciated the glimpse the souvenir booklet provided of the "tradition of gracious southern hospitality." Of the 150 recipes Virginia had gathered over decades of housewifery, those chosen for the booklet included many of the southern dishes she had eaten while growing up in North Carolina: vegetable soup, creamed spinach, mashed peas, yeast rolls, doughnuts, and fried chicken. These were interspersed with recipes for a number of "Victorian" dainties— brandied cherries, oyster soup, and Charlotte Russe (a molded dessert made with ladies' fingers)—and home remedies with names and ingredients that evoked "the Good Old Days."[26]

In producing the booklet, the CHF sought to translate old-time housewifery into the vernacular of modern housekeeping while at the same time solidifying the established narrative of the house. This led to a number of curious contradictions. For example, the book celebrated "making-do" and a middle-class style of housekeeping while talking obsessively of elegant entertaining during a time when "living was luxurious."[27] The cover design brought these apparently incompatible ideas into a kind of uneasy partnership: museum officials chose a florid, stereotypically "Victorian" style for the phrase "Virginia Campbell's" (probably also meant to evoke her "elegant" handwriting) and a utilitarian block lettering style for the phrase for "Cook Book" (which resembled that used on the covers of popular domestic advice books of the day). Likewise, the content was a blend of folksy, commonsense advice and easy-to-follow instructions and precise measures that had been popularized—some say invented—by Irma Rombauer in *The Joy of Cooking* (the St. Louis author's immensely popular book already in its third edition in 1943). Thus, Virginia's old-style "receipts" became "recipes" wartime housewives might themselves prepare, though significant alterations might have been required to meet the rationing guidelines imposed by the Office of Price Administration (OPA).[28]

Would St. Louisans actually make Virginia's custards and soufflés with their rationed eggs? Many local observers seemed to think so. In an *Advertising Club Weekly* article promoting the new museum (fig. 11), CHF president Gordon Hertslet acknowledged that while "meatless days, eggless days, high prices and other factors make it virtually impossible for any of us to become epicures," there was still much to be gained by studying the "social traditions of leisurely and stately St. Louis living."[29] His review included reprints of several of Virginia's recipes, and like other interpreters, he depicted her as the resourceful housewife of her day, describing her kitchen as a site of conscientious, even frugal housekeeping. With some imaginative work, the traditions of "gracious living" could inspire new thinking about modern cookery or even alleviate the drudgeries of "making-do" during a season when most Americans found nearly every aspect of their household routines affected by shortages and increasingly complex OPA guidelines.

"Luxurious living" was a thing of the past, and cookbooks authors and advice columnists were increasingly preoccupied with the dilemmas of "keeping house"—a phrase that referred not just to physical maintenance of one's home and provision for one's family but the preservation of an

Living Was Luxurious in the Good Old Days at the Campbell House

Virginia Campbell's Cook Book — containing the favorite recipes of Mrs. Robert Campbell. Available at the Campbell House — price 25c.

By G. Gordon Hertslet, Vice-President, Campbell House Foundation

MEATLESS days, eggless days, high prices and other factors make it virtually impossible for any of us to become epicures these days. But in the files of the Campbell House is the original copy of Virginia Campbell's Cook Book which shows that menus were full and varied, back in the 1850's.

As mistress of the Campbell House, Mrs. Campbell united her tradition of gracious southern hospitality to Colonel Robert Campbell's tradition of generous Irish hospitality. In this house, which has now become an oasis in downtown St. Louis, centered the social traditions of leisurely and stately St. Louis living. Here as hostess Virginia Campbell entertained guests of such heroic stature as General U. S. Grant, then President of the United States, and as humble as Father De Smet, the black-robed friend and apostle of the Indians.

By permission of the Campbell House Foundation, owners of the copyright, we reproduce on these pages some of the recipes which made the Campbells famous for their table. The complete cook book has been reproduced in Mrs. Campbell's own hand-writing and this collector's item can be obtained by any visitor to the Campbell House for 25 cents.

32

FIGURE 11. Cover of *Virginia Campbell's Cook Book,* from "Living Was Luxurious in the Good Old Days at the Campbell House," *Advertising Club Weekly,* 1945. Campbell House Museum, St. Louis, MO.

"American way of life." Thus, alongside practical tips on meal-planning, sustaining Victory gardens, home-canning, laundry, and hundreds of advertisements for products that would aid in family nutrition, cleanliness, and well-being, magazines published articles on traditional foodways that were meant to reassure American women of their wholesomeness and continued relevance to daily life. In July 1943, for example, *Good Housekeeping* editors announced that the war had ushered in a "New Cookery" defined by creative adaptation and a "return to basics." Acknowledging that readers faced a "wit-sharpening game of stretching rationed foods and their point values," and that scarcities narrowed the parameters of the possible, the writers encouraged a reexamination of existing resources, including practices handed down from those who had survived the Great Depression, the Civil War, and even earlier periods of hardship.[30]

To inspire this kind of modern yet reassuringly traditional cookery, *Good Housekeeping* ran a series of sample menus with new versions of "classic" dishes, including tweaked (or radically altered) recipes with substitute or "stretcher" ingredients in place of eggs, oils, and meats. Each issue described new approaches to weekly meal planning, new uses of unfamiliar ingredients and inexpensive meats such as liver, new strategies for frugal shopping, and all kinds of time-saving recipes (for example, quick breads that required no yeast but were "just as satisfying as great-grandmother's kneaded bread"). This "new cookery" did not preclude traditional favorites or celebratory meals; it simply asked for care, selectivity, and moderation. A large and satisfying midday meal such as a roast with potatoes and carrots could be served on Sunday, as it would have been in the past, and then leftovers could be used to prepare small weekday meals (extra meat, fat and bones that might previously have discarded used as a base for soup or turned into hash and mixed with beans, rice, or other stretchers).[31]

These efforts at adaptation would not only provide a modicum of comfort but allow home cooks to preserve their traditions and past lifestyles (or even to try out new ones). They mirrored the obsession with other tropes of Americanness during the war, among them baseball, family, and technological innovation. The well-tended household came to represent economic and social order as a result of individual sacrifice, ingenuity, and "making do" without giving up one's sense of identity. This was highly paradoxical given that rationing and related practices were a top-down mandate of the OPA and posed challenges for the average household, not to mention thousands of women who in this new "servantless age," as Boo called it, when "the helping hand of dusky Minnie or sturdy Hilda is helping defense instead," found themselves learning new household tasks.[32] Others who had always done their own housework struggled to maintain a sense of control in straightened domestic situations. Women were repeatedly told that these represented a kind of "home-front" where they were the "first line of defense" against threats to the "American way of life."[33]

In St. Louis, these were the same women who took tours of the CHM and were the presumed audience for much of the local promotion. On the day that Boo's column ran in the *Censor,* the *Globe-Democrat* published a review by Harry Burke that celebrated the museum's souvenir booklet for offering "some amazing glimpses of the contrast between a plenty in provisions and a poverty of things to do with [them]." Acknowledging that Virginia was a "poor little rich wife," he added that "the mistress of the [Campbell] house was actually looking ahead almost a century to anticipate the best of modern cookery." Cognizant of the thousands of advice columns and practical tips for penny-pinching housewives that ran in newspapers across the country, Burke went on to explain that, while there was "no rationing in those years of ominous peace just before the civil war and after the Mexican war . . . Virginia Kyle Campbell . . . faced by problems of 'do-without' that would drive a modern housewife to distraction." He pointed for example to food scarcities and the challenges of working in a "primitive" kitchen. The servants who endured most of these drudgeries in the Campbell household fell out of the picture; he focused on Virginia, a "methodical woman as well as a charming and generous hostess," who, like the wartime housewife, believed in "preparedness against the common ills." He even suggested readers would find solace in the glimpses the receipts provided of a bountiful life that could be reclaimed after the war, when "duck with potato stuffing" and "fish timbales with creole sauce" would no longer be out of OPA bounds.[34]

Such interpretations seem to have captured the public imagination and secured a place for the receipt book—and the folklore of Victorian domesticity—in the museum narrative for decades to come. Even as the concern for making-do fell away and resourceful housekeeping ceased to be such an obsession in the popular press, CHM interpreters continued to conjure the glories of antebellum St. Louis by describing Virginia's home-spun hospitality and the meals prepared and served under her guidance with recipes from her collection. The ideals of nineteenth-century living had been pressed through the screen of late 1930s and early 1940s idealism and subtly infused with wartime anxieties and fears. As time passed, more and more visitors (a record 1,200 in one summer month of 1946), most of them white, middle- and upper-class St. Louisans, paid homage to these ideals on their tours and took home copies of her recipes.[35]

For this audience, the receipt book signified wholesomeness and tra-ditional values, and allowed for some smoothing out of the class and economic disparities that not only were built into antebellum household life in Lucas Place (where families relied on small fleets of servants) but in fact persisted into the mid-twentieth century. As the next chapter shows, the stories associated with the receipt book legitimized claims about the Campbells' ostensible middle-classness and pointed to nineteenth-century analogues of middle-class consumption that came to dominate postwar America. As we have seen with Boo's account of her tour, the allure of the receipt book depended on multiple, at times contradictory understandings of domestic life—a symbolic richness that, as Celeste Olalquiaga has argued, commonly gives souvenirs their "fetishistic poten-tial," their power as emblems of cultural heritage and social identity.[36] In the coming decades, CHM officials would seek to harness that potential through all manner of promotions, including alternative versions of the souvenir booklet (which itself went through four editions) and a host of events inspired by Virginia's receipt book, often featuring food and drink she had once served her guests.[37]

The public's investment in this unlikely heritage object partook of a compensatory logic by means of which they could lay claim to the material evidence of the past without cognitive dissonance of the kind museum officials must have felt when faced with interpreting a site of luxurious living as a symbol of American identity—even of democratic experience—as the nation descended into war. The receipt book became the most well-known of all the Campbell possessions because it was a hieroglyph of social privilege but also an emblem of national (and local) character traits—steadfastness, frugality, resourcefulness, sturdiness—that were cherished and nurtured by St. Louisans throughout midcentury.

CHAPTER 6

THE DINNER PARTY

All of St. Louis knew that . . . President Ulysses S. Grant would dine
at the palatial residence of Robert Campbell that night.
—*Selma Robinson, "The Magnificent Campbell House"*

THE LIGHT OF the day was fading as Virginia peered through the lace
curtains of her bedroom window. A handful of carriages had lined
up on the street below, and coachmen bustled about, tending the horses
and trying to manage a growing crowd of onlookers. Delicious smells
wafted up the back stairs, and she sighed a bit as the maid fastened the
hooks on her mulberry satin gown. In the adjoining bedroom, Robert
pulled out his heavy gold watch, checked it yet again, and gave the cover
a little polishing before he put it back in his pocket. It was nearly time.
Virginia straightened her diamond cross pendant and stepped into the
hall. Behind the voices of servants and the scuffling of the horses she
could make out the strains of a violin: a Philadelphia band Robert had
hired for the occasion was tuning up in the back parlor. She ran her hand
along the bannister as she descended, following the butler into the dining
room for his hundredth "final check" of the day.[1]

The room was aglow; dozens of candles and a pair of gasoliers emit-
ted flickering light that reflected in the mirrors. The butler straightened
a yellow rose and studied the centerpiece, a silver epergne anchored by a
gleaming pile of grapes, pineapples, pears, and pomegranates. The table
settings were like immaculate shrines: each place had its own cut-glass
finger bowl, specialty forks, and Baccarat crystal goblets, and each was
topped by a linen serviette shaped like a cardinal's hat. The staff had
spent days preparing the room, adding leaves to the oak table, laying out
dozens of pieces of hand-painted Limoges porcelain and crystal, draping

flowers from the light fixtures, and choreographing a twenty-course meal. The Campbells' guests would dine on tongue of buffalo, prairie hen, smoked fish, roasted haunch of venison, raw oysters, and lobster interspersed with cheese and nuts, tomato aspic, roast vegetables, and fine spirits: champagne, Roman Punch, claret, native wines, sherries. Dessert was a Charlotte Russe *á la modern,* an assortment of fruit ices and pastries, and chocolates in the shape of harvest fruits. Each item on the menu had its counterpart in the parlor furnishings—carvings of fish and game and grape leaves on the oak sideboard; fruits and nuts painted on the china; a wall-hanging featuring dried fruit and flowers.

When at last the front doors were opened, Robert and Virginia greeted Ulysses S. Grant, his wife, Julia, and the dashing General William Sherman in person. A roar of welcome rose from the crowd as the honored guests climbed the steps to the house. The band struck up a patriotic anthem, and they were greeted in the parlor by the Honorable Henry T. Blow of the U.S. House of Representatives and Captain James B. Eads, among other Lucas Place notables. This was not the president's first visit, but the Campbells were known for their lavish hospitality, and the event quickly became the talk of the town.[2] In less than two decades, St. Louis had been transformed from an outpost town into a genteel "gateway city," and Robert Campbell had been instrumental in that process. Many saw him as "one of the noblest men" around, celebrating his exploits as "fur trader, explorer, merchant prince, public benefactor, humanitarian," and husband to the charming and accomplished Virginia Kyle of North Carolina. The evening's festivities—which included an elaborate dinner, a "young people's reception" and dance, and a midnight serenade of the president by the Arsenal military band—gave expression not only to his own achievements but to the ambitions of a city "destined for greatness."[3]

"Our Living Heritage"

The festivities described above occurred in 1957, not 1874, and the esteemed guests were not the Reconstruction president and local dignitaries but costumed reenactors recruited by the Junior League. The scenes of household preparation and the elaborate table-settings; the eager anticipation by Robert and Virginia and their household staff; the "sizeable crowd" that gathered and "stood . . . chattering excitedly or looking up at the impressive house with the red carpeted stoop"—all of it had been conjured by *McCall's* based on newspaper accounts and other sources. When editors of the popular lifestyle magazine heard about this legendary episode of Midwestern hospitality, they decided to stage a full-scale reenactment for their series "Our Living Heritage," the first of its kind at the Campbell House Museum. The script took nine months to develop, much of it produced from a distance (*McCall's* was headquartered in New York City), but in close consultation with CHM officials, period cookbooks, and in the final weeks, a fleet of specialists—lighting and costume technicians, culinary experts, makeup artists, even florists.[4] The resulting ten-page article ran in the July 1957 issue of the magazine: it included sixteen color photos, a historical narrative (including fictional flashbacks to early life in frontier-outpost St. Louis), and reprints from Virginia's receipt book, including recipes for stuffed leg of veal, floating island, and duck with potato stuffing. These were dishes said to demonstrate "that the St. Louisan housewife of late Victorian days set a fine table."[5]

McCall's was by this time among the top sellers in the fashion and lifestyle magazine industry, and they knew such a feature would have broad appeal—particularly for an audience already primed to think about the nation's past as a repository of national values.[6] Print culture had for decades been laced with allusions to American history, as for example in thousands of advertisements that deployed allusions to the past—both to celebrate American heritage and to promote certain behaviors and products. Many were set at iconic historic sites that, in colorful scenes of reenactment, became the stage for middle-class consumption. Thus, Priscilla Alden expressed delight at the durability of Armstrong Linoleum ("Early American Plank—but with no splinters!"), restorers fantasized about repainting a shabby-looking Mount Vernon with products manufactured by National Paint and Varnish, and a young Abraham Lincoln espoused the virtues of hard work and progress (from a cot in his Kentucky log cabin) in a General Motors public service announcement.[7] The notion that one could study the past to learn about modern national character—and in turn discover in consumer goods a means of reclaiming this character and "traditional" American values—had taken firm hold in the popular imagination, and the Campbell House seemed ripe for such treatment.

But there were other contextual factors at play that made this particular historic house appealing to *McCall's*. In recent years, the CHM had come to be known as a site that "exemplifies the maturing of the frontier, [and] the lush, mid-nineteenth-century urban taste of the wealthy," as historian Charles van Ravenswaay asserted in *Antiques* magazine in 1945—thanks not just to national publications like *Antiques* and *Life* but to the zealotry of local boosters.[8] While the postwar city had experienced disinvestment, population loss, and overall economic decline, CHM's interpreters continued to assert connections between the city's past glories and its future aspirations. Tour guides increasingly paid attention to the particulars of life during and after the Civil War—a far more tangible period than the generic "Victorian age" privileged by 1940s preservationists—and even to some details of the Campbell history. With time, the site's interpretive center of gravity underwent a perceptible shift from the "front" to the "back" of the house, such that by the late 1940s, guests spent far less time rhapsodizing about parlor furnishings than they did contemplating "daily life" as depicted in spaces like the family bedrooms and kitchen.

Promoters also invested increasing energy in the precincts of domesticity. As we have seen, Virginia's receipt book—an artifact of family and regional heritage—was a symbolic pivot point between the Campbells' public and private worlds. Throughout the war years, this especially popular artifact was displayed in the kitchen, a space where the "cook-hostess" was said to have been most at home and where it became the anchor for a narrative about Virginia and her legendary hospitality. The receipt book reminded visitors of their own home-making practices—of "making-do" with little and celebrating family and country. Robert soon joined Virginia at the center of this mythology: like a returning GI, he gained heightened visibility after the war, his heroic service to country (during the Mexican War), as well as his leadership in business and politics, garnering new attention in museum narratives. These biographical details supplanted early vagaries of "frontier life" and turned Robert into a flesh-and-blood father and husband. By the time *McCall's* decided to recreate the Grant dinner party, Robert was back at the head of the table, as it were, despite the fact that he had actually been absent from two of the three historical Grant dinners that inspired their reenactment.

Outside of these new emphases, museum narratives underwent relatively few revisions in the postwar years. The CHF sustained public programs that reinforced the site's heritage appeal, and museum traffic remained steady; in some months, the museum hosted as many as 1,000 or even 1,200 individual tours, including school groups.[9] But the number of visitors began to taper off in the early 1950s, a period when the demographics of the city were continuing to shift, with middle-class flight being a major cause. Indeed, St. Louis seemed to be experiencing growth everywhere *except* in the central corridor, as planning and traffic studies from the late 1940s demonstrated. An *Expressway Plan for the Saint Louis and Adjacent Missouri Area* (1951) suggested these issues would have to be addressed with new and improved roads.[10] As the locus of public culture shifted from the Civic Center and downtown to points west (Forest Park, University City, and Creve Coeur Lake Memorial Park, among others), the CHF began to express concern over declining interest in the museum and in the history of the city more broadly.

In its effort to attract younger visitors but also to hold the attention of core supporters (white suburban women), the CHF began moving outside the target timeframe of the house's history, prioritizing the acquisition of "period costumes." The interest in historic clothing went back to the founding of the museum: Grace Ashley's fundraising gala at the Chase Hotel and other events of the early 1940s had often featured social elites wearing Virginia's dresses, basking in the sense of connection with the past that such activities encouraged. But the new (non-Campbell) acquisitions altered the shape of the permanent collection and confounded the logics and motives of display that dominated the CHF's work at the time of the museum's opening. A formal Costume Room exhibit installed in 1946, for example—which was dedicated to Grace Ashley and used by members of her St. Louis Fashion Creators (SLFC) for educational and entertainment purposes—led to vigorous new fashion-oriented interpretation of the house.

In 1949, the SLFC unveiled "St. Louis Heritage Fashions," a modern clothing line inspired by dresses recently "found in the attic" of the Campbell House. The line featured designs that adapted the "slim basque waists, bustles, flounces and other elegant fashion details of the 1860s and '70s," and was launched in a curious show that combined Virginia's gowns (shown on mannequins) with modern fashions (on live models who posed throughout the house). One model wearing a "patterned pique dress [suited] for summer dancing in 1949," which, "like Mrs. Campbell's brocaded faille ball dress, has [a] full skirt, tight pointed bodice," and taffeta bustle, was photographed in the master bedroom. Another in a fitted dress-suit inspired by "Mrs. Campbell's formal gown of cut velvet" posed next to the mannequin in the parlor. When the live fashion show was done, the heritage fashions were installed in an upstairs bedroom that the SLFC had "transformed into a Victorian parlor" to serve as "a more authentic setting for the costumes."[11]

Virginia's brocade, lace, and taffeta certainly bespoke the elegance of the Lucas Place lifestyle that had been so frequently highlighted in early museum interpretation. But in these new interpretive contexts, such finery took on different associations entirely. It gave a distinctly modern—one might say even commercial—aura to the house, while, paradoxically, confirming the heritage appeal of the original gowns. But the point of the costume room and related promotional events seemed to be to associate the CHM collection with the "lifestyles" of local debutantes and socialites rather than the other way around. The costume room exhibit resembled nothing so much as a department store display or fashion advertisement. Stix, Baer & Fuller (SBF) promotions from the same period (see chapter 4) similarly turned the Campbells' possessions into consumer goods and laid claim to their heritage associations in order to promote postwar lifestyle consumerism.

Around this same time, the Campbell children made their first significant appearance in museum lore, though always as young children ("aging bachelors who never threw anything away" hardly fit the story the CHF wished to tell). Their childhood portraits, saved at auction and hung in the parlor but mostly ignored, now received mention on every tour, often in the context of a discussion of family life. And some of the children's surviving possessions inspired a semi-permanent "Children's Room" exhibit dedicated to the museum's patron saint, Jesse P. Henry, which opened in 1950.[12] Like the Costume Room, which is discussed more fully in chapter 7, this display featured just a handful of original Campbell objects supplemented by "period" artifacts from local collections, and was almost certainly a response to trends in popular culture, which is to say, an effort to boost visitorship.[13] As children gained visibility in the museum, they became an established feature of the Campbell family of the public imagination—established enough that, years later, *McCall's* felt the need to hire a child actor for its dinner party reenactment.

While these new exhibits created local buzz, a general sense of anxiety pervaded the board's discussions during this time. The house had begun to show signs of its age, and between 1951 and 1956, the CHF was forced to pursue "refurbishments" throughout the house: not only deep cleaning but patching of wallpaper; moth prevention treatments; repair of faulty wiring (essential given the number of public events that were being staged); and exterior improvements such as repair of gutters and downspouts, replanting of the garden, and the purchase of new signage. Much of this work was paid for by longtime benefactor SBF, while special projects were funded by local groups like the Ad Club and SLFC. But the to-do list kept growing, and in the months leading up to *McCall's* dinner party, the CHF president warned that positive publicity would not be enough to sustain the house long-term.[14]

In response, the CHF pursued a new media campaign, publishing endorsements for its new exhibits in local hotel guides and Automobile Club weeklies, and promoting the museum with help from the Ad Club and local interest groups such as the Junior League. The National Society of the Colonial Dames of America sponsored special tours of the house aimed at women, including one focused on fashion and home decor that was a favorite of the SLFC. And events such as garden parties thrown in honor of the secret society the Veiled Prophet's "Queen of Love and Beauty" and her "Maids of Honor court" in the mid-1950s gave the museum a boost among local elites (the society's membership overlapped with debutante and country club sets) and the general public.[15] The board also vigorously promoted short-term exhibits, many featuring objects unrelated to the Campbells (for example, Grace Ashley's collection of Victorian valentines). These activities reflected a new pragmatism about how to showcase the collection and an effort to rekindle affection for St. Louis heritage.

Bringing the Past to Life

The Campbells had hosted many grand parties over the years, and they visited with dignitaries like the Grants whenever they came to town. Hugh Campbell continued the tradition after his parents passed away, and the last big social event at the family residence seems to have been a party hosted for Nellie, Ulysses and Julia Grant's daughter, at the time of the St.

Louis World's Fair in 1904.[16] But the 1870s dinners with President Grant and his wife were especially storied occasions that were still recounted at the turn of the century, usually as marvels of fashion and hospitality, with well-dressed guests and resplendent table settings. An 1888 *Post-Dispatch* account was typical: it described Lucas Place as "the Belgravia of our Western metropolis" and remembered fondly a time when "dinner parties were stately affairs." Virginia's "ceremonial but brilliant" performance as hostess was especially celebrated.[17]

Memory of these stately affairs became fuzzy in the Depression, when the various Grant dinners, now effectively merged, received only passing mention if any. A 1941 article on the "Rise and Fall of Lucas Place," for instance, remembered the "dignified elegance" of a neighborhood that was now just "a phantom," explaining that its "lavish" dinners and balls were "peculiar to the period" but "justified by the wealth and taste of its leaders." It was the tragic "fall" of Lucas Place that was the real subject of the article, which ended by describing efforts to save the Campbell House. Grant never came up, his reputation having suffered in the decades after he sold off his Missouri property and moved to New York.[18]

But the Grant dinner stories were dusted off again in the 1950s, mainly for use in promotional material. A placard on display in the downtown Visitor's Bureau starting in 1950 urged visitors to the city to come "see how prominent St. Louisans lived in the 1850s. . . . See the dining room where President Grant was entertained." The slogan served mainly to confirm the site's (and the city's) historical significance, a message reinforced by the inclusion of a black-and-white photograph showing the "famous double parlor as featured in *Life* and *National Geographic*."[19] The unthinking conflation of two distinct eras—the 1850s and the 1870s—reveals the less-than-stable interpretive frame that had taken hold at the CHM. Visitors of the period certainly left the house with a sense of the Campbells' social and historical influence: political figures visited often, Grant among them, and such events were common in genteel old Lucas Place. They just did not know precisely when the dinners occurred.

These event were often said to epitomize the grandeur of life in "lush, mid-nineteenth-century," usually in the context of claims that the Campbell mansion had once been the "center of St. Louis [high] society."[20] But the details, as well as the timeframe, had become muddled in translation. Some of this was a function of slippages inside the museum itself. While WCS preservationists had chosen a bounded period ("the 1850s"), they developed period-room-style displays that incorporated objects from more than fifty years of family history and encouraged visitors to celebrate them as part of a generic "golden age." The influence of these choices is evident in *Life's* photograph of the parlor, where a handful of artifacts dominate the composition and the costumed women are ghostly figures who seem to feel not a sense of connection to the past but unbridgeable distance and loss. *McCall's* editors operated on a totally different assumption, one half-articulated by early visitors like "Boo" and more directly advanced in the 1950s: that the Campbell House was a place to make contact with a *living past,* not just ghosts or mute treasures of the dead.

To these interpreters, as we have seen with the SLFC show, the house was a stage on which history could be felt, or more precisely inhabited, even reenacted. They believed, furthermore, that the past spoke to ideals of material well-being and cultural vitality that might inspire visitors and be linked to their own lives. These arguments were not wholly new: some early museum backers seized on the house as an emblem of old St. Louis, which they retooled for their own purposes. SBF, for example, incorporated images of the house (and in its stores, artifacts from the collection) to advance its brand identity, encouraging customers to engage with local heritage as a tangible thing. Taking possession of the site on behalf of the public, which SBF initially framed as a tasteful ceremony of remembrance keyed to the ethos of wartime austerity, came with time to look like a more assertive claim on the house and the city's history. With SBF's influence, new tropes of ownership, security, and social order took hold in everyday museum practice, and *McCall's* may well have been drawn to the site because of these efforts.

The idea of a reenactment of the Grant dinner was conceived by *McCall's* food editor Helen McCully when CHF president John A. Bryan sent her a copy of *Virginia Campbell's Cook Book*. The magazine's editorial staff saw in the collection of recipes what wartime reviewers had seen: a kind of heritage of everyday life and entertaining that would be of interest to their readers. Searching out historical cookbooks and newspaper coverage of the original Grant dinner, they began to develop a picture of the Campbells' social universe. They pursued additional details with anthropological curiosity, exchanging letters with CHF members and the Junior League over a period of six months about everything from menu to clothing to atmospherics. The dinner quickly took on the complexity and symbolic significance of an actual state dinner.[21]

McCall's staff believed performative engagement with the material practices of the past would collapse the distance between then and now and provide readers with a concrete sense of *being there*—of deep connection to, and immersion in, the past, or what contemporary reenactors call "period rush."[22] Close attention to historical particulars notwithstanding, the event would require elaborate staging. While many of *McCall's* articles involved "production," reenactment was far more involved than the standard onsite photo shoot. The magazine had to write a full script, hire actors, borrow suitable costumes, and prepare the site for a media event. Given the age of the home, this last task was no small matter: floors had to be scrubbed, waxed, and polished (McCully insisted that even the inside of the oven and horse-drawn carriage be cleaned); furniture freshened and repaired; plaster and paint touched up; and new electrical circuits added (*McCall's* would need mounted stage lighting as well as every fixture in the house).[23] And the period clothing they borrowed from a theater company would have to be tailored to fit fifteen actors recruited by the local Junior League. This was not to touch on makeup, food prep and plating, the choreography of the shoot, and the archival research required to produce the accompanying narrative.

Toward the end of the long exchange between the editor and the CHF president, McCully apologized for giving so many orders to her St. Louis correspondents: "I feel as though I were acting like a general in the army. . . . But I hope you will understand that we are trying to show the Campbell House in its best possible light—as wonderful and beautiful *as it really is.*"[24] The metaphor turned out to be apt given the full-scale refurbishment of the house that was expected, second only to the initial "restoration" the CHF had pursued a decade earlier. When the *McCall's* team arrived, the staging continued. They reconfigured the rooms extensively, showing little concern for existing setup or museum practice. Seeking to conjure a sense of what they called Victorian "sumptuousness," they combined existing furnishings with objects pulled from elsewhere and added a layer of greenery—houseplants and fresh flower arrangements. The stark grandeur typically seen on museum tours (fig. 12) was made more visually

FIGURE 12. Parlor scene photograph in "The Magnificent Campbell House: Our Living Heritage," *McCall's*, July 1957, 44. Originally published in *McCall's® Magazine*, July 1957. Campbell House Museum, St. Louis, MO.

complex and more inviting. The magazine photos captured a depth of color and texture that none of the earlier images had shown, and indeed that would not be seen again until the house was restored based on the 1880s photos (discussed in chapter 8).

Once all this setup was complete, the "dinner" could begin. The team staged a sequence of household preparation and dining scenes that corresponded to stages of ceremonial hospitality; each was captured "live" by *McCall's* photographers, who positioned their cameras at near eye level. Their spotlights illuminated the high-ceilinged rooms in ways they never had been before: hulking furniture and architectural elements that dominated earlier photos seemed harmoniously blended and more human-scaled. And despite the formality of the furnishings and costumes, the atmosphere was now almost homey. While the photos look like film stills, the elaborately coiffed reenactors lounge about on furniture, sipping drinks, laughing, and generally performing mirth like experienced Hollywood extras. They show none of the awkwardness exhibited by the women who donned Virginia's gowns for the *Life* magazine shoot—probably due in part to coaching by *McCall's* staff, who seem to have been involved in every last detail. They seem to have pushed past beyond playacting, experiencing the event "as it really was."

McCall's chose to make two photographs showing the dining scenes the centerpiece of the article. The first, a frontal shot of the dining room as it might have looked to the butler as he made last-minute adjustments, shows a table "profuse with roses . . . and banked with fruit, typical of the 1870s." The flower arrangements command attention: they are taller than the people about to be seated, the silver epergnes in which they are set branching like fruit trees in a Victorian garden. And they seem to gesture artfully toward tasteful bouquets on the mantle, as well as the medallioned floral wallpaper and an oval-framed wall-hanging behind, with miniature ladies' bouquets by each plate. The second photograph (fig. 13), an action shot taken from just above the heads of the diners, presents the Campbells' guests socializing animatedly, some lifting their forks or munching food. The butler stands at the sideboard carving meat; his head is the apex of the scene.[25]

Here again, the table is the primary focus. We are meant to study the textures and colors of the meal that the staff have prepared with Virginia's recipes: game hens and lustrous creamed spinach; gelatin molded into the shape of two giant strawberries; mounds of shiny fruit, including a pineapple, the symbol of hospitality, conspicuously placed atop heaps of grapes, bananas, pears, and even tomatoes; goblets of red wine; and enormous roses framed by bright green foliage. "Sumptuousness" is brought to its fullest, most dramatic expression in the table, a luxuriant assemblage meant to express "hospitality dispensed on the largest scale." The

FIGURE 13. Dinner scene photograph in "The Magnificent Campbell House: Our Living Heritage," *McCall's*, July 1957, 45. Originally published in *McCall's® Magazine*, July 1957. Campbell House Museum, St. Louis, MO.

caption notes that the Campbells' table was often so full that "there was barely room for the customary bouquet at each lady's place." It describes a typical menu of "twenty or more courses . . . [including] buffalo tongue, prairie hen, venison."[26] Many of the foods mentioned are visible on the table. *McCall's* editors had done their homework.

And yet, this was a Victorian dinner party of the 1950s middle-class imagination. The dining table photo was taken in the style of room portraiture made popular by the more upscale *House Beautiful* and commonly used to showcase professionally decorated suburban homes in decorating magazines. The high-detail, high-contrast image calls attention to architectural and design symmetries and underscores intentional placement (as well as ceremonious use) of meaning-laden objects that are meant to express conviviality, casual conversation, and unapologetic consumption. Readers of *McCall's* could take the same pleasure in the image that they did in articles explaining modern home decor trends or pool parties. People were key elements, their costumes, facial expressions, and gestures communicating "hospitality dispensed on the largest scale." Their fancy clothes aside, they might be guests in hundreds of illustrations depicting festive occasions, including Norman Rockwell's iconic *Freedom from Want* (which first ran in a 1943 *Saturday Evening Post* and has a similar composition). The guests' faces fairly glow with good cheer: each is attentive to his or her fellow companions (who seem to be telling great stories), and each seems to be genuinely enjoying the event.

The narrative accompanying the photos heightened the pleasing effects of tangibility and sociability. It was filled with sensory description of the food and decor and snippets of "actual" dinner conversation that contributed to a sense of immediacy and historical specificity. While some of what *McCall's* editors chose to include came from museum lore or was wholly fabricated (the bit about Virginia's dress having been "made to match" the porcelain dinner service, for example, was a favorite apocryphal story told by tour guides), much of it was gleaned from historical sources. The whole thing had the sheen of verisimilitude associated with period drama. A being-there quality of the reenactment trumped anything museumgoers got on the standard tour.

"A Time of Wealth, Pleasant Social Life, and Important Cultural Beginnings"

McCall's editors knew the thrill of vicarious engagement with such a meticulously reconstructed past would be all the stronger if readers grasped its symbolic significance—that is, if they understood what the 1874 Grant dinner meant for the family and the city. Thus, alongside her account of household preparations and up-close views of the meal, the author, Selma Robinson, served up the rags-to-riches story of Robert's life, starting with his arrival in St. Louis in the 1830s as a "penniless" teen from "County Tyrone in Ireland" confronted by the "fascinating and varied parade" of "St. Louisans" commonly found on the riverfront, who at the time included "bearded, long-haired fur trappers, savagely attired in beaded buckskin . . . mincing ladies, like hourglasses with their pinched little waists, their Negro slaves carrying market baskets . . . farmers . . . [driving] mule-drawn wagons," and "sun-browned Creole boatmen from the New Orleans."[27] This was not, in Robinson's telling, just the place where a fur trader launched his remarkable business career; it was the very seedbed of industrial capitalism in the West—a locus of growth made possible by vigorous mixing of cultures. Robert was considered one of St. Louis's "greatest citizens" not only because of his bravery and ingenuity but because of his generosity to the poor, immigrants, soldiers, and Indian trade partners. *McCall's* was celebrating these not just as St. Louis history but as American heritage.

The Grant dinner of 1874 thus served as the other bookend of Robert's public life—a kind of crowning achievement ("the high moment in the life of a man who could still remember" his difficult start) and also, not incidentally, the fullest expression of his considerable wealth. Editors undoubtedly felt drawn to the dinner party because it signified economic power and political celebrity, but they chose to represent the event itself as something more: as part of public culture (the daily marketplace) and private housekeeping (the kitchen); as both a ceremonial ritual (guests assembled in the parlor) and a familial practice (owners dressing in their bedroom). They were especially concerned to capture the Campbells' home life, including Robert and Virginia's "long and happy marriage" and well-run household, which reflected ideals suburban readers themselves were expected to long for.[28]

These ideals were captured in the other photographs from the spread. The very first image, which shows the kitchen as it looked during preparations for the dinner party (fig. 14), follows closely on the aforementioned description of the 1824 St. Louis riverfront. Together, they evoked both the possibility of westward expansion and the quality of life enjoyed by those who were leading it. On the plain wooden table we see "local" goods (eggs, tomatoes, green beans, potatoes), a loaf of homemade bread, and "turkey at ten cents a pound (screened here from flies)," as well as

FIGURE 14. Kitchen photograph in "The Magnificent Campbell House: Our Living Heritage," *McCall's*, July 1957, 48. Originally published in *McCall's® Magazine*, July 1957. Campbell House Museum, St. Louis, MO.

luxury goods imported by riverboat, including oysters and red snapper, a box of Chinese tea, a ceramic teapot, and several pieces from the Campbells' French porcelain dinner service. The room's simple decor, its cast-iron stoves and a copper-lined sink (which, readers would learn, provided the only running water in the house), communicated the idea of humble roots and sincerity.[29]

The other meaning-laden artifact in the image was a large tome in the center of the table: it is meant to represent Virginia's receipt book (although it looks more like *The Joy of Cooking* than the real thing). No cook was shown or even mentioned in the narrative; readers were instead invited to imagine Virginia herself sitting in the chair (though she likely did no such thing). It is "her" dishes that grace the dining table; "her" recipes that appear at the end of the magazine; "her" labors as "gracious hostess" that are praised throughout. The intimacy of this perspective reinforced the sense that *McCall's* had pulled back the curtain on domestic life in the nineteenth century (although not so far as to expose the extent of their own stagecraft), and that readers were seeing a real Victorian household.

Robinson anticipated her readers' questions about this household: How could a meal fit for a president have been prepared in such a primitive kitchen? How many people were involved in the staging of a twenty-course meal? What did Virginia actually serve? She matter of factly explained that the family had two kitchens (the second one was in the basement); that servants worked day and night to keep up in such a household; that the food was bought in nearby markets stocked by steamboats. This too was familiar territory for women's magazines of the time, which were forever posing questions (Just how does the lady of the house pull off such a splendid meal each night when she has her hands full with the children all day?) and then answering in the form of advice, step-by-step instructions, or reviews of labor-saving products. But Robinson took readers someplace new: "Bowls of dark, shiny watercress stood ready to garnish the haunch of venison sizzling in the oven. The huge soup tureen waited for the savory consommé simmering on the stove. The butler sniffed deep of the many odors. One of the cooks whipped the heavy cream for the cakes so fast that her arm was a blur of movement."[30] The passage reads like *Good Housekeeping* fiction about the "new wife's first big dinner party" but with the tantalizing descriptions of a modern food blog. Is this a magazine expert's careful explanation we are reading? Or a reenactor's sentimental imaginings? Or perhaps Virginia's own reminiscences? In reenactment, all three come together to express a sense of intimacy, of "being there." Readers might even draw connections between the historic event and one they had staged in their own home (if only to register that they had been outclassed!).

In many ways, *McCall's* suspended the famous Grant dinner between past and future: readers could become vicarious participants in a meal at once aspirational and already finished whose significance had been established. The meal the magazine staged, painstaking in "historical" details down to the position of serving platters and olive forks, was also symbolic, with all the associations of a ceremonial feast: material abundance, social belonging, and wish-fulfillment through consumption, all of which took on new meanings in the postwar period. The (historical) Grant dinner might have been remembered for its "lavish hospitality," but in 1957 it also undoubtedly expressed a collective sense of recovery and relief from the strife of (that other) war—a "return to normalcy" and social order, as a war general and president returned to the "Compromise" state and dined with both Union and Confederate sympathizers. As a state dinner, it might also have been a kind of ceremonial potlatch or even the First Thanksgiving, or a new version of Rockwell's *Freedom from Want*, where ideals of hope, community, the family home, and individual flourishing were embodied in the bounties of a harvest. *McCall's* managed to evoke all of these without explicitly naming any of them.

"Faith in the Future, Glories of the Past"

St. Louisans who were involved in the *McCall's* reenactment, and the many who read the magazine after it came out, had their own reasons for embracing such a beautiful vision of their city's past. As we have seen, urban life was fundamentally reshaped by postwar renewal in a series of projects whose scale—and effects—would have been unthinkable before the war. This was in many respects a new era of frontier expansionism for St. Louis, but one fueled—or haunted—by "city problems" from deteriorating streets and industrial plants to urgently needed highways to critical shortages in low-income housing. A widely read *Post-Dispatch* series from the beginning of the decade posed the problem of compromised expansionism as a question that answered itself: "Progress or Decay? St. Louis Must Choose." Echoing city planners and their reports, the article noted that "more than a third of the city" was "blotted by areas of blight and of progressively worsening slums," and warned that the suburbs were "no longer . . . isolated from the unpleasant parts of the community. Fine homes and . . . pleasant white collar dwellings . . . are within hailing distance, if not actual sight, of obsolete dwellings, overcrowded subdivisions or downright misery."[31] The solution seemed plain, and it involved changes so radical that planners used surgery metaphors to describe the excision of "cancerous" parts of the city—aging neighborhoods increasingly seen as cesspools of crime and poverty and barriers to progress.

The surgeries were well underway when *McCall's* began laying its plans for a feast. Chestnut Valley, an African American district just west of downtown known for its ragtime bars and cheap housing, had been quickly cleared in 1953, and nearby Mill Creek Valley (MCV), another African American district that lay in the path of the new interstate, was next: its demolition began in 1955, right as the CHF was starting to fret about the fall-off in attendance and deterioration of the house, which was the same age as the "slums" in question. The uncomfortable parallels continued, though few chose to acknowledge them: while twenty thousand MCV residents were being forcibly relocated, many to segregated districts outside the city limits, their arrival triggering fears of a "negro invasion" in the county, *McCall's* was reconstituting the social world of white, urban elites of the previous century and celebrating their "hospitality" for a primarily nonlocal audience.[32]

The Campbell House occupied a position at the symbolic crossroads between past and future and the literal crossroads of business, residential, and civic St. Louis. In the hands of *McCall's,* such a site offered confirmation of the city's (and nation's) past accomplishments and a glorious vision of its future—a kind of aspirational consumption that, it was believed, would bring community and social harmony. The sizzling venison and shiny watercress, the filet of beef and red wine and cigars, had the aroma of an authentic historical past, but their real pungency lay in the ideals that they were said to represent—ideals of community and sociability that the growing metropolis was at that moment struggling to maintain.

McCall's expressed those ideals in a vocabulary known best to white, middle-class readers and museumgoers: it performed the city's best-known historical feast as a suburban dinner party and infused the Victorian town house with a 1950s suburban social aesthetic, a sense of order and well-being that certainly was available to the Campbell family in the narrative but had little to do with "life as it was lived" by the Campbells. The "new" Campbell House was no longer the domain of high culture and formal manners—an ironic fact given the high formality of the culture that produced it and the event being reenacted. Instead, it was a site for imaginative engagement with the past, a screen on which to project middle-class fantasies of domestic and social life. *McCall's* meant for readers to identify with those dinner guests—a fantasy "Boo" and others longed for—but not as historical figures so much as vicarious participants. The power of reenactment lay in its apparent innocence, of being *in* but not wholly *of* the past; of indulging its material excesses without being implicated by them; of being *in* but not *of* the ruling class, who in modern times was busy remaking the city.

The Return of the Repressed

The translation between the old world and the new was not entirely straightforward, however. As *McCall's* staff laid claim to scenes of the past, they could neither entirely escape their own sensibilities nor cast off the problematic elements of the past. Both informed a range of elements of "The Magnificent Campbell House," but the representation of "daily life in the Campbell house" merits special consideration, particularly given the racial politics of the city at the time. As noted, the magazine opted not to represent the cook, leaving readers to imagine Virginia working in the kitchen instead. Likewise, it showed little interest in the family's large staff, which was known to have included many servants who hauled ice and groceries, ran errands, fetched horses, and did a range of things to support the household, especially during events such as the Grant dinner. The butler, however—who is here something of an editorial confabulation, since the Campbells never had a butler—was prominently featured; he even got something of a voice, or at least a point of view, in the fictional narrative, which highlights his efforts to prepare the house (apparently without help from footmen and kitchen staff).[33]

There might well have been practical reasons for not showing other servants, such as lack of appropriate costuming, lack of knowledge about how to represent their activities, or a sense that they would not appeal to readers. The only other "help" shown in the photographs is a chamber maid, who was played, revealingly, by a young African American girl. She appears in two separate images: one that shows her adjusting a parlor lamp above the head of a curly haired white boy sitting on a Belter chair looking at a family album, and another that pictures her filling a small tin bathtub in a corner of the master bedroom. A caption explains that "every drop of shaving and bathing water was carried to bedrooms and down again. Understandably, [the] family could take very few baths."[34]

In these representational choices we see a drift toward something distinctly new in Campbell House folklore: a concern with power relations.

In these images, and indeed throughout the *McCall's* spread, (white) women anchor the social and domestic scenes and perform symbolic household labor (eating, playing piano, sewing, pouring tea, administering a dose of cough syrup, studying pictures of far-off places), while (white) men are shown as authority figures. In nearly every image, men are standing, while the women sit; in the dinner scene, where everyone is seated, the butler's authority is expressed by his position at the center and his reflection in the mirror. Yet while the women do not exert themselves, the fruits of "their" household labor are in evidence everywhere in the article: in allusions to Mrs. Campbell's "southern woman's traditional charm, and graciousness" and her "superb and imaginative food" (which, while she did not prepare it, came from her cookbook); in the fine embroidery and other evidence of tasteful decorating shown in the photographs; in the healthful glow of well-dressed children and well-planned meals. Who performed all this labor in a wealthy home? In the modern household, readers of *McCall's* well knew, it was the housewife; in the preceding era, it would have been the help. The account invited readers to revel in the conflated experiences of both. To what end? we might ask.

The presence of the housemaid offers another answer: an unconscious desire to give expression to white privilege of a sort achieved through symbolic as well as actual dominance. We see this kind of sublimated dominance in the SBF advertisement and *Life* photographs, and more in the "renewal" policies that authorized clearance of MCV and other "slums." The presence of this girl in the photo *could* be read as an intentional reference to the keeping of slaves during the nineteenth century, which had been a common feature of elite white society in St. Louis right up to and during the war, and which would have been visible in the earlier period at the Campbell House—the years that were privileged in museum interpretation. Still, a slave would not have been present in the moment supposedly being depicted: research would have shown *McCall's* editors that the Campbells emancipated their inherited slaves two decades before the Grant dinner and did not hire black laborers. Most of their servants were Irish. The housemaids at the time of the dinner were named Hannah Roke, Ellen Maney, and Nellie Mean, all recent immigrants in their mid- to late teens, part of a long line of Irish individuals that Robert hired out of a sense of loyalty, as Hugh continued to do in later years.[35] Tellingly, *McCall's* makes no mention at all of either slavery or domestic labor (besides the butler's fussing) anywhere in the long article; the images are the only place where such imaginative work takes place.

And yet the casting of a black child was intentional: she was the only person of color in the entire reenactment operation and the first one mentioned in official Campbell House interpretations since the opening of the museum. Putting her in that role "made sense" to those who planned the event, staged the house, and shot the film—if not because of what they knew of the history they were representing, at least because black domestics were still common in the white households at the time, where they cleaned, cooked, and helped stage dinner parties. In any case, her presence suggests the degree to which symbolic dominance and control were tied with actual social and economic conditions in the city of St. Louis and communities like it throughout the country. Readers of *McCall's* were being invited into a vicarious experience of ownership and control, here coded as the pleasure of high-society entertaining, of hospitality. This was a racialized cultural heritage that St. Louis's urban (and increasingly suburban) elites had reclaimed and reimagined in the post–World War II years and that, with *McCall's* help, was given new lifelikeness and palpability.

CHAPTER 7

TWO BUCKSKIN SUITS

Striking an Authentic Note

IN THE FIRST two decades of the Campbell House's operation as a public museum, official interpretation attended to heritage of "Old St. Louis." Members of the museum foundation and its local promoters urged visitors to commune with the house as a gloriously intact remnant of the city's "golden age," when it was still a cultural, political, and mercantile powerhouse—an experience that required a degree of willful denial of the realities on the ground across the city.[1] In much of the interpretative work explored in preceding chapters, including that associated with the *Life* magazine spread, Stix, Baer & Fuller's promotions, and *McCall's* dinner party, as well as standard museum tours, visitors were invited to imagine themselves as invited guests of the Campbell family, "crossing over" into a world of material abundance, ritual feasting, or ceremonial remembrance. The sense of imaginative transport, and the security and well-being that the "intact and integral" site exuded—the house's distinctive heritage mystique—were reassuring to many during the 1940s and 1950s, a period substantially defined by dramatic material and social change for the gateway city.

Such an encounter with the past and the marvels of intact materiality depended on engagement with "meaning heavy" artifacts associated with nineteenth-century gentility, such as fine china, Belter chairs, and silk brocades, as well as select everyday things said to evoke "simpler times." One set of Campbell possessions, however, had a different suggestiveness: a pair of buckskin suits that had belonged to Robert, probably acquired in the 1830s. While associated with the Campbells' social and domestic worlds and sometimes displayed inside the house (alongside Virginia's dresses), the suits retained strong associations with the world outside—with frontier adventure and even the romance of Hollywood. And with time, they came to be more directly linked with a specific "mountain man" past, one not yet fully appreciated at the time of the opening of the museum but that had appeal to many in a later period defined by suburban expansionism.

The "Indian Costumes," as members of the William Clark Society (WCS) and Campbell House Foundation (CHF) called them, had been secured during the 1941 Selkirk's auction. At the time, their acquisition was front-page news because of their singularity: two suits, one adult- and one child-sized, each with fringed elk-hide trousers and matching waistcoats, beading, quillwork, and fancy linings of patterned silk, in near-pristine condition. Made by tribal artisans or possibly the Métis of Canada during the height of Robert's early career as a fur trader, they were unlike anything most St. Louisans had seen.[2] Their design combined the brain-tanning and applique perfected by the Blackfeet, Crow, Cherokee, and other Plains tribes with the European tailoring favored by white traders, and even a few elements of "mountain man" garb (fig. 15).[3] These particular suits may have been gifts from Robert's trade partners in the mid- to late 1830s or ceremonial objects acquired somewhat later, when he served as an Indian commissioner. Or perhaps he had purchased the suits from a trading post near Fort Pierre, or even in St. Louis, which did stock such goods for a time.[4] Even without knowing their provenance (which was murky then and remains so today), the WCS knew enough to be "jubilant" about their acquisition (they paid just forty-five dollars). These were some of the most evocative objects yet salvaged for a museum devoted to "early St. Louis life," and everyone agreed they would "strike an authentic note" in an exhibit devoted to "the Indians and the early fur trade."[5]

But this was something of a new tack in their thinking given that the fur trade, and indeed the bulk of Robert's biography, had been almost wholly absent from early preservation rationales. The details of his early career were just being reconstructed in probate court when the suits floated into view like a pair of frontier apparitions, conjuring a world far more exotic than the "citadel of social significance" known as Lucas

FIGURE 15. Adult-sized buckskin coat, photograph, ca. 2000. Campbell House Museum, St. Louis, MO.

Place.[6] For the WCS and its supporters, St. Louis's early history as a "frontier city" was a kind of remote abstraction, as evidenced by its decision to display the suits alongside Virginia's satin and silk gowns—first, at fundraisers, including one where Boy Scouts wore the "costumes" on stage, and later in early museum exhibits. The members were unsure what they were dealing with, speculating that Robert brought the suits home "to please his young sons."[7] Unlikely as it was that the clothing had been purchased primarily as playthings, the idea aligned perfectly well with commonly held notions about childhood and the Victorian home. It also helped to domesticate what might otherwise have been categorized

as exotica. Other such goods that the WCS saw fit to save at auction but
were unsure how to interpret included a miniature alabaster Taj Mahal,
a group of Chinese teakwood tabourets, fragments of Roman terra cotta,
and several leather-bound albums filled with images of European landmarks and historic figures, among them twenty-one 1860s photos of
Native Americans taken by William Soule.[8] Likewise, while they saved
many of the "western" objects owned by Robert (a bearskin rug, a pair
of watercolors of bison grazing by Alexander Barclay [1850], and Thomas
McKenney's *History of the Indian Tribes of North America* [1836]), the
group did not put them together with the "Indian costumes" or try to
think about how they might be linked historically or biographically.[9]

Even those looking ahead to exhibits devoted to "Indians and the
early fur trade" had little concrete knowledge on which to build such
interpretations. Much of the material evidence of St. Louis's role in the
trade had been sacrificed to the priorities of urban renewal: as noted in
earlier chapters, forty blocks of the riverfront mercantile district—where
Robert's dry-goods outfit had been located and trade goods were distributed to points east and south—had recently been cleared for the Jefferson
National Expansion Memorial. Many observers perceived the irony of
erasing the city's banking, shipping, and trade history to build a memorial to national expansion, and indeed the initial interest in the Campbell
residence followed such a vein of thinking. More than any conviction
about its salience to western or trade history, however, it was general nostalgia that dominated public discourse about saving the house.

This began to change in the weeks leading up to the auction, when
several historically minded citizens spoke their minds. A letter sent from
a Missouri town named for Daniel Boone (whose house was one of the
few fur-trade relics to survive into the twentieth century) that ran in the
Post-Dispatch was representative.[10] The writer warned St. Louisans not
to disregard the Campbell House's national significance in the name of
more provincial concerns: "Does the memory of Ashley, the fur trade,
that terrible battle at Pierre's Hole . . . his work with Father DeSmet and
others in many Indian councils—do these things no longer have meaning? Surely they must. Here, then, is your memorial to national expansion, a unique, living, personal memorial, not the Dunkerque of your
riverfront."[11] Another editorial by "J. B. Middlewesterner" that ran the
same week accused authorities of negligence, anticipating the loss of this

"landmark of historic St. Louis" to "another parking lot or weed patch [that will only] help spread the blight of downtown" further west. Why did St. Louisans care so little about "the American scene" represented in the homestead of a true "hero of the Battle of Pierre's Hole . . . [and] one of the greatest figures in the fur trade and early St. Louis"?[12]

Some in the WCS joined in the outpouring of enthusiasm for this heroic past, critiquing St. Louisans' habit of "sit[ting] silently by while time and other forces have worked destruction to its most significant historical survivals, and then wail[ing] loud and long because they are gone."[13] Still, the group's understanding of the period in question—beyond what they gleaned from grammar school lessons on the "opening of the west" and Lewis and Clark—was weak. In their heyday (1820–1840), "mountain men" trappers and traders had been folk heroes in St. Louis, where many caroused during the off-season. Their daring acts were fondly recounted across the region, as were stories of hedonistic rendezvous rituals for which they became known. Many of the most accomplished (or notorious) among them—Kit Carson, Jim Bridger, Pierre Chouteau, and General William H. Ashley—were special favorites of the public throughout the nineteenth century.[14] But these stories had been forgotten in recent decades. To the extent that the fur trade was known at the time of the Campbell House campaign, it was seen through the filter of popular culture: a flitting sequence of images "recollected" from Buffalo Bill's Wild West shows, biographies of Kit Carson, and Erastus and Irwin Beadles' dime novels.[15] These were dim shadows of a "closed" frontier that had been nearly eclipsed by stories of the Dust Bowl and early western film. With two early exceptions—Hiram Martin Chittenden's *The American Fur Trade of the Far West* (1902) and Theodore Roosevelt's sweeping, multivolume frontier history, *The Winning of the West* (1885–1894)—historians had not taken up the fur trade with seriousness until the mountain men folklore penetrated popular culture in the 1940s.[16] Davy Crockett would become a household name long before the "most often studied and least understood figures in American history" achieved anything like a full historical treatment.[17]

This sleeping element of local historical memory had, however, been slowly nudged awake during years of legal proceedings that followed Hugh Campbell's death, which made Robert's "fur trade fortune" a subject of public interest. Attorneys digging through family records learned of his notable military and economic successes in the mid-1840s, for example, when he reinvested a modest fortune that he had secured through risky fur trade dealings in Missouri real estate. His land holdings included "much of the site of [present day] Kansas City," speculations that paid off handsomely, allowing him to finance other sectors of the frontier economy: railroad, steamboats, and hotels.[18] In addition to a large cash fortune and the house on Locust, Robert bequeathed his sons property throughout St. Louis—investments seen as evidence of business savvy, self-determination, and economic optimism. In recounting such biographical tidbits, the press fixated on the size of his fortune and his Horatio Alger–style rise from sickly immigrant to millionaire, or as they liked to say, "from Fort Laramie to Locust Street."[19]

Robert's evenhandedness and generosity were likewise celebrated. Newspaper accounts from the 1930s were filled with stories of his provision for "sufferers in the Irish famine of 1846," which motivated his kinfolk back in Ireland to "erect a triumphal arch and salute him with a cannon" in the 1850s, and of his legendary friendships with political opponents and Indian trade partners.[20] One often-recounted episode involved a delegation of Native chiefs stopping to call at his Lucas Place residence on their way to Washington, D.C. (Robert was not at home; they were welcomed by Virginia, who served them "fire-water," which they drank sitting cross-legged on the fine carpets in the parlor.)[21] Such stories were tied metaphorically to the endangered Campbell mansion, whose unlikely persistence in the face of widespread commercial development now could be seen to reflect Robert's resilience.

These narratives were, however, complicated by the presence of the "silent heir" inside the house.[22] Hazlett was a sickly figure whose invalidism and mental incompetence haunted the frontier myth. The last heir to the "fur trade fortune" was an uncanny inversion of heroic figures past and a reminder of how far genteel Old St. Louis had fallen since the reign of the mountain man. A 1935 *Post-Dispatch* feature on the vexed inheritance of the "Locust Street Campbells" presented Hazlett as a figure of physical and moral ruin—a mere shadow of his more vigorous "Indian fighter" father. Whereas Hazlett fought psychological demons and was beset by the "subtle, gratuitous obligations," his father had faced real danger and "debated every step with enemies human and elemental."[23] Exaggerated though this description was, the wilderness-parlor dichotomy was rooted in facts recently divulged in court (for example, in testimony about Hazlett's dementia, "infant-like" dependency, and paralysis). The more his infirmities were known, the more preoccupied with his father's "Frontier Deeds" and St. Louis's status as one of "the most cosmopolitan [cities] in the world" locals seemed to become.[24]

Robert had come to be known as a man of purpose, ingenuity, and strength, one whose leadership extended from frontier outpost to battleground, diplomatic post to boardroom. To justify its paeans, the *Post-Dispatch* disclosed previously unknown biographical details—for example, that Robert had conducted an Indian council in Wyoming in 1851 which "resulted in a treaty that served for years," and been part of a commission established by President Ulysses Grant "to bring about more amicable relations" with Indians. While Campbell suffered from a lung condition in his early years that might well have been passed on to Hazlett (or his other children who died young), Robert's labors as a plain-dealing trader were the most celebrated facts of his life. He was neither "barbaric aborigine" (apparently meaning local natives of French origin) nor "ultra-sophisticated newcomer[s]" nor an emasculated son. In this compensatory mythology, the pale-faced accountant became a hearty frontiersman and civic leader who enjoyed deep ties with the West and a "long friendship with General [William T.] Sherman."[25]

Apart from the tinge of sentimentalism, the mythology had the advantage of being mostly true: Robert *had* earned a reputation as an honest businessman, and along with William Sublette and others in General Ashley's Rocky Mountain Fur Company (RMFC), kept the firm—and the city's trade networks—viable during a competitive period. Under their leadership, the RMFC *had* innovated new approaches to frontier provisioning in rugged country and developed trade partnerships based on trust rather than coercion. And they *had* turned a modest fortune into much more (Campbell through dry goods and real estate, Sublette through investment in a plantation). Both men eventually left the trade and its bodily dangers to the likes of Kit Carson, whose perilous adventures seemed in hindsight to confirm their level-headedness. At the time that the WCS was campaigning to save the Campbell possessions, a newspaper glossed Campbell's career thus: investing in "trade infrastructure" at the right time and "diversifying" his holdings "when the fur and buffalo dwindled and other goods came to the fore," he became "prosperous beyond all his early dreaming," modeling "the strength of character, the firm purpose, the shrewd shrift and the patriotic devotion . . . of his age."[26]

To justify the "strength of character" arguments, observers noted that Campbell lacked typical mountain-man aggression and the take-no-prisoners mindset of other venture capitalists, especially his rival, John Jacob Astor of the American Fur Company (AFC). Still, Campbell acted courageously when circumstances required it—most famously during the skirmish that became known as the Battle of Pierre's Hole (1832), where he proved an able combatant and commander. Such actions were described in terms of the positive energies of innovation and trade rather than brute militarism, just as his interactions with Indian trade partners were said to reveal his humanitarianism.[27] Thus, while he and his partners benefited from (and participated in) territorial aggression and violence, in the retelling, Campbell's fur trade exploits took on the innocuousness of historical drama or children playing with "Indian costumes."

Local investment in these narratives did not, however, preclude celebration of Campbell's material ambitions and successes, which were the primary reason anyone remembered him at all. His St. Louis had been a city on the make, and he asserted dominance at a time when trade markets—like the territory of the West itself—came to be contested again and again. Boosters like Thomas Hart Benton defended St. Louis's interests through verbal aggression, performing political dominance on the floors of the state legislature and U.S. Congress, while Campbell and Sublette defended them "in the field."[28] Together they soon controlled major frontier markets, nurturing "The Opposition" (those who resisted the market dominance and shared a "violent hatred" of the AFC and other East Coast traders) and thus advancing St. Louis's economic autonomy and self-determination.[29] The Opposition eventually forced the partitioning of the western trade zone, which advantaged many local trade partnerships and the city as a whole.[30]

In remembering all of this a century later, St. Louis could claim mercantile innocence anew, including the values of respect, honor, and strategic partnerships (as opposed to brutalizing competition and monopoly). The general outlines of this revisionist frontier history were visible in some of the earliest CHM promotional materials. In a speech delivered during the 1943 dedication ceremonies, which aired on the radio and was reprinted in museum pamphlets used for more than a decade, CHF president Arthur Hoskins argued that "the story of the Campbell House" was at its heart a story of its "distinguished owner," whose "career is linked with the explorers, fur traders and great mountain men of the early far West who, from St. Louis as a starting point, were makers of the history of our Western America. More than a hundred years ago [Campbell] did what many a boy once dreamed—crossed the plains to fight Indians and win his fortune in the West. Beaver pelts, trapped in the Rocky Mountains and carried over the prairies in long caravans, built the Campbell Home."[31] Hoskins recapitulated the narrative of progress from "Fort Laramie to Locust Street," noting that Campbell's fortune had been "won" through physical and commercial dominance and that he helped turn St. Louis into a metropolis where furs were the "coinage of the era." The magazine *Antiques* presented much the same account a year later, adding that Campbell's house "exemplifies the maturing of the frontier, the lush, mid-nineteenth-century urban taste of the wealthy" but also his rise from "fur trader, [to] banker, merchant . . . landowner," and trusted public servant.[32]

These stages of Campbell's career—corresponding as they did with the defining elements of his character—came also to be associated with the buckskin suits themselves. These clothes evoked both heroic action in the West and youthful innocence, both mercantile dominance and domestic consumption, both narratives of ascendancy and of declension. More generally, as matching suits "passed down" from father to son, they represented investment in local heritage and reminded St. Louisans of their forebears' adventuring "way of life." The suits also conjured Campbell's special relationship with his Indian trade partners and a sense of the sacred trust forged through trade or diplomacy. Even without knowing the particulars of his interactions with various Plains tribes, museumgoers could perceive in the suits a sense of their owner's "Indianness." As Philip Joseph Deloria has argued, such conceits historically have corresponded to whites' at-once utopian and destructive impulses, as well as contradictory longings for idealized "aboriginal liberty" and complete security (through control of Native lands).[33]

The Campbell House itself represented analogous contradictory desires. But the buckskin suits, which embodied so powerfully the white fantasies of "playing Indian," made the desire for domination curiously visible. This desire was also expressed in other, quieter ways in museum narratives about the Campbells' wealth and power and uncritical displays of their possessions. The house was repeatedly declared an emblem of the "maturing of the frontier, [and] the lush mid-nineteenth-century urban taste of the wealthy," and the suits aligned with these claims.

The "Indian Costumes" found new visibility after World War II, including during two episodes of new publicity for the museum: the airing of a radio program based on Campbell's exploits as a trader in 1948 and the publication of *Across the Wide Missouri,* Bernard DeVoto's historical account of the fur trade, which was awarded the Pulitzer Prize in 1949 and made into an MGM film released in 1951. Both of these works offered a more historically minded account of the frontier past, albeit one tinged with postwar sentimentalism. And each conferred upon the Campbell House a deeper moral suggestiveness, legitimizing its function as a site of cultural heritage at a time when the city faced growing evidence of its economic and material decline and diminished national standing.

"Robert Campbell's Romance"

GEN. ASHLEY: Oh . . . I'm not worried about the money. . . . I just don't want to see you lose it. To tell you the truth . . . I'm getting out of the fur trade because it's too risky. The Indians are worse than ever . . . the American Fur Company is bigger than ever . . . and the demand for beaver is falling off.

R. CAMPBELL: It's been a panic year. . . . The demand will pick up when money is freer.

ASHLEY: Yes . . . and if it does . . . John Jacob Astor will try to hog the whole trade.

W. SUBLETTE: I believe we can keep him from doing it.

ASHLEY: You can?

CAMPBELL: Yessir . . . I know we can.

ASHLEY: Well . . . if you're wrong . . . you'll be ruined. . . . You might be able to give old John Jacob a run for his money . . . and make a fortune yourselves. . . . I've done it . . . but then times have changed.

SUBLETTE: Gin'ral . . . I . . . wish yuh'd give us a chance. . . . I'd rather go broke in a good fight . . . than just set back [and] see the American Fur men take everything.

ASHLEY: Allright . . . allright. . . . I'll sell to you . . . and what's more, I'll help you all I can until you get organized. By jingo . . . we've made St. Louis the fur capital of the world . . . and we'll keep it that!

CAMPBELL: With your Rocky Mountain Fur Company . . . we can do it, sir.

ASHLEY: No . . . no . . . not mine. . . . From now on it'll be the Rocky Mountain Company . . . Will Sublette . . . and Robert Campbell . . . owners and partners![34]

This revealing exchange comes near the end of "Partners in Adventure," the first of a two-part KMOX radio program about Robert's early life that aired in January 1948 as installments in the St. Louis–based program sponsored by Union Electric, *The Land We Live In*. Recorded before a live audience in a studio three blocks east of the Campbell House, both segments broadcast to a regional audience numbering in the tens of thousands. The jingoistic style of the program reveals something of the sponsor's agenda: to animate forgotten events and characters while engaging the folklore of Old St. Louis. *The Land We Live In* scripts were produced by a husband-and-wife team, Alice and Ken Jones, using documents from local archives. But Union Electric maintained the right of editorial review, and while the shows had a strong historical flavor, they functioned as an audio Walk of Fame that fostered local as well as national pride.[35] Robert Campbell's frontier biography fit this local-history-as-public-heritage model beautifully.

Loosely based on an actual exchange that occurred in 1827, shortly after Campbell joined the RMFC, the conversation was inspired by letters and other material from the CHM archive. Earlier in the program, the audience learned that when he arrived in St. Louis as a teenager, he suffered from a lung inflammation (possibly tuberculosis). When his doctor warned him that the lack of "decent air" in the city would kill him, Campbell responded to an advertisement inviting "young men of enterprise" to join the next RMFC expedition and signed on for two years—despite the fact the fur trade was a "dangerous, rough life." In an early scene that foreshadows events from the second segment, Ashley warns Campbell to write home before he leaves so his relatives "don't . . . blame me for what happens to you . . . drownin' or scalpin' or freezin' . . . lots of things might happen in two years to a tenderfoot."[36]

But the "tenderfoot" promptly proves his mettle. During Campbell's first overnight stint as camp watchman, Jim Bridger decides to give him "an Indian scare" by sneaking up and making noise like a scrounging coyote. Campbell anticipates the ploy and then saves the camp from an Indian scout looking to steal horses. Much to the surprise of the old stalwarts, Campbell shoots the scout on sight, and when a couple dozen Blackfeet warriors retaliate—apparently with the encouragement of the AFC, who have taught them "a new way of fightin'"—he again proves he has good fighting instincts.[37] He winds up rescuing William Sublette, who otherwise would have died, and the event solidifies their comradeship.

Campbell's battlefield bravery is not the main reason for his status as a hero, however. The playwrights highlighted his resilience, trustworthiness, and gentlemanly courtesy, which he brings to bear on business dealings and diplomacy, and on the wooing of Virginia. His resilience is evident in his uncomplaining attitude toward the harshness of a frontier lifestyle, while his courtesy is seen in deference to his mentors, whose callousness and swagger he tolerates. He reads *Hamlet* to Sublette by the light of the campfire, and their discussion of its meaning bridges class and age divides. The adventures they would have in the years following become the basis for the "famous friendship" that later was "immortalized by a great American writer," Washington Irving.[38] Perhaps inspired by CHM boosters Arthur Hoskins and Ellwood Douglass, the playwrights argued that Campbell and Sublette's history as business partners was formative to St. Louis history and emblematic of the city's economic, political, and moral dominance.

Despite eagerness to lay hold of this legacy for the city, the radio play could not wholly resolve contradictory elements of that history, which combined dominance and egalitarianism, treachery and honor, frontier aggression and domestic tranquility. Part 2 explores Robert's decision to enter the fur trade in the late 1820s and leave it a decade later—subjects captured in correspondence with his older brother and future business partner, Hugh, that had come to light during the Campbell estate hearings. The tension between the frontier lifestyle and a desire for domestic security (as represented in the views of Robert's family) fuels the romance between Robert and Virginia, which begins with a visit to Philadelphia, where Hugh and Robert's sister-in-law Mary have been discussing his motives for settling in St. Louis—seen as "an outlandish place," the very "outpost of civilization"—with Mary's teenage cousin Virginia. Hugh explains that his brother has come to "prefer" frontiersmen to polite company and made a name for himself by winning "concessions from John Jacob Astor." But why, Hugh wonders, would any self-respecting merchant seek his fortune in such a backwater? And what had ten years in such an environment done to Robert? Perhaps he had become "half savage"! Virginia contemplates further, speculating with horror that Robert "probably paints his face like an Indian."[39]

Indulging spurious "savage Indian" tropes, these observations point to a matter of seriousness: just what would the brutalizing trade economies of the West do to its participants? What would it mean for citizens in a "civilized" city and nation? Hugh put it this way in a November 1828 letter that the *Post-Dispatch* reprinted in its entirety a month after the estate auction in 1941: "Can it be possible, Robert, that you, who were raised amidst peace and quietness, should devote yourself to a course of life nearly allied to one of bloodshed and rapine? And for what? The gratification of a love for adventure, or the excitement of staking life and liberty against fortune. For shame, my brother. For the honor of our good mother, desist and return to me. I beseech you to return to civilization and security."[40] The radio play never quite shakes the concern over "bloodshed and rapine." When Virginia meets Robert, he is dashing (she had expected a "frail" man) but "dark"—that is, both weather-beaten and morally tainted from years "in the rough company of mountain men." He falls ill within a few days of arrival in Philadelphia ("I can't understand it," he tells Hugh. "For ten years I didn't have a sick day . . . out in all kinds of weather . . . swimming rivers"), stricken by something like neurasthenia, and rashly proposes to Virginia from his sickbed: "I offer you life in a rough, frontier town . . . but Virginia I love you with all my heart." She balks out of fear at what it would mean to be married to such a man, and he heads back to St. Louis alone.[41]

The playwrights compress Robert and Virginia's on-again, off-again courtship of many years to a couple brief scenes, focusing instead on his business maneuverings. Upon returning to St. Louis, Campbell tells Sublette he wishes to leave the RMFC partnership to "build up our outfitting store," a seemingly pragmatic business decision that turns out to be an excuse: he means to marry Virginia. Sublette reveals that he has sunk all the RMFC money in an unusually large stock of goods for the next season's trade, a kind of final gamble, he explains, given that the demand for beaver is dwindling. Happily, they enjoy a windfall trade season and earn enough for Sublette to retire and buy a "farm out West of St. Louis . . . over 1,000 acres . . . with sulphur springs in the middle of it." Campbell is able to secure a "fine house" for Virginia.[42] This is a turning point in the play and an inversion of the dispersal process that the Campbell estate had recently undergone, as many in the audience would have known.

Even more than proof of his accomplishments as a fur trader, Campbell's new home represents his hoped-for "civilization and security." Virginia accepts Robert's hand in marriage, but as soon as they settle in St. Louis, Sublette brings news of "trouble out West with the tribes." Campbell protests that he is "out of the trading business," but Sublette implores him to return, turning the image of a happy homestead, the thing they both long for, into a metaphor of citizenly obligation: "A lot of people out there have already built homes. . . . They might have 'em burned down if a treaty isn't made with the tribes." Virginia is deeply affected by this image, and she urges Robert to join the diplomatic corps, adding, "I'd never been away from the East until I came here with you . . . and as we came up the Mississippi . . . saw farms and villages and cities . . . I couldn't help but think . . . they wouldn't be there if there weren't men like you . . . and Mr. Sublette to clear the way. That's why I think you should go. We can get our home later." Emboldened by her support, he vows to buy the "most beautiful [house] in all of St. Louis" when he returns.[43] The audience knows that he means the house on Locust Street.

Thus emerged a vision of the Campbell House as evidence of their "arrival" in St. Louis society and of Robert's conquest—his ability to "clear the way" for frontier trade (presumably that of whites threatened by Indian aggressors) and stake a claim for the city. To soften the theme of conquest, the playwrights emphasized his integrity and longing for a return to domesticity. The narrator explains that the Treaty of Fort Laramie (1851) "was accomplished largely through the efforts" of Campbell and a St. Louis–based missionary named Father Pierre-Jean De Smet, and "brough[t] a long period of peace to the West . . . cleared the way for settlers . . . gave security to the sod huts and log cabins on lonely homesteads."[44] The convergence of treaty-signing and home-buying is metaphorically significant and constitutes the play's moral crux: giving up a life of adventure, Robert finds love and the makings of a kinder, gentler capitalist enterprise. Peace and prosperity are knitted together and handed to St. Louisans as a fictive mantle of innocence.

The play ends with twin images of that innocence: the Campbell House and Sublette's estate in the valley of the River des Peres near St. Louis. The former was for decades "synonymous with gracious living" and hospitality, as listeners likely knew, while the latter was turned into a hot springs resort with an "outdoor zoo" stocked with buffalo, antelope, and other wild animals. Both, in a sense, were cultural heritage: one a "unique memorial to an age past," the other a monument to entrepreneurial creativity. There is no mention in the play of the fact that Sublette's 779-acre plantation inluded a coal mine worked by slaves (visitors to the resort reported seeing slaves' cabins on their way to the clubhouse).[45] Neither does the play mention the exclusivity of Lucas Place. But the egalitarian style of hospitality at both sites is loudly proclaimed. Plantation visitors include St. Louis elites and retired traders, trappers and their ilk (Sublette's own social set), while at the Campbells' well-appointed table "the great and near great of the day" dine alongside "Indian chiefs and senators . . . [the] buckskin clad trapper and silk hatted business man . . . missionaries . . . and army officers from Jefferson Barracks."[46] The play ends with a utopian vision of a burgeoning trade city that boasts urban sophistication and agricultural abundance, and is symbolically fulfilled not just in the friendship of Campbell and Sublette but in Robert's marriage to Virginia and his decision to reinvest his fur trade fortune in industrial ventures. The age of flourishing that resulted can still, the announcer reminds listeners at the close of the play, be experienced in person.

Hundreds of St. Louisans poured into the museum in the weeks following the radio play's airing, their interest apparently spurred by the "colorful presentation of the story behind the house."[47] Besides the handful of exotic and "western" objects, however, there was still relatively little in the CHM collection that conveyed information about Robert's frontier experience—except the buckskin suits, of course, the adult version of which was now on view in the Costume Room dominated by Virginia's gowns (fig. 16). That left a gaping hole in museum interpretation between the "lush" interiors of "civilization and security" and the fur trade frontier. How could the fur-trading and treaty-signing stages of Robert's life be linked, and ultimately reconciled, with those

FIGURE 16. Photograph of "the newly-opened 'Costume Room' at the Campbell House, with mannequins gowned in the elegant 19th century dresses of Mrs. Robert Campbell." *Advertising Club Weekly*, December 1949. Campbell House Museum, St. Louis, MO.

of home-buying and entertaining of heads of state, much less the more recent phase when the family because reclusive and their house was "shuttered and inhospitable"?[48]

One answer that emerged in the coming years was a narrative of family and children, which extended the marriage and partnership plots introduced in the play. The Campbell sons had never been given more than a passing glance (and then, only as the adults who saved their parents' possessions), but they now seemed viable, even necessary, features of museum narratives. Within a few months of the radio program, CHM officials converted one of the servant's bedrooms into the Children's Room, which featured donated Victorian playthings, including two pull-toys (a cow and a horse) and the "buckskin beaded jacket . . . presented to Robert Campbell for his son, James."[49] Held on the anniversary of Robert's birth, the room's dedication was attended by some of his heirs, including a fifteen-year-old great-great-grandniece who cut the ribbon, and a bevy of local elites.[50]

The press obligingly noted that the exhibit evoked the charms of "older St. Louis" during its heyday as a gateway to frontier markets and the heights of power of one of its founding families. One columnist, adopting the same logic Hoskins had used years earlier, described a day gone by when "boys used to play with animals on wheels . . . in a day when all wheels moved more slowly," and "eastern comforts had caught up with the western frontier, even [for] children." The buckskin jacket "given to Robert Campbell by Indian friends," alongside the "splotched cow on wheels," now expressed sanitized ideals of frontier capitalism through literal and symbolic domestication, as well as Victorian childhood and innocence. Even nostalgia itself was acknowledged as a possible meaning of the display: the columnist told readers that "the cow on wheels waits, on the floor . . . attached to a long string [t]hat looks as if it needs pulling" by museum visitors.[51]

The buckskin suits officially represented Robert's character traits and frontier adventures, details of his biography that were now woven together with the history of the city and Lucas Place. An advertisement for Home Insurance Company that ran in *Time, Newsweek,* and the St. Louis press in 1950 literalized this set of associations and tightened the linkages between Campbell's fur trade experiences and the history of capitalism, with a memorable tagline: "The Campbell House: *Bought with Beaver Pelts.*" The ad's key visuals—a black-and-white photograph of the Campbell House facade taken from the north, a small photograph of a tuxedoed Robert taken in late middle age, and a hand-drawn sketch of two mountain men on horseback—serve as pictorial emblems for the story of Campbell's success, including leadership of "an important fur trading company" and of troops at "the famous battle with the Blackfeet at Pierre's Hole," where he "displayed great bravery by carrying his wounded friend to safety under fire." Despite "hostile encounters with the Indians," the ad maintains, he "won their last respect" through "integrity." Having "amassed a fortune in beaver pelts," he "became one of the town's most influential citizens, serving as president of two banks, owner of the Southern Hotel and much real estate."[52] The "Fort Laramie to Locust Street" career had become the very backbone of the Campbell mythology.

In the well-chosen metaphor of beaver pelts, the currency of frontier trade, but also in its vision of the material and moral substrate of the city's (and Campbell's) great "fortune," the ad conferred mysterious power to the buckskins suits and their owners. While this power was conceived in cultural-historical rather than economic terms, the logic of modern (not just frontier) capitalism was evoked, for "beaver pelts" were symbols of luxury, and one could easily see in them the motivation to labor for the well-being of the city. Indeed, Campbell's remarkable biography was a kind of shorthand for the material and moral motivations that drove business and planning in the city. Sometimes the connection was quite literal: employees from the Universal Match Company headquartered across from the CHM took tours of the museum to admire the possessions of an "early St. Louis millionaire" they had seen described in their company newsletter as a man who "provided himself with a stake by fur trapping and fur trading," and was "known for his fair dealings and just practices."[53] They could lay hold of this legacy—and also of the reassuring ideal of a city "built with beaver pelts"—simply by walking across the street.

Across the Wide Missouri

As St. Louisans were reclaiming this frontier legacy, *Across the Wide Missouri*—Bernard DeVoto's "fast-paced account of the western fur trade"—became a national bestseller, and in 1948 was awarded the Pulitzer Prize in history.[54] Within months, MGM announced plans for a movie version of the book. The studio, which had been enjoying box office dominance due to several immensely successful adventure films, committed more than a million dollars to its production—a huge sum at the time. Much of it would be needed for onsite filming in the Rocky Mountains (whose scenic wonders DeVoto had captured through elaborate description and dozens of illustrations) and a large cast.[55] MGM hired the aging but ever popular Clark Gable to play Flint Mitchell, a Kentucky fur trader who bargains for an Indian bride during a mountain rendezvous seeking to forge ties with the Blackfeet. He was a composite of several historical figures treated by DeVoto, including some in Campbell's and Sublette's network. The supporting roles, representing a range of roustabouts from DeVoto's history, would be played by some of the industry's best character actors. While not precisely a "cast of thousands," as the studio claimed, it was an ambitious film on nearly every level. Executives raised expectations by billing it as a "Stupendous Drama of Adventure in the great

Northwest!" whose "spectacle" and "rich sentiment" would capture a "frontier history never before presented on the screens."[56]

Members of the CHF and their supporters were positively ecstatic when word of the film reached them in 1950. DeVoto had been to St. Louis twice in recent years—first during his book tour in late 1947, and then as the guest of honor at a May 1948 reception at the museum that included dignitaries and the Kansas City art collector who "discovered" Alfred Miller, the illustrator whose field sketches are reproduced in DeVoto's book. The latter appearance, which occurred just days before DeVoto's Pulitzer was announced, went entirely unreported by the local press—a snub the CHF struggled to explain to the revered historian.[57] But the author endorsed the museum as "extraordinarily interesting and valuable [and] . . . culturally important both to St. Louis and the country at large," and CHM officials used his comments to curry favor with the national press.[58] At long last, Robert Campbell would be added to the pantheon of mountain-men heroes! Perhaps, too, St. Louis's significance as a gateway to the West would register nationally (as it had done years earlier with *Life* magazine) and fuel new investment in the city. Campbell's exploits lie at the very center of DeVoto's "fast-paced account of the western fur trade," and locals anticipated that *Across the Wide Missouri* would advance the recovery of regional history, giving this story a grandeur—and Technicolor vibrancy—that only Hollywood could afford.[59]

Museum officials were so emboldened by enthusiasm for DeVoto's work that CHF president Gordon Hertslet contacted MGM directly in 1950 to inquire about a joint publicity campaign. He proposed that the studio "focus attention on Robert Campbell and his home," which had already been nationally publicized (a point he underscored by sending copies of the *Life* article and other publicity materials).[60] The notion was not totally farfetched given the positive press the city had recently enjoyed. But MGM declined, explaining that Robert had been "written out" of *Across the Wide Missouri* entirely—a kick in the stomach hardly softened by the studio's polite concession that "some benefit could be derived for both of us if your organization were tied in with the opening of the picture when it plays in St. Louis."[61] The hoped-for "St. Louis connection" (as it is called today, often ironically, for instance when residents make fanciful local connections to national news stories) had no significance to studio executives concerned primarily about catering to a national and increasingly international audience.

Crestfallen but undeterred, Hertslet tried one last strategy—this time writing to Loew's, MGM's sales and promotion company, to ask how the CHM could be made a "focal point for launching [the] picture." He emphasized that "as a starting point for the fur trading exhibitions to the West, [St. Louis] offers unusual tie-in possibilities," and offered to make the "luxurious doeskin jacket . . . [given to Robert by] his Indian friends" available to the studio for whatever purposes they might name. He closed by reiterating that DeVoto himself had "visited the House on several occasions."[62] Loew's officials professed uncertainty about when the film would be released, showing little interest in tie-in possibilities. It was becoming clear that Hollywood had moved along without Campbell and St. Louis, although they were not above pandering to a regional audience, as Loew's final response made clear: the film premiere would take place in "Jefferson City . . . and the two metropolises of your great state—St. Louis and Kansas City," after which they would "blanket the state" so that "all across the wide Missouri territory your people can see this fine picture prior to its presentation nationally."[63] But when MGM's test audiences responded negatively to the film, studio executives retooled it, cutting thirty-five minutes of "complicating" historical background to underscore the romance plot (a decision that enraged both director William A. Wellman and Gable), and launched a vigorous promotional campaign. When the ultra-hyped, over-edited film finally opened, it received tepid reviews, and CHM officials were deeply disappointed.

Trying to blend historical drama—a "Sweeping Saga of the Mountain Men . . . Who Blasted Their Heroic Way into a New Empire!"—with romance and comedy, MGM had reduced the complexities of the fur trade represented by DeVoto to a half-dozen plot points. Indeed, the main character, a mountain man from Kentucky named Flint Mitchell, seems not to fully grasp how the trade works or what the stakes for his actions might be. By turns a heartthrob and a drunk, a naïf and a savvy businessman, a brawler and a military strategist, a bigot and a humanitarian, he is a highly unstable hero. Gable performs the role with trademark swagger that at times verges into buffoonery.[64] The central conflict in the film involves a trade partnership-truce with the Nez Perce that Mitchell stumbles into during a trade rendezvous. In a drunken act of machismo, he offers a large dowry for Kamiah, a Blackfoot woman whom the Nez Perce kidnapped years earlier; it is a self-interested, not a diplomatic act, for he wants to regularize relations with the Blackfeet, who are known for fiercely protecting their "hunting grounds." But the treaty falls apart and people are brutalized by careless vengeance on both sides that Mitchell does not try to prevent. In a grim but affecting scene shot on a windswept plain full of tree stumps, the mountain men bury Kamiah and Peg Leg Smith (both recklessly killed by the Blackfeet) and stand, contemplating their fresh graves, heads resting on downturned muskets in a quasi-military ceremony of tribute. Someone plays a mournful tune on the bagpipes, and Mitchell stands by with his infant son in his arms. What does the "bloodshed and rapine" of the trade signify? Will Mitchell give his men words of hope to spur them to action?

The film demurs. Mitchell resists his men's entreaties to return to Blackfeet territory (whether to seek fortune and vengeance is even unclear) and commits to raising his son Chip among "his own people." *Across the Wide Missouri* ends with an unexpected sequence of happy scenes, including one where Mitchell teaches Chip to tan buckskin, while an adult Chip provides a sentimentalizing gloss on his father, who "belonged to the Indian country now, heart and soul." And while he could never return home with his biracial son and empty pockets, he could take solace in the fact that he had "helped open the west for new trappers—for men who loved the country as much as he did"— and would secure new "outposts of civilization."[65] In sharp contrast to the partnerships portrayed by DeVoto and celebrated by the Joneses in the radio play, however, these so-called "giants who walked the west and became part of our history" show no business savvy or capacity for political leadership. Mitchell's marriage to Kamiah fails to have lasting political meaning—in fact, it triggers more violence, a tragic element the film does not explain—and the glorious fur trade, where it is made visible, is trivialized, its ultimate meaning never articulated. In fact, nostalgia is the primary means by which characters and actions come to be given moral significance.

Like the 1940s accounts of Robert Campbell's career, the film depends on the contrast between then and now, between the heroism of an older generation and the feeble efforts to reclaim that heroism by the younger. Of course, *Across the Wide Missouri* makes no direct allusions to him, William Sublette, or any others in their cohort, and it shows little interest in the fur trade partnerships that DeVoto found so fascinating and argued had played a vital role in securing those "outposts of civilization" for future trade. Trading is everywhere and nowhere in the film: a few scenes show trapping-related activities, but the complex political and procedural elements are given little attention at all, much less careful study of the sort that DeVoto saw fit to provide. While the real prototypes of some of his characters—mostly the flamboyant ones—are legible, the film does not render them with confidence.[66] To be fair, DeVoto's study was a mixed blessing of a source: sprawling in scope, over-rich in narrative detail, lacking in unifying core arguments, it aimed "to report everything that happened in the mountains and to keep half a dozen fascinating rings going at once," but was unable to deliver, as early reviewers observed.[67] DeVoto praised traders' bravery and business ingenuity, and seemed to revel in their masculine excesses, but acknowledged that the trade was built on compromising, illegal, and often violent practices— that the mountain men did in fact blast their way across the frontier, pursuing imperialistic, morally questionable advantage.[68] Their actions were neither as autonomous nor as noble as was commonly assumed, and they often became the tools of big-city capitalists.[69]

The main problem for MGM was simply that DeVoto's detailed account of the fur trade was history, not romance. Even its most romantic elements did not conform to the public imagination of the West as a domain of outlaw-heroes who resisted authority and modeled frontier-style masculine integrity. There were many discrepancies between these ideals and the difficult realities of Campbell's and Sublette's fur trade, but perhaps the one most challenging for Americans of the 1950s to confront lay in the perception of the trader as a "free agent"—that is, a wholly self-determining freelancer (or "buckskinner") who found economic opportunity in the West by asserting his will and, like Robin Hood, outfoxing the ownership class (and sometimes the federal government). The free agent ideal was not borne out by historical evidence; while buckskinners resisted regular employment by big outfits, they often struck deals with competing firms to get ahead, and the business model was not sustainable after about 1840. Neither was the dynamic of resistance to monopolizing firms romantic; many died or lost their shirts or were forced to seek out partnerships with larger firms. Some trappers spent years in indentured servitude to these firms to get their footing, and few enjoyed the great successes of Campbell and Sublette.[70] It has been estimated that three-fifths of the men who worked for William H. Ashley and successors (Campbell and Sublette) were killed by Indians, rivals from other firms, or wild animals.[71] Those who endured often left the profession within a decade.[72] The real fur trade, in all its messy contradictions, lacked the picturesqueness and nostalgic appeal *Across the Wide Missouri* sought to impose.

The film discloses these contradictions both in its central plot element (the failure of its hero either to succeed in the trade or transcend its brutality) and its overall narrative instability. But the movie's dominant mode is that of compensatory bravado: inscrutable acts of violence and the bombast of empire-building dominate subtler ideas about the frontier. MGM had chosen a formulation of fur-trade heroism that, while it attended to actual historical events and actors, was so steeped in a nostalgia for the age of "giants" that it struggled to communicate clearly about what those giants had achieved or indeed what had been lost with the "closing of the frontier." Its mountain-man mythos was uncomfortably suspended among romance, self-satirizing comedy, and historical realism à la DeVoto. So while *Across the Wide Missouri* stimulated public interest in the fur trade and other subjects essential to an understanding of Campbell history, it obscured as much as it illuminated.

Yet predictably, it helped to further raise the profile of the museum as a site of frontier heritage. In one two-week period in November 1951 alone, 2,364 visitors took the house tour, many of them viewing the Alfred Jacob Miller watercolor *Snake Indians Testing Bows* (c. 1837), which was among the many reproduced in DeVoto's book, in a centennial year exhibition that emphasized Robert Campbell's exploits as a fur trader as they had never been before.[73] The museum continued to see a steady stream of visitors in the years to come, thanks not only to the good publicity associated with DeVoto's book and the film but to general postwar economic growth, which benefited public heritage sites and tourist industries nationwide. The *McCall's* dinner party reenactment would also provide a boost, reinforcing the sense of positive local association with the house.[74] And a steady stream of donations by the usual array of business and cultural elites committed to the museum would allow for targeted new acquisitions and maintenance of the house, and some small-scale restoration work, during this period.[75]

Most of the CHF's interpretative energies within the house now revolved around family possessions and household decor that dated to the period between when Robert and Virginia Campbell first moved in and furnished the town house with the very best a fur trade fortune could buy and the early 1860s, when a major expansion of the house created the gracious double-parlor everyone celebrated. The official tour narrative was now firmly tied to this early period—tethered to it, in fact, as we see in the next chapter. Officials seemed reluctant to depart from this symbolic turning point in Campbell's career, when, riding the wave of fur trade success into great mercantile wealth, he became a humanitarian-capitalist. This would be seen increasingly as St. Louis's "high-water" moment—one the radio play had given a certain visibility and moral legitimacy, and that gave the museum its legitimacy as a regional and national landmark.

Across the Wide Missouri, with all its deficiencies, exposed the fallacies of this mythologizing work. As DeVoto's study made clear, the apogee of the fur trade had in fact been in the early 1830s, when the near-extinction of the beaver and buffalo and reckless Indian removal policies led to the increased competition and violence of the late 1830s and 1840s, a period of far more "bloodshed and rapine" than is generally appreciated. Yet this knowledge had been so successfully sublimated that even a pair of buckskin suits—which had been made from hides sewn by Indians at the height of that period—could be seen as children's playthings. The suits had been liberated from the political and social realities that produced them and transported into a later, happier age. As some of the museum's most distinctive heritage objects, they now seemed the very embodiment of St. Louis's economic and political might, as well as its integrity and honor.

CHAPTER 8

RESTORATION

I N DECEMBER 1965, the *St. Louis Post-Dispatch* published an elaborate photo essay in its Sunday *Pictures* section documenting historic neighborhoods of St. Louis that had been "Caressed by the Years" and given the city a "quiet, dignified harmony." It featured dozens of images, some in large format, a few in full color, highlighting the city's worthiest features: distinctive vernacular building forms constructed by German artisans in the 1870 and 1880s; gracious old homes and parks showcasing the talents of nationally known architects; landmarks and specimen buildings, including the Old Courthouse, the Anheuser-Busch Brewery, Bellefontaine Cemetery, and the Campbell House; and charming streetscapes full of pleasing contrasts between residential and commercial, historic and modern construction—all "The Harmonies That Time Makes," as the article was subtitled. It was an impressive "sampling of visual pleasures found in the city's neighborhoods," meant to counter the declension narratives that had come to dominate the public imagination—to remind those fixated on "venerable buildings" lost, old trees "slaughtered," and "rivers [turned] into sewers" that St. Louisans had much to celebrate, and to urge "respect [for] the marks that time makes" on a city.[1]

The editors acknowledged the primary context for their efforts near the start of the essay: the ongoing rehabilitation of huge swaths of midtown, several square miles starting just west of the Civic Center and Union Station. Recent projects included LaClede Town (an experimental integrated housing complex built on an unruly patch of ground at the southwestern corner of what once had been the sprawling Mill Creek

Valley neighborhood, near St. Louis University) and the West End Urban Renewal Project, a large-scale renovation plan for which city officials had secured $20 million in federal funds, much of which would be spent on demolition of slum housing. The very same Sunday edition of the *Post-Dispatch* also had two front-page articles critiquing the latter project, which had been hampered by delays, mismanagement, and a range of abuses perpetrated by the city's Land Clearance Renewal Association (LCRA). One of the articles called out the LCRA and the premise of its work as a "massive problem of renewal." In their effort to "rehabilitate" several predominantly African American neighborhoods (the *Post-Dispatch* calls them "Negro areas"), planners had in the columnist's view *compounded* blight, or the spiraling problems of "rot," as he put it, suggesting the reality was one not only of material but of moral violation. Neglect had begotten neglect; condemnation of properties had hastened devaluation of neighboring properties; and the erratic process of "rehabilitation" through eminent domain had fueled what he called an "I don't care attitude" among landlords and residents and a certain brazenness among "vandals and wholesale people" (and some thieves) across the region. In the case of the West End, the most astonishing outcome of these patterns had been the dismantling, "piece by piece," of entire buildings in the renewal zone without the owners or mortgagers knowing—some discovering their properties had been condemned only after demolition. Whether the work of LCRA agents or thieves (and it was becoming difficult to tell the difference, the article argued), the negligence had contributed to the loss of buildings that could have been saved and ruined whole neighborhoods.[2]

These were the effects not of natural decay or "blight" as commonly defined by planners, but of willful neglect and violative *taking*—patterns that have continued in midtown and the Central West End to this day, and are particularly rampant in African American neighborhoods, as for example in Paul McKee's Northside Redevelopment holdings, which are described in the introduction. Neglect and taking were the opposite of the "caressing" and respect for "the marks that time makes" the *Post-Dispatch* wished to affirm in its way: they represented a grotesque inversion of the ideals of stewardship and historic preservation.[3] Bringing them together served to acknowledge something of the dynamics of what I have been calling the memorial unconscious, whereby remembering was rooted in darker preoccupations and impulses—and at times patently aggressive acts—that so often defined the politics of public life and planning in the city. By the same token, drawing an association between the acts of "saving" and showing care and respect with acts of destruction involved its own compensatory logic of nostalgia.

As the preceding chapters suggest, this same logic dominated the history of the Campbell House both before and after it became a museum. Here was a site that had enjoyed decades of fond "caressing" and been buoyed along by collective nostalgia (and pangs of regret) for longer than many 1965 observers knew. From the time that it was built—the first in a private neighborhood whose designers aspired to protect and control space and elevate the city's status—the town house at 1508 Lucas Place (and then 15th and Locust Streets) embodied "venerable" materiality and later the "marks that time makes," and indeed was enshrined as a specimen of the city's "Continuing Grandeur," to use the words of the *Post-Dispatch* in 1965, for some fifty years in the late nineteenth and early twentieth centuries. By the Depression, it had already come to be known as one of the city's greatest "visual pleasures," again using the *Post-Dispatch*'s characterization, and within a decade would be transfigured, reconstructed, and interpreted as a local and national heritage commodity.[4]

While it had been transformed thus, many of the CHM's advocates still found the experience of visiting the house—of crossing the threshold between past and present—as unsettling as it was uplifting. As for the editors of the *Pictures* photo-essay, their cognitive dissonance was palpable: the "indiscriminate use of the headache ball" and the celebration of the "harmonies that time makes" could not be reconciled by one gloriously intact specimen, even if the celebration of aesthetic and domestic order at times served as a distraction from all the loss the city had suffered, all the "Departed Grandeur" that it could no longer experience. Early interpreters had not attempted to make visitors feel "at home" in the Campbell House, although they rhapsodized about the pleasures of "stepping back into another time" and exploring a lost social and domestic world. Instead, docents served up period-room-style displays featuring showpieces whose status as heritage objects was self-evident—at least for white, middle- and upper-class patrons who showed interest in the site. Their choices reflected the curatorial sensibilities that *Post-Dispatch* editors (adopting the perspective of the "urban explorer" who takes "leisurely morning tours of the city's diverse neighborhoods" in search of hidden architectural gems) modeled in the *Pictures* article, those of the political and cultural elites who had "a proper regard for history and tradition—and beauty, too."[5]

During the war years, when there were no funds to do more than express a proper regard for history and tradition, the house's condition as an "intact" historical site became a primary (and self-fulfilling) argument for keeping and admiring it. Interpreters devoted little time to the story of the family, much less to the servants, social networks, and broader historical and political dynamics; they focused instead on the house itself— its unlikely persistence, its aptness as a symbol of a golden age of material comfort and gracious hospitality. These claims were evolving ones, and they took on new dimensionality in the postwar context, which produced the Costume Room and Children's Room exhibits, the *McCall's* reenactment of 1957, and dozens of garden parties and high-society teas.

These same sensibilities prevailed during the late 1960s and early 1970s, a period when some of the original museum foundation members were still active but losing the strong sense of purpose they once had. As they fussed over private events and exhibitions featuring their favorite objects, and sometimes their own personal collections, the tenancy of the central business district and the number of visitors to the museum continued to decline. The CHF faced daunting maintenance issues in this period as well, and spent much of its time and energy debating the best strategies for stabilizing aging infrastructure. With the 1967 hire of Theron Ware, a decorative arts specialist and seasoned antiques collector, to the newly created role of museum curator, the board acknowledged the complexity of their situation with respect to stewardship and the pressing need for more specialized care both of the interiors of the house and its collections. Ware would have an enormous influence on the museum's exhibition and curation practices in the coming three decades, laying the groundwork for future museum staff who carried out targeted restoration work in the 1990s and a full-scale restoration of the exterior and many of the interior rooms during the early 2000s.

Much has changed since the time of Ware's strongest influence (the 1970s and 1980s—he retired in 1993), both inside the house and out. While the CHM remains a loved and well-protected site whose significance to public memory and ongoing preservation are predicated on claims of persistence and intactness, these concepts have been redefined to suit professionalized curatorial and preservation practices and evolving public sensibilities. The visitor experience is no longer dominated by tightly controlled tours and exhibits or the feedback loop of local media hype, and few who visit today have preconceived notions beyond those they would bring to any historic site. They are often surprised, even staggered, by what they discover inside, and instinctively declare the site a "hidden gem," unconsciously echoing what *Post-Dispatch* editors had declared about "the rewards awaiting those who take the side streets instead of the expressways."[6] Why don't more people know about this remarkable place? they wonder. One answer is simply that many St. Louisans have low expectations about the city's "half-empty" downtown—a tenacious narrative that is the product of more than a half-century of botched "renewal" efforts. Thus, the visitor's sense of disjunction—between inside and outside, industrial and residential, no place and hyper-defined place—may be striking, but it is short-lived, like the unanticipated delight of discovering a "hole in the wall" restaurant with great food but spending no time in the surrounding neighborhood. But it seems not to have significantly altered local regimes of place.[7]

The obvious lack of "quiet, dignified harmony" between the house and its surroundings is not precisely painful but neither is it fully understood. This problem of indecipherability is one every docent recognizes and seeks to manage. The mission of today's CHM is no longer simply to showcase specimen objects and architectural features but to *historicize* them—to tell the story of the site itself, and by extension of the city that created it.[8] Most tours start with an invitation for visitors to study an enlarged segment of Rich J. Compton and Camille N. Dry's remarkable topographical atlas of the city, *Pictorial St. Louis* (1875–1876) which has been laminated to the wall near the front door. It shows a birds-eye view of Lucas Place and environs as it might have looked to someone in a hot-air balloon (supposedly how the artists who produced the atlas got their information) after the Civil War, offering a historically specific version of "quiet, dignified harmony" that no longer exists, not on Locust Street or indeed anywhere in the downtown area.[9] Thus begins the difficult act of imagining how much has changed since the family lived in this house.

But in addressing the problem of decipherability, today's interpreters have distinct advantages their predecessors did not. Decades of research about the house, the neighborhood, the family, and the contents of the collection now inform their narratives; they have a much fuller sense of context to provide and, one must acknowledge, a fuller imagination for local history, including the darker elements of the city's past that are also part of the site's history. Most importantly, they have the circa 1885 photo album. Visitors usually hear about this remarkable artifact within the first ten minutes of their arrival. Whether directly engaged as a visual aid or simply described, the album informs most of the tour. And it *is* a remarkable and significant artifact, full of high-resolution albumen photographs showing both exteriors and interiors of the house, each shot with great care and professionally mounted on heavy paper in a fancy leather album. Some of the images are almost poetic in their framing and sensitivity to light; others are stunning simply in their documentation of minute details—the sheen of upholstery, the position of personal items on bedside tables, even the titles of some of the books come through (figs. 17–19). All of them have granularity most museum curators can only dream of. And while a few, including frontal shots of the front and side of the house, seem straightforwardly documentary in their approach, no one would confuse them with photos taken by the press in the late 1930s and 1940s. They have a richness of texture and shadow, a quality of "expressiveness," that high-quality printing captures especially well. And they provide a distinctive and authoritative view of the house—that of the *owner,* but also, perhaps, of one who has "a proper regard for history and tradition—and beauty."

In the context of today's tour, the photographs are treated as uniquely important historical evidence—images commissioned or possibly taken by Hugh Campbell, who was known to be an amateur photographer (he owned a camera that could produce such images and could easily have afforded the expense of producing it). They date to around 1885, a significant moment for the family: shortly after the death of Robert and Virginia, which signaled the end of the older generation's hold on the estate and coincided with the expiration of Lucas Place deed restrictions.

FIGURE 17. "Southwest corner of 15th Street and Lucas Place showing the front façade of Campbell House and the garden gazebo." Photograph, ca. 1885. Campbell House Museum, St. Louis, MO.

FIGURE 18. "Parlor looking southeast into the Morning Room showing the bay window and the pair of Cornelius and Baker gasoliers." Photograph, ca. 1885. Campbell House Museum, St. Louis, MO.

FIGURE 19. "Home of General William Harney at the southeast corner of Lucas Place and 15th Street. Central High School in the background." Photograph, ca. 1885. Campbell House Museum, St. Louis, MO.

Some speculate that the photographs were taken primarily for insurance purposes, the level of detail serving as a means of documenting the value and breadth of the family's possessions. But it was unusual, even among the well-to-do, to take so many and such elaborately staged photographs of one's own house. Hugh took a second set around the same time that show the interiors of a house near Cambridge, Massachusetts, that the family rented while James was attending Harvard, and assembled the photos, as well as some others showing family possessions (including their plot at Bellefontaine Cemetery), around the same time. In any case, the circa 1885 photos are generally assumed to have had personal significance—at the very least, to express Hugh's sense of commitment to his parents' memory and his general caretaking impulse, which at times verged into fetishism of their possessions.

That the photos were purportedly "salvaged from a dumpster" only adds to their evocativeness as memory objects and historical artifacts. The story of their discovery is now a central element of the Campbell House folklore, extending and deepening the origins myth that began during the 1930s and took deeper hold during the estate auction, as the "mystery house" became the "unlikely survivor" of the city's glorious past and then an object of heritage: the most "integral and intact display of . . . [Victorian] furnishings" found in the country.[10] That story goes like this:

> Sometime in the early–mid 1960s, an unassuming St. Louisan (possibly a local barber?) went to discard his trash in a local dumpster, and was amazed to find a fancy photo album inside. It was a remarkable find: the photos inside documented the property at 1508 Locust and its environs, including a handful that depict what looked to be heirloom objects (family portraits and sculpture). Fortunately, he saw fit to bring them to the museum, where someone determined they must have been discarded by staff at Kirby and Orrick, the law firm that handled the Campbell estate. The photos slipped from public view and museum records for a decade (during which time they were apparently at the home of architectural historian and CHF president John A. Bryan), but resurfaced in 1973, when they were officially donated to the museum, and began to inform internal research.[11]

To these later interpreters, the salvaged photographs' significance as historical evidence registered as powerfully as did their sentimental value. The album seemed to offer as complete a view of the Campbell estate as one could hope for from before the auction dispersal and early 1940s "restoration"; before the slow disintegration of the neighborhood and the loss of the city's oldest precincts; and before the deaths of James, Hazlett, and Hugh, when the house was still a hub of social activity and influence. Putting the house "back the way it was" in this time "before" would become a driving priority for much museum interpretation starting in the mid- to late 1990s.

Today, HC-8, or "Hugh Campbell Photograph Album—1508 Locust, 1973.1.1" as it is designated in the CHM catalogue, is rarely on display, spending most of its time in an acid-free box inside a fireproof office closet on the fourth floor. But its images are reproduced just about everywhere: in CHM newsletters and brochures; on the website, blog, and social media; in educational resources and plastic-coasted reprints throughout the house; and in tour narratives and exhibits, which are forever being compared, and calibrated, to the photos. Even though the building's restored interiors are brightly colored, Hugh's photos dominate much of the print material used to tell the story of the house. Curators chose, for example, to include several of his images alongside full-color shots of the Campbell dining room and scanned pages from Virginia Campbell's receipt book in *The Gilded Table,* a book about Victorian food and entertaining that the museum saw published in 2015.[12] And the photographs are forever being mentioned in media profiles of the house. It is no exaggeration to say that the album is now a foundational premise for the house's ongoing interpretation and for most claims about the building's significance as a site of public history and memory.

The Campbell House as a Site of Memory

Photography is associated with the work of memory, as today's CHM visitors intuitively understand. Indeed, since its invention, it has served as a metaphor for the act of remembering itself (snapshots being conceived as "imprints" of a given moment in time). As Alan Trachtenberg has argued, the analogue camera came to be understood as an actual "instrument of memory," the means by which individuals not only recorded the past but made everyday life memorable. While today's digital photos bear almost no resemblance to nineteenth-century photographs (the mechanics and chemistry of transfer having been replaced by a totally different process), we continue to understand them as the domain of a specific kind of "truth" that such transfer implies. They are the traces of lived experience, and as Trachtenberg notes, the "old regime photograph" in particular is still seen by most "as a certifier of authenticity, an assurance that here at least was a sign that matched a referent. The power of photographs as cultural memory, the memory of persons or events we could not have experienced firsthand except through photographs, derives from the ingrained belief that every photograph contains at least the raw material of memory, and thus show what memory is."[13]

The special allure of old photographs, furthermore, lies in their seeming "awareness" of, or at least capacity to document, this transaction of meaning. They seem in their uncanny way to "speak" of this transaction and of their own work of carrying into the future resonances of the past. They are mechanical eyewitnesses to a domain of private experience that, while it is sealed off from the future, can nevertheless be glimpsed in the traces—the imprints—left on the photographic plate. Photos are thus in multiple senses "ghostly": they capture living realities in "dead" (chemically fixed) form, and they conjure up the dead and their pasts with tremendous "lifelikeness." Sometimes too they express the past as a ghostly or shadowy realm, as we see in some of the circa 1885 photographs, the image of Hugh Campbell featured on the Locust Street banners, and even some of the *Post-Dispatch's* records of the "harmonies that time has made" in St. Louis. Here lies much of their pathos as records of a lost, or otherwise violated, material world.

Hugh's photographs are ghostly in yet another sense: they document the house and neighborhood in all their material splendors but are devoid of the people. The one exception is a photograph of General William Harney's residence (located right across 15th Street from the Campbells'), which includes a child sitting on the curb, an apparent stowaway from the past (see fig. 19). The boy is barefoot and dirty, and he looks directly at the camera while he pets a dog lying on the street next to him (perhaps one of the Campbells' beloved spaniels). The high-quality camera has captured all of this and more: the intricate dental molding at the roofline, the floral curtains and shutters in the upstairs windows, the urn full of plants on the front walk, and even—remarkably—the haze in the sky and the weeds and debris that fill the street. But this is an exceptional case; the boy and the weeds seem accidental, or at least superfluous, details in a set of photographs otherwise concerned with scenes that express composure and a sense of material well-being. In general, Hugh's photos appear to participate in a mode of domestic photography that was popular during the Victorian period, that is, minus the accustomed human subjects reading or sewing or studying a photo album beside the fire. He was evidently more invested in the house and its contents, documenting them with middle-distance shots that suggest a well-ordered domestic universe suspended in a pristine state of tableau. In this respect, they are more analogous to estate portraiture of the late eighteenth and early nineteenth centuries and period rooms of the twentieth.

In their scale and visual tropology, however, the images more closely resemble a type of documentary photography from a later period—the so-called threshold or doorstep photos made famous by Jacob Riis in *How the Other Half Lives* (1890), and later used to great effect by Depression-era photographers such as Dorothea Lange, who documented the domestic realities of commoners as if peering through the open doors of their homes. St. Louis's own Civic League used such images to document the myriad "evils" of tenement housing, including crowding, inadequate plumbing, and "complete decrepitude" in 1908.[14] As Didier Aubert has shown, twentieth-century photographers working in this genre often engaged self-consciously with "the issue of access, and the boundary between publicity and privacy in social photography," exploring how their subjects—many of them extremely destitute—attempted to negotiate with their social-domestic realities, their public image, and the gaze of the photographer. In the case of Riis's *Other Half* photos showing the squalid environments endured by immigrant communities in New York City in the late 1880s, taken around the time Hugh Campbell was shooting his second set of estate portraits (of the rented mansion outside Cambridge, Massachusetts), we see families crowded into public-private spaces such as stairwells, doorways, dangerous-looking back porches, basements, parks, and alleyways. Many are framed so as to interrogate the problem of violated privacy, although it is unclear whether Riis understood himself as an intrusive presence.[15] Hugh's photos have a similar preoccupation with threshold spaces; many are shots of bedrooms and sitting rooms as seen from hallways or doorframes, as if being viewed by someone in search of human inhabitants. But they are an inverse of Riis's images in that their inhabitants elude the gaze of the photographer, and the world of material coherence they capture expresses inviolate security and privacy of a sort enjoyed by the wealthy.

Strange as it seems to compare photos of the interiors of a Gilded Age mansion with those showing tenement apartments set up as sweatshops, the two sets of images have qualities in common beyond their fascination with 1880s urban domestic spaces. Despite their divergent material conditions, both Hugh's and later threshold photographs engage the private residence as a domain of autonomous selfhood, seeking expression of character and dignity, even a kind of moral integrity, that viewers are presumed to be able to interpret. Aubert argues that in this implicit exchange, the threshold photograph "caters ultimately to the values of an essentially-white, liberal middle-class public" by representing the ideals of individualism and bourgeois homeownership (even when it aims to expose the everyday cruelties of poverty).[16] Hugh's photographs partake of this ideology, documenting the family's home not just as a material asset but as the domain of character and memory. But whereas for Riis and Lange and the Civic League of St. Louis, the lower-class domestic realm had a vexed relationship to morality, their subjects struggling to overcome fundamental hardships evident in material disorder, for Hugh the domestic was a domain of heightened order and security. In those former photographs, the home is always, if troublingly, a semi-public zone: the alley, the rickety porch or fire escape, and the shanty are places where privacy is violated. In Hugh's, by contrast, the home is sacrosanct, and even the streets and rooflines become extensions of his private world and memory. Again, the lone exception seems to be the barefoot boy, who may indeed be one of Hugh's "own" (a street child or orphan of the sort he would have supported through various acts of kindness over four decades).[17]

Visitors confronted by the floating fragment of history that is today's Campbell House, like those who stumble upon the banners along Locust Street discussed earlier, must find the existence of these photographs reassuring. They offer a coherent vision of the past, an orderly domestic universe that corresponds to received notions of the "Victorian household," and whose objects have recoverable meanings. What is more, they appear to document the home *as it really was*, complete with that palpable sense of pastness that photographs offer, which Roland Barthes has famously described:

> To recognize the *studium* is inevitably to encounter the photographer's intentions, to enter into harmony with them, to approve or disapprove of them, but always to understand them, to argue them within myself,

for culture. . . . The *studium* is a kind of education (knowledge and civility, "politeness") which allows me to discover the *Operator*, to experience the intentions which establish and animate his practices, but to experience them "in reverse," according to my will as a *Spectator*. It is rather as if I had to read the Photographer's myths in the Photography, fraternizing with them but not quite them.[18]

"Fraternizing" with historical photographs involves engaging with the details of that past and with a sense of its meanings—meanings we long to understand and symbolically reinhabit, or even possess. When viewed alongside other material remains (the furnishings and physical environment) of that same past, as happens during the CHM tour, the photographs serve as corroborating evidence of the house as a fully "authenticated"—and decipherable—historic site.[19]

Getting the House in Order

Of course, having the photographs in hand did not guarantee decipherability. Nor did it immediately produce the remarkable verisimilitude and material integrity that today's Campbell House seems to offer. These took nearly three decades, millions of dollars, and intensive restoration to accomplish. But the rediscovery of the photographs was a major boon— perhaps the most significant episode in the museum's history since the public auction, which it resembled in many ways. The circa 1885 photographs opened up the private household to scrutiny by all manner of "spectators" and promised the symbolic wholeness of a "complete record" of material-historical facts—of not just engaging but *re-collecting* these facts, and thereby putting the house back in proper order. In a very real sense, *studium* became the primary domain of and mechanism for rehabilitative and interpretative work at the site. The earlier mythology of the house as a symbolic whole achieved through the careful selection of specimen artifacts understood as "ancestral objects" (see chapters 4 and 5) gave way to a mythology of "actual" intactness—that is, to an intact interior restored to reflect not a nostalgic sense of "how it was in the golden days of yore" but "how it *really* was" in the historical sense, which is now understood to be knowable.

This new mythology—which was in fact a major paradigm shift that anticipated many of the broader changes in the preservation industry—took hold over years, not months. And it introduced a host of new contradictions that would not be hashed out until the mid-1990s, when a long-range plan and accompanying architectural study were conducted. When the photographs were donated in 1973, the CHF was attending to urgently needed repairs, security concerns, and declining receipts; it would take time to develop the motivation and means to pursue larger projects based on photographic evidence.[20] The initial tweaks to museum interpretation were small: docents began to describe decorating changes made in the later period alongside those made during the 1860s renovation of the house, which invited visitors to imagine the material evolution of the house over more of its full lifetime. The shift also eased Hugh and his brothers back into the story. Likewise, objects were slowly "put back in their proper places"—sometimes against strong objections by members of the Campbell House Foundation board, who had always enjoyed the freedom to dictate how rooms were configured and frequently indulged an "antiquarian bias" similar to that of their predecessors in the William Clark Society.[21]

By the late 1970s, the photographs had come to inspire a more-strategic approach to restoration, and the CHF began to prioritize the care of artifacts "actually owned and used by the Campbells" and to approve only restoration and repair that was based on evidence.[22] So, for example, in 1977–1978, decisions about repairs to the carriage house and a collapsed section of the morning room ceiling, as well as the replacement of a fireplace mantle in the dining room and some bedroom carpeting, were made based on study of physical remnants alongside the photographs. Theron Ware was especially attentive to such evidence and to local archives and family papers as well. He conducted targeted "excavations" throughout the house, largely to seek new insight about changes made over time—especially during the 1860s renovations, which greatly impacted core infrastructure (that associated with, for example, the installation of central heating). Ware also revised the docent handbook to incorporate new information he gathered, and developed a list of proposed restorations and repairs that would help put the rooms "back as nearly as possible to their earlier appearance."[23] These activities were pursued systematically during the 1980s, and his ongoing "detective work" in the house informed the CHF's growing commitment to the use of "as much documentation as possible to make [the house] authentic."[24]

The photographs gave the CHF board a sense of perspective when serious maintenance problems were uncovered or disaster struck—for example, in the summer of 1988 when an electrical fire broke out in a third-floor storeroom that damaged the costume collection. No one expressed hysteria—or even much sadness—about the lost artifacts, which were not Campbell possessions. The fire had not damaged the "historic section" of the building, and it led to changes in the museum's fire prevention strategies, storage and loan practices, and insurance policy.[25] Before long, the remaining costumes were deaccessioned—a decision that would have enraged some CHF members a decade earlier (especially those behind the Costume Room). Likewise, when exterior repairs to the roof, windows, and woodwork were done, the board increasingly favored careful restoration of original features over stop-gap repairs. Care-taking was predicated not on appearances and structural intactness but on notions of material-historical integrity. But it would be impossible to reverse the effects of time throughout the house, much less the extensive changes made before the opening (the replacement of carpets, the painting-over of stenciled ceilings and wallpapered walls, the removal of doors, and many other projects) without extensive study.

With the photographs in hand, Ware and his docents slowly moved in the direction of a mixed-period interpretation of the house. While certain rooms such as the parlor continued to be discussed in terms of mid-1850s furnishings and styles that had been such a focus for early preservationists, and the house was still characterized as a "Civil War mansion," the later renovations and styles of decor were now also mentioned, allowing visitors to think in terms of evolving tastes and uses of space, and sometimes even the decisions that had produced a given change. This expanded material history led to some confusion, for visitors were asked to imagine distinct periods in the very same or adjacent rooms, and often in the face of radical, historically inappropriate changes made by the museum in earlier decades. But Ware and his colleagues did their best to clarify, emphasizing changes in design and infrastructure as they related to broader social history. He also advocated that non-Campbell objects once used to fill visual and interpretive gaps be stored away, thus loosening the institution's grip on period-room-style display.[26]

This new way of interpreting the house was formally articulated in an application to the National Register of Historic Places (submitted in 1977) but would continue to evolve over the coming decades, culminating in the drafting of a formal restoration policy (adopted in 1999) that named "target" restoration periods for different parts of the house. The National Register application began with a systematic assessment of the property's defining features inside and out, its construction and evolution, its siting and contextual history, and its significance. This required new contextual research on changes to the house and neighborhood between the 1860s and 1890s, as well as new documentation by the Historical American Buildings Survey (HABS) department of the National Park Service in 1975 (HABS had also documented elements of the property in 1936, 1940–1941, and 1959).[27] The final application narrative again deployed the mythos of the house as a "miraculous survivor" of 1850s St. Louis, but it also documented a longer history, and a more complex heritage, than had previously been claimed—one informed by multiple architectural and decorative styles, changing configurations and second-generation ownership of the house, and the ultimate decline of Lucas Place.[28] And, needless to say, this more complete material history of the property was deeply informed by study of the circa 1885 photographs, which provided Ware and his colleagues with a conception of the residence as it appeared before all the changes visible in the accompanying HABS photographs, such as the neglect of the house's exteriors and garden and the deteriorating neighborhood, occurred.

The National Register application represented the first public statement of institutional commitment to period-appropriate restoration, and its success was motivating. When members of the CHF board were not attending to collapsed ceilings, rusted fence posts, or broken downspouts, they continued to strategize about the growing list of desired repairs and refurbishments, which they intended as elements of an "ongoing restoration" that would move toward fuller historical specificity. The biggest challenge they faced was uncertainty about which items to pursue first, especially given the pressing need for exterior repairs, such as a new roof. Should their commitment be to maintaining and preserving what was there, including the refurbishments pursued by the Campbell sons, or to restoring the "original" fabric of the house, circa 1865, after its first major expansion was completed? And what about the initial restoration done by the CHF in the 1940s, and the Costume Room and Children's Room exhibitions the earlier board had installed, which obscured or damaged as much as they revealed and restored? Should all of this be undone? Perhaps the current board members should aim for a more incremental approach, reversing some of these changes and slowly returning the house to a circa 1885 state? The board's uncertainty hampered progress on various smaller projects, although in the late 1980s it managed to conduct a partial restoration of the dining room and morning room that included installation of circa 1885 reproduction wallpapers, art glass windows, and carpets (all of them still present in the house today).[29]

If the photographs suggested a hundred new priorities for future restoration, they also triggered a slow-detonating crisis of mission. One long-serving member of the CHF, Mimi Kerth, used the occasion of her resignation in 1991 to describe the stakes of this crisis. Reminding the board of the seriousness of their responsibility to the "public good"—namely, to "educat[e museumgoers] with the truth" of history—she urged against what she disparagingly called "redecoration" schemes based on "speculation." In her estimation, such ill-conceived restoration work would undermine the mission of "one of the finest museum houses in the country," a site made distinctive by its "98%" original contents and the circa 1885 photographs, which allowed for more "truthful" interpretations of those contents.[30] It was a striking statement—implicitly an argument against the erratic forms of rehabilitation that had been pursued elsewhere in the city—and one the board evidently found persuasive. A "Commission on Planning" was established early the following year whose charge was to wrestle with these matters.[31]

In working to develop a long-range plan, the Commission on Planning reassessed the museum's existing mission and vision statements as they related to restoration. They also commissioned a "comprehensive and integrated" historic structures and architectural assessment of the property inside and out, including mechanical systems, that would "guide a major capital improvements campaign" they hoped to complete "before the 150th anniversary of the building in 2001."[32] They underscored the need to "protect and accentuate the historic fabric of the building," urging the architects who did the assessment to "take into consideration preservation of prior restoration work" and avoid "intrusive solutions and demolition." Most importantly, from their perspective, the exteriors needed to "be restored to reflect the mid-1880s appearance found in the family's period photograph album," which was taken to be the point at which the property stabilized (in other words, when all the major renovation inside and out had come to an end).[33] A local architectural firm, Kimble A. Cohn & Associates, took the job and within a few months produced a report in which they advocated for a comprehensive restoration to be pursued in one five-year period so as to minimize disruption. The estimated cost for the first (exterior) phase was between $1.5 and 2 million.[34]

Their recommendations were promptly endorsed by the CHF. Raising funds would take time, but they anticipated success on this front. The lingering worry was methodological and philosophical: how strictly should they define periodization? The museum's collections, and especially the revered photographs, made multiple readings of the same site possible. And as Theron Ware had long argued, the house's persistence through a number of "aesthetic and stylistic movements popular during its occupancy" allowed for its interpretation as "a continuum of one American family's residence."[35] A "continuum" is precisely what members of the Restoration Committee had come to believe in. They drafted a new restoration philosophy/policy in 1995 that argued the house represents "an invaluable cultural resource that provides significant insight into the history of the nineteenth and twentieth century." They emphasized further that the "abundant visual and physical documentation" in the CHM archives (and especially the photographic evidence) represents "a unique opportunity and challenge to meet the highest level of authenticity and scholarship in the restoration and preservation of this building."[36] They had embraced a new standard of material-historical intactness and integrity, although without fully understanding the implications.

The committee members acknowledged that any restoration plan would necessarily evolve with time but named target dates that made sense to them: the exterior of the house, including the carriage house and the garden, as well as the morning room, back hallway, and bathroom, should be restored to circa 1885 conditions based on Hugh's photographs, while the rest of the rooms should be returned to 1855, 1867, circa 1870, 1875, or even (in the case of the kitchen) 1900 conditions, depending on features and available evidence. The group's logic was inconsistent, but their approach had a certain pragmatic appeal, especially given the uneven curation practices of the previous thirty years. The new plan took into consideration the quirks of the house and the private fascinations of its two generations of owners (and indeed several generations of CHF members and volunteers), which, as I have argued in preceding chapters, shaped the collection, as well as the realities of the house as an experience, in numerous ways.

The plan had to be modulated, however, when the nation's foremost historic homes experts were called in to offer their analysis in 1997. Gail Winkler, a Philadelphia preservationist whom the CHF wished to consult on the interior restoration and furnishings, was suitably impressed with the evidence provided by the committee and affirmed the proposed restoration as an opportunity to move the house toward rigorous, historically grounded interpretation, noting that the photographic evidence in particular illuminated processes of change over time that were valuable to restorationists and curators. The "complex overlay of finishes and furnishings [that was the result of such a] long occupancy by a single family" was a palimpsest that would be difficult to interpret, but she believed that "visitors would find it extremely rewarding" and that the CHM would soon be seen as "one [of] the most important house museums in the Upper Mississippi River Valley."[37] But Winkler strongly objected to the committee's preassigned target restoration dates, which, while they reflected the CHF's "laudable desire to memorialize Virginia and Robert Campbell," did not correspond to the "physical evidence" and "pictorial documentation."[38]

After some tense discussion, Winkler agreed to produce a preliminary furnishing plan for eight rooms in the house and to review completed restoration work elsewhere in the house. She and her colleague Roger Moss came to the CHM in the summer of 1998 and spent several days conducting onsite research during which time she delivered a public lecture on the subject of Victorian interiors.[39] The approach that she and Moss advocated in their final report took some members of the CHF board by surprise—in particular, the stringency of the target-date logic for restoration of furnishings. In discussions that played out over several months, the CHF struggled with but eventually came around to the idea that "c. 1880 was the period for which there is the most evidence, such as the existing photographs." Given that it was also a high point for the family, "before the death of Virginia and the deterioration of the neighborhood," and that key improvements such as the porch enclosure happened at this time, the chosen period was a locus of stability on many levels.[40] It was difficult to argue with the need to avoid a "muddled" approach that would cause delays and confusion, and the choice of the 1880s certainly had its appeal. Yet to achieve this degree of consistency much of the previous restoration work would have to be reversed. In addition, many objects would have to be relocated, reconditioned, or deaccessioned.

What was most persuasive about the approach Winkler and Moss recommended was that it represented a clear strategy for engaging that impressive but daunting "98% original material" at the site. The furnishing plan emphasized the revelatory nature of the collection, with its "rich, dense layering" of three generations of the family's experiences, decorating choices, and sensibilities. It was encouraging to be told that the circa 1885 photographs, which they, like so many others, saw as the most important evidence in the collection, could help them excavate those layers to figure out how things had really looked, thus forestalling the need for "speculation" and erratic rehabilitation that Kerth was concerned about. It was also reassuring to hear an expert declare the photos as evidence that "the Campbell sons honored their parents' memories."[41] Winkler and Moss conceived of the photos as the key to unlocking the domain of the past both in a material and an epistemological sense—that is, as "certifiers of authenticity," as Trachtenberg would say, and reliable source-texts for restoration and ongoing heritage work at the site. Their report pointed back to a kind of material-historical integrity the museum's founders had long ago named as defining characteristics of the site but had failed to deliver.

Restoration

Of course, *total* material-historical integrity would be impossible to achieve, even with the circa 1885 photographs and millions of dollars in hand. Too much inside the house had been altered or dispensed with (or never saved in the first place), and many details in the photographs were simply too ambiguous to be relied on for restoration-related decisions. But the furnishing plan provided a framework that would draw exclusively on evidence of the house "as it was" at a moment of psychic and material stability of the sort the city longed to reclaim, if only in symbolic form. This framework was all-encompassing: it conceived of restoration as a reconstitution of all of the house's material elements, top to bottom, from structural, architectural, decorative, organizational, and even atmospheric perspectives. Winkler and Moss of course advocated only period-appropriate furnishings and fabrics, color schemes, and materials. But they also argued for a host of not-so-small "tweaks" to existing infrastructure and decor: raising or lowering of light fixtures (which often required rewiring); removing "false" finishes and reconditioning woodwork on hundreds of windows and shutters; relocating and replacing objects, from missing tie-backs to house plants to transom windows; and reordering the contents of every single room, even those that had already been restored, based on evidence from the photographs.[42]

While there was wiggle room with some of these recommendations, and much local interpretation (and additional research) would be required to actually achieve them, the goal was an overall integrity that depended to a great degree on fidelity to the target date in all spheres of household decor, inside and out.[43] The new Campbell House would depart from the old both in form and content—or, we might say, body and soul. Becoming an "authentically restored" historic site required complete material transformation suited not only to all the pomp and circumstance of a sesquicentennial year but to the discriminating sensibilities of the experts. The restoration the CHF ultimately pursued would take about six years and cost more than $3 million, and depart in nearly every respect from "the first restoration" in 1941.[44] There would be minor setbacks and unanticipated discoveries (dozens of revealing objects were found between the walls, in crannies beneath the floorboards and chimneys, and in the basement); fundraising challenges and unexpected windfalls from private foundations; and hundreds of the kinds of compromises that a limited budget imposes, including scaling back or modifying key recommendations by Winkler and Moss.[45] But for the most part the furnishing plan (with data from a finish investigation and analysis report of 1998 and several smaller finish and fabric studies) dictated the terms on which the restoration was performed.[46]

Accordingly, the house was completely emptied out, a security fence was erected, and thousands of Campbell possessions were once again crated up and put in storage. As the scaffolding on the outside of the house went up, the layers of the inside—and with it the layers of time— were slowly peeled back and the "bones" exposed (see, e.g., fig. 20). In such a state of "undress," core features of the house could be studied closely, yielding a range of insights about the "original" structure (which now meant present from the start in 1851 or added in 1865). While some of the decisions about structural reinforcement, such as the need to replace floor joists and stabilize the main staircase, effectively imposed themselves, many others had to be negotiated along the way as funds were raised and decisions about scope were made. The contractor's punch list was an endlessly evolving document. But with quick fundraising success, a large number of electrical, plumbing, and code-related updates could be completed, many of which involved still more demolition and reconstruction (for example, a mantle in the parlor had to be removed when the chimney was opened so electrical systems could be run through the flue).[47] This subsequent peeling away of layers continued for months and was conceived as a thoroughgoing investigation—a more vigorous version of Ware's "detective work"—and an effort to access the "heart and soul" of the building.

As with historic homes like Mount Vernon and Monticello, which are often cited as models of true preservation integrity, the restoration of the Campbell House involved as much new fabrication as repair and reconditioning. "Original material" had to be reinforced structurally, which required repainting and repair and in some cases total resurfacing. In most of the rooms at least some compromised woodwork and cracked plaster had to be fixed, and new outlets, switches, and sprinkler heads installed. Portions of wall had to removed and sometimes reconfigured to accommodate modern ductwork and insulation. Restoring the circa 1885 finishes required the stripping—or at least the revarnishing—of doors and trim throughout. Traces of earlier paints, wallpapers, or fabrics (dating to the 1850s or 1860s) discovered throughout the house were

FIGURE 20. Front and east facades of the Campbell House during renovation, photograph, ca. 2001. Campbell House Museum, St. Louis, MO.

typically removed (though notably, archival samples were taken wherever possible—choices that the WCS had not considered).[48] Once these more invasive procedures were completed, the remaining layers could be put back: reproduction carpets and fabrics installed; wall stenciling and wood-graining hand-applied by specialists; original furnishings, including 258 boxes of smaller objects, returned; and selectively chosen new (non-Campbell) objects, such as furnishings for the servants' rooms and a cast-iron range and wood icebox for the kitchen, were put into place.[49] It was a long and painstaking process that gave tangible expression to the complex ideals of material integrity and intactness.

As Winkler and Moss had recommended, the restoration process was incorporated into public tours as soon as was feasible. Visitors were invited to participate (vicariously) in the scraping away of layers of paint and time—and to discover the house's hidden "secrets" by taking limited-time "behind the scenes" tours in which they could study "peeling wallpaper, chipped paint, [and] small uncovered sections of original stenciling" alongside sketches of the stencil patterns and wallpapers that would be installed.[50] They were told of the "historically accurate wall-to-wall floral motif Axminister or Wilton carpeting" being replicated based on evidence from "Hugh's photographs," which would be installed as soon as the paint dried.[51] And they could watch as artisans applied forty-two different paint colors in the parlor, imagining the elaborate "decorative display" that was being put back, layer by layer (see fig. 21). The museum's quarterly newsletter and local press reported on the latest findings by the restoration crew, and described the tours as a chance to "step back in time," and possibly to spot some new evidence the experts missed. In one such account, the *Post-Dispatch* included a supplemental column advising readers how they too might "play detective and uncover the secrets of [their own] old house."[52]

Besides educating the public about the house and its history, these restoration-related accounts had other important benefits for the museum. They asserted claims of the house's significance as an unusually complete, palimpsest-like record of the past, now confirmed by "historical documentation" and industry experts. And they turned the restoration process

FIGURE 21. Restored parlor, with all custom finishes and details reconstituted based on the furnishing plan and related studies, photograph, 2010. Campbell House Museum, St. Louis, MO.

into something of a ritual of local remembrance. Central to this process was the emptying out and filling back up of the house, which was an unconscious reenactment of earlier moments of near loss and symbolic recovery in the museum's history, including the discovery of the photo album, the buying back of Campbell possessions at auction, and the first restoration. It also (of course only symbolically) reversed what had been going on for decades across the city, and especially in the central corridor, from the systematic clearance of the riverfront and whole neighborhoods, to the piece by piece dismantling of houses in "Negro areas" in 1965 and the demolition of Pruitt-Igoe. Indeed, the restoration presaged the ongoing dispossession of residents in McKee's NorthSide Regeneration district and the National Geospatial-Intelligence Agency's development zone, whose homes would not receive recognition as local heritage.

But the ritual involved repetition with a crucial difference, for this new CHM restoration was in material respects more "complete," more fully "authenticated," by the art and science of preservation. Disclosing the house's "secrets," pulling back the curtain of time to see the past "as it was," served to update the core fantasy of restorative nostalgia that had so long animated the work of preservation at the site. As Svetlana Boym notes, restorative nostalgia entails the imagined return to "original stasis" or even some "prelapserian moment" through recreation of "emblems and rituals of home and homeland . . . [that] conquer and spatialize time." In these rituals, the past becomes "a perfect snapshot," an "eternally young" image that resists "decay."[53] The newly reconstituted Campbell House was an emblem of just this kind, and its restoration was part of the ritual of caretaking that Hugh had begun in the 1880s, which now had a different symbolic significance for a city that, to put it lightly, had failed to "caress" many of its neighborhoods and residents.

Including the public in the house's reconstitution was a central part of the ritual of caretaking. It instilled confidence in the techniques and outcomes of restoration. Guides continue to describe both—for example, by explaining how spectroscopy can be used to figure out all those colors of paint and by showing cutaway sections of the wall where samples of plaster were removed for analysis and faint outlines of original *trompe l'oeil* decoration still appear. Both have been covered with Plexiglas to serve as permanent exhibits—perhaps especially intended for a public that finds the science behind shows like *History Detectives* (DNA "ancestry" kits, photographic aging software, and the like) compelling. But even for those who do not, seeing the "man behind the historic preservation curtain" is reassuring, as many twenty-first-century interpreters understand: it reinforces belief in material-historical integrity, including its apparent ability to resist decay and its suitability as a symbolic home.[54] Alongside such exhibits, the circa 1885 photographs are the other centrally important artifact in restoration-related interpretation. Among other things, they are now understood to reveal the material-historical particulars—what Roland Barthes calls "the very raw material of ethnological knowledge"—that restoration uses to "bring the past back to life."[55]

While most do not think of restoration as an extension of ownership in the material sense, this is what it amounts to: a symbolic act of repossession. Hugh's photographs served to legitimize material and moral claims over his family's wealth and well-being—and over the ideals of home. These associations have infused decades of preservation work that made different but analogous claims over the history of the city and the nation. Restoration ritualizes such acts of ownership, encoding them as cultural labor and memory work, rather than as efforts to control space, resources, the meanings of the past, or local regimes of place. But it necessarily builds on these other more overt acts of possession, including those pursued by previous caretakers—the preservationists who sought historic district status for parts of Locust Street; the William Clark Society and its successors in the CHF; the Campbells themselves; even those who platted Lucas Place on a tract of farmland, previously covered in Indian mounds. And it requires continued labor, as we have seen with the cleanup after the burglary and many other episodes in the museum's history.

Restoration continues even today, as more and more of the house's "original" contents are put back into their places based on photographic evidence. The museum regularly receives offers from owners of former Campbell possessions, many acquired at the 1941 estate auction and passed down in the family. Recently repatriated objects include a monogrammed nightshirt worn by Hazlett during the later years of his long illness; a porcelain cup and saucer made in Naples by Capo di Monte, once part of a whole set; twelve large sterling silver punch goblets the Campbells used for entertaining; and Virginia's silk and woolen "Kashmir" shawl, which appears in a large portrait of her that now hangs in the parlor.[56] Members of the CHM community relish these "homecomings," for each has a hint of the pathos of more pivotal acts of salvage, such as pulling the album from the dumpster. And each serves as an opportunity to tell some part of the fascinating story of the house, to draw the public into behind-the-scenes activity of the sort that is now a special emphasis on museum tours: the cataloguing and cleaning of objects; the research on those objects, which invariably begins with Hugh's photographs and other key archival sources such as Selkirk & Sons' *Dispersal Resumé;* and finally the many considerations curators must give as to how best to display them.[57]

CONCLUSION

NO PLACE LIKE HOME

T HE CAMPBELL HOUSE is a site laden with contradictions. As the first
house built in Lucas Place and its last surviving remnant, it evokes
all the aspirational grandeur of frontier capitalism while pointing to its
limits, and the inevitability of change and loss. Once the heart of a "citadel of significance," the house and its contents had to be actively "saved"
from dismantling and then painstakingly recovered and protected. And
while it has survived various cycles of growth and decline—and the end-
less rehabilitation of the city—the house has become a floating fragment
of the past, one that, like the bend in the road, holds mysterious allure but
frustrates the desire for continuity or complete historical understanding.

If the house has been a site of "living history," it has also been a reli-
quary of the dead—a repository of family possessions tended as lovingly
as a mausoleum and with the same dark mystique. Yet these possessions
have repeatedly been made to "speak" for the city and its past, giving
expression to a distinctive local heritage characterized, variously, in terms
of its owners' refined tastes and gracious hospitality, of the city's economic might and political influence, of frontier heroism and domestic
order, of urban humanitarianism and hospitality, and of historic remembrance and the collective work of preservation. The Campbells' things
have spoken, in other words, of St. Louis's "better nature"—of ideals such
as hope, happiness, honor, and community.

In coaxing forth these rich and varied associations, the house's caretakers have most often privileged ideals of *heritage* and material *intactness*. Both are vital elements of historic preservation as a practice and
philosophy: their adherents past and present have found in them a sense

of fulfillment, even transcendence, and a whole range of uplifting social effects as well. These positive ideals fortify a sense of place and identity, security and belonging. They also motivate selfless acts of caretaking and stimulate the historical imagination, both of which reinforce local commitments to place. But as we have seen, the ideals of heritage and intactness have often become entwined with the logics and aggressions of urban planning, commercial capitalism, and possessive individualism. And thus, at times they have given expression to certain darker elements of the local character as it were, including conceit, provinciality, opportunism, self-protection, aggression, and bravado. The mythos of intactness in particular has been rooted in acts not only of caretaking but of appropriation; it is a philosophy premised on the work of *taking possession* of the past in both material and symbolic senses, and it is often accompanied by acts of *dispossession,* all manner of violative takings and acts of disregard whose effects, perversely, reinforce the commitment to selective preservation. The claims of heritage made by the house's many agents of care, furthermore, have justified other forms of interpretive aggression and amnesia such as those explored in chapters 5 through 7, and supplied new narratives of exclusive ownership and social-material order.

"Saving the Campbell House" involved pursuit of both intactness and heritage, and acts of caretaking and taking. Indeed, from the beginning, the William Clark Society conflated these ideals and actions, employing selective curation and assertions of control over the house and its history to construct what they understood to be "a truly representative Victorian period museum." The "best things" of Virginia and Robert Campbell in turn represented "enough" to merit further public support and fill period room–style displays. In the early years of its operation as a public museum, "enough" came to mean other things as well, including a "representative sampling" of specimen artifacts and a curated set of meaning-laden objects meant to give tangible expression to an innocent national past. In short, "enough" amounted to legitimation of the objects and the house as cultural heritage.[1]

With time, the mythos of intactness became more dynamic, and interpreters treated the Campbell House less like a curio cabinet than a stage where one might engage imaginatively—performatively—with the past. In these contexts, the ideals of heritage and intactness were confirmed through live "encounters" with material remains of history, albeit remains curated as vigorously as specimens under glass. Initial encounters of this kind were tentative, full of apologetic or compensatory gestures, but interpreters soon found confidence in the house as a site of "crossing over." Many people besides CHM officials—corporate executives, commercial artists, local business and cultural elites, magazine writers, professional historians, and everyday visitors—claimed the right to do so, and in its early decades as a museum, the house became a portal to many different idealized pasts. As initial experiments in display and choreography gave way to more sweeping dramatizations such as the *Land We Live In* radio-play and the prize-winning history of the fur trade *Across the Wide Missouri* and its related Hollywood film, and as period rooms became more elaborately staged reenactments of the materialized past, such as the *McCall's* dinner party and St. Louis Fashion Creators' exhibits, new (or perhaps just imaginatively invigorated) conceptions of "gracious living" and genteel urban life emerged—ideals that were calibrated to the sensibilities of white, middle-class suburbanites, many of whom had abandoned the city. While these ideals may not have been overtly linked to the acts of violative taking we now associate with the period (for example, the construction of an interstate highway and segregated public housing, and the "rehabilitation" of historic neighborhoods across the city), as I argue in chapter 4, they promoted a white spatial imaginary and treated the city as a heritage commodity.

In recent decades, the mythos of intactness has continued to evolve alongside urban renewal practices, which have given the house added poignancy. Its unaccountable *persistence* contrasts starkly, peculiarly, and unsettlingly with all the disfiguring material changes that have occurred in the region, especially in the city's central corridor. Ironically, while the CHM collection has come to be more fully historicized by docents and curators who show eagerness to engage the city in all of its political and material complexities, the site itself has become more enclosed and self-referential, both in material and symbolic senses. The early 2000s restoration of the house depended on elevated notions of historicity and material intactness, yet "returning" it to a more fulsome state of integrity involved enshrining the house anew, which imposed a kind of psychic distance.

Whereas early interpreters privileged aesthetic and affective registers of interpretation, today's museum staff privilege rational ones: they describe the house as a site of cultural, archaeological, and even scientific labor rather than as a cabinet of wonders, emphasizing expert views and seemingly incontrovertible evidence of "what's there." Yet the sentimental language of intactness and heritage persist, and the "time capsule" metaphor seems more apt than ever. Encounters with the past are not only still possible but encouraged. Tea parties have given way to "drink-up, tweet-ups" and historical food events, and today's visitors know to avoid romanticizing, preferring "facts" to "quaint notions" about the city's past. But many still celebrate the house's "miraculous survival" as an opportunity for discovery, one defined—now less sensationally—as a fuller understanding of the city's and the nation's history.

Having "enough" has morphed into a standard of having (just about) "everything," and a new degree of intactness is presumed to yield fuller decipherability and thus more *history*, more *meaning*. The meaning of the Campbell House lies not in heroicizing narratives of the sort privileged in the World War II decades, which have undergone thorough critique, but in "real" encounters with the materialized past. We can recognize in these changes the pivot from restorative to reflective modes of nostalgia as described by Svetlana Boym, whereby acts of remembrance—making contact with the past—come to be infused with irony, uncertainty, and feelings of ambivalence.[2] Indeed, the qualities of heritage significance and intactness that have been so vigorously celebrated, and that made the site a symbolic home, are shot through with the *unheimlich,* the uncanny.[3] Intuitions of the uncanny lurk at the edges of the site—quite literally, since the first thing visitors must confront today is the incongruity of the house, which looks like it fell from the sky. What accounts for its presence here—how has it survived when so much has been lost? How should we reconcile its marvelously intact interiors with the desolation and neglect we see outside? And what does its unlikely persistence mean?

While these uncertainties have always haunted the work of preservation, they are especially disconcerting here, on this particular corner, in this particular city. Here we find the uneasy convergence of aging mercantile, civic, residential, and industrial districts; here landmarks and memorials alternate with parking lots and abandoned properties; here the city is everyone's (a home even to the homeless) and no one's, and regimes of place break down, with alienating effect. Visitors must confront all of these facts and more—subtle but distressing signs of disinvestment, aggressive policing, and increased privatization of public spaces, and the general problem of indecipherability—just as they enter the Campbell House. Whether or not they experience the cognitive dissonance many before them have described on crossing the threshold, they cannot deny that such remarkable vestiges of the past as the house and its contents "acquire resonance through their relationship to something forgotten" or lost, indeed, to many somethings.[4]

Perhaps because of these unsettling realities, and broader feelings of uneasiness about the political, social, and material conditions of the city, the ideals of heritage and intactness require constant policing. We see such policing in the history of the Campbell House itself, which has been so vigorously "protected" against all manner of incursion—crime, disease, pollution, mental and physical degeneration, commercial devaluation—since it was built. And we see it in the work of museum interpreters, who have "saved" the house, ritually, again and again—not only from the depredations of time, the courts, and urban planning, but from the more insidious effects of forgetting, disregard, and shame. The 2012 burglary described in this book's opening pages, a memorable episode in the material history of the house, was likewise seen as an incursion; it motivated swift reaction, symbolic as well as literal protection, and restoration.

The destruction of the etched-glass window was experienced as a violation for many reasons. In a literal sense, it involved loss of an original feature of the house, one that would be difficult to replace, especially given the high standards of integrity that have been adopted in recent decades (fig. 22). In a more symbolic sense, the burglary involved a rupture of the membrane between past and present that adherents of restorative nostalgia seek to keep intact. The front door of the house has long been experienced as a threshold of departure, a point of access to the "historical" realm; it has also (as we see in the Stix, Baer & Fuller advertisements) been an emblem of the house as a site of heritage and a corporate-philanthropic brand, and by extension, a symbol of the city of St. Louis itself, at least during that period of heightened publicity.

FIGURE 22. The violated front door of the Campbell House Museum, photograph, August 2012. Campbell House Museum, St. Louis, MO.

But there is more to the front door as a symbol still: by mythical logics, it is a liminal zone, where life and death, continuity and change, certainty and dread, can be felt simultaneously—and also the space where the ideals of heritage and intactness come into view. In another sense, the door-as-threshold might be seen as the outer shell of the house and the family therein, a kind of protective skin; violating that skin amounts to an act of willful disregard for both the house and the ideals it represents, or at least what seems so to those who hold them dear. Given its mythical (as well as material) qualities, we might think of the window as analogous to the glass bell jar that has protected the Campbells' taxidermied pets. The jar could easily have been broken, and yet for more than a century it has kept the bodies of the family's smallest members in suspended animation, apparently protecting them from decay. The glass preserved and kept them for the work of memory, like the rest of the family's possessions.

For many observers in 2012, of course, the broken window was something else entirely: a reminder of "city problems" such as crime and homelessness, and disregard for public property. A relatively modest crime, to be sure—one whose only violence was inflicted on the glass, and whose motive was a small pile of cash. Yet it inspired a vigorous, angry reaction full of rhetorical violence of the kind that has come to be associated with policing (the chants of police a few blocks away: "Whose streets? OUR Streets!") and politics more broadly; it hardly reflected the supposedly disinterested nature of public history.[5] In other words, broken glass engendered compensatory aggression.

Revealingly, the aggression was followed immediately by vigorous efforts at recuperation and protection of the site, which point directly back to the ideals of intactness and heritage. In post-burglary blog updates on cleanup and restoration, for example, Campbell House officials described efforts to find an artisan skilled enough to "reassemble the glass from the broken pane" and duplicate the original design in a new window, which would be both a "daunting task," and an expensive one, given the museum's high standards of intactness. The accompanying images have the intimacy of a PBS special on fine craftwork, though one looks like a crime-scene photo (fig. 23), its caption directing our gaze to the "point of impact" on the window, a locus of almost bodily violence (again, like the piercing of flesh). Readers were invited to marvel at the acid-etched design and the painstaking efforts to bring the delicate leaves and stems back to life, the hand-made template destroyed by sand-blasting, the "hand cramps" of the artisan. They were expected—like the craftspeople who assessed the window and were "nothing short of appalled"—to lament the irreversible nature of the damage. In other words, they were asked to acknowledge a material violation as a moral one.[6]

Well-intended as the defense of the house and replacement of the window certainly were, they involved mixed feelings and motives, as we can glimpse in the rhetorical violence of the "string them up!" comment quoted in the introduction. The fact that it was followed by the "beefing

FIGURE 23. The "point of impact" on the shattered front door of the Campbell House Museum, photograph, October 2012. Campbell House Museum, St. Louis, MO.

up" of security at the CHM is even more revealing. In the months following the repair of the front door, Hackett Security Company installed hefty new inside door locks, an ultra-loud alarm, and other high-tech surveillance tools, measures that the board of the museum described as deterrents for "knowledgeable professionals" (that is, high-class art thieves, not petty burglars) who might come after its valuable decorative and fine arts collections. One blog post gaily reported that the fortified museum is now a "small—but impeccably decorated!—version of Fort Knox!"[7]

The joking reference to Fort Knox, the most militarized of all sites on the U.S. National Register of Historic Places, is telling.[8] It suggests that some feel the CHM, a site already protected by an alarm, a fence, a sprinkler system, a live-in caretaker, and various federal statutes, and supported by a large donor base, a paid staff, and a fleet of volunteers, is *still* vulnerable. "We were burgled!" the house's defenders protested; they felt dismay over the compromise of the house's "impeccably decorated" interiors. In such reactions, we can also see moral indignation and defensiveness on behalf of the city's treasures of a sort that have been present since the founding of the museum, and that are periodically reactivated. Like the WCS officials who compared the potential loss of the Campbell House to the bombing of European villages, or city boosters who came out in force when National Football League owner Stan Kroenke announced his intention to move the St. Louis Rams to Los Angeles, those speaking on behalf of the Campbell House at this moment expressed concern about something far more serious than material loss.[9] They were defending the city's good name, its history and heritage, and other, less tangible elements of public memory: the sacred qualities of home.

NOTES

Introduction: The Burglary

1. After the other burglary on July 30, 2012, which also involved theft of cash, CHM officials conducted an inventory to see if there was some pattern; their findings were inconclusive but revealed evidence that several small items had disappeared in recent months or years. Board of Directors meeting, minutes, September 17, 2012, box CHF-2I, folder 5, Campbell House Museum (CHM) Collection, St. Louis.

2. "We Were Burgled," Campbell House Museum, August 7, 2012, https://camp bellhousemuseum.wordpress.com.

3. The NLEC was shut down by court order in early 2017. See Doug Moore, "Rev. Rice Loses City Appeal, Must Close His Downtown St. Louis Homeless Shelter April 1," *St. Louis Post-Dispatch,* January 13, 2017.

4. "About Us," Campbell House Museum, http://www.campbellhousemuseum.org.

5. Racialized violence has been a defining element of local history for nearly two centuries, the most notorious case being the May 1917 massacre in East St. Louis in which a white mob terrorized and killed dozens (some say as many as one hundred) African Americans, many of whom fled to and ultimately resettled in St. Louis. See, e.g., C. L. Lumpkins, *American Pogrom: The East St. Louis Race Riot and Black Politics* (Athens: Ohio University Press, 2008).

6. Tim Edensor explains this concept in "The Ghosts of Industrial Ruins: Ordering and Disordering Memory in Excessive Space," *Environment and Planning* 23, no. 6 (2005): 831. Other geographers have offered influential theories of place that have informed this project. See, e.g., Delores Hayden, *The Power of Place: Urban Landscapes as Public History* (Cambridge, MA: MIT University Press, 1995), and Larry Ford, *The Spaces between Buildings* (Baltimore: Johns Hopkins University Press, 2000).

7. In February 2016, St. Louis–based news agencies reported that the city had

been named the "murder capital of the U.S." based on policing statistics collected by the Brennan Center for Justice. See Sarah Fenske, "St. Louis Has the Highest Murder Rate in the Nation," *Riverfront Times* (St. Louis), October 1, 2015.

8. Daniel Fisher, "America's Most Dangerous Cities: Detroit Can't Shake No. 1 Spot," *Forbes,* October 29, 2015, https://www.forbes.com; Erik Eckholm, "Rise in Murders Has St. Louis Debating Why," *New York Times*, February 10, 2015. See also Richard Rosenfeld et al., "Peering into the Black Box: The Criminal Justice System's Response to Gun-Related Felonies in St. Louis," St. Louis Public Safety Partnership, University of Missouri–St. Louis, July 2014, http://www.umsl.edu.

9. Some of the earliest analysis of the causes helpfully distilled Ferguson's complex prehistory. See, for example, Robert Rothstein, "The Making of Ferguson: Public Policies at the Root of Its Troubles," *Economic Policy Institute,* October 15, 2014, http://www.epi.org, and Larry Buchanan et al., "What Happened in Ferguson?" *New York Times*, August 10, 2015. More recent analysis, including Rothstein's book-length study, *The Color of Law: A Forgotten History of How Our Government Segregated America* (New York: Liveright, 2017), and the widely read "For the Sake of All" reports on health disparities in the region (Jason Purnell, Gabriela Camberos, and Robert Fields, 2015, https://forthesakeofall.org) have contributed to a fuller understanding of the racialization of Ferguson and across the region.

10. Both episodes were widely reported, including in the national press. See, e.g., Susan Hogan, "St. Louis Officers Chant 'Whose Streets, Our Streets' While Arresting Protestors," *Washington Post,* September 18, 2017, https://www.washingtonpost.com, and Yasmeen Sherhan, "St. Louis to Remove Its Confederate Monument," *Atlantic Monthly,* June 26, 2017, https://www.theatlantic.com.

11. For more on St. Louis's futile efforts to keep the Rams from leaving, see Joe Nocera, "In Losing the Rams, St. Louis Wins," *New York Times,* January 16, 2016, and George Lipsitz, "The Silence of the Rams: How St. Louis School Children Subsidize the Super Bowl Champs," in *Sports Matters: Race, Recreation, and Culture*, ed. John Bloom and Michael Willard (New York: NYU Press, 2002), 225–245.

12. Benton made his arguments in late 1849 and 1850, positioning the cause of building a national railroad, which he believed should be hubbed in St. Louis, as a means of preserving the union. Newspaperman Logan Reavis extended this argument after the Civil War when he proposed relocating the national capital to St. Louis. See, e.g., Adam Arenson, *The Great Heart of the Republic* (Cambridge, MA: Harvard University Press, 2011), and Kenneth H. Winn, "God in Ruins: St. Louis Politicians and American Destiny," in *St. Louis in the Century of Henry Shaw: A View beyond the Garden Wall*, ed. Eric Sandweiss (Columbia: University of Missouri Press, 2003), 19–50.

13. Jens Brockmeier, "Remembering and Forgetting: Narrative as Cultural Memory," *Culture and Psychology* 8, no. 1 (2002): 18–19. See also David Lowenthal, *Possessed by the Past: The Heritage Crusade and the Spoils of History* (New York: Free Press, 1996).

14. Tourist maps showing these landmarks are widely available and have been reproduced in a range of promotional contexts. See, e.g., "Route 66," Explore St. Louis, http://explorestlouis.com.

15. For example, Busch Memorial Stadium was built in 1964–1965 where "Hop Alley," St. Louis's Chinatown, had been. The area was cleared through eminent domain in the late 1950s. See Huping Ling, *Chinese St. Louis: From Enclave to Cultural Community* (Philadelphia: Temple University Press, 2004).

16. These planning visions are more fully described in Eric Sandweiss, *St. Louis: The Evolution of an American Urban Landscape* (Philadelphia: Temple University Press, 2001); Colin Gordon, *Mapping Decline: St. Louis and the Fate of the American City* (Philadelphia: University of Pennsylvania Press, 2009); Mark Abott, "The 1947 Comprehensive City Plan and Harland Bartholomew's St. Louis," in *St. Louis Plans: The Ideal and the Real St. Louis*, ed. Mark Tranel (St. Louis: Missouri History Museum, 2007), 109–150; and Joseph Heathcott and Máire Agnes Murphy, "Corridors of Flight, Zones of Renewal: Industry, Planning, and Policy in the Making of Metropolitan St. Louis, 1940–1980," *Journal of Urban History* 31, no. 2 (2005): 151–189.

17. The house was named a "Local Landmark" at the time of the CHM's opening in 1943, documented by the National Park Service in the Historic American Building Survey (1936–1941), added to the National Register of Historic Places in 1977, and awarded a National Trust for Historic Preservation Save America's Treasures grant in 2001. Its application for National Landmark status is currently pending.

18. Joseph Heathcott, "Harland Bartholomew, City Engineer," in Tranel, ed., *St. Louis Plans,* 99; Joseph Heathcott, "The City Quietly Remade: National Programs and Local Agendas in the Movement to Clear the Slums, 1942–1952," *Journal of Urban History* 34, no. 2 (2008): 221–242.

19. "Society Formed to Collect Objects of Early Midwest," *St. Louis Post-Dispatch,* January 10, 1939.

20. On the clearance of the riverfront for the Jefferson National Expansion Memorial, see Sandweiss, *St. Louis,* 221–229, 233–234; Heathcott, "The City Quietly Remade," 221–224; Arthur W. Mehrhoff, *The Gateway Arch: Fact and Symbol* (Bowling Green, Ohio: Bowling Green State University Popular Press, 1992), chapter 3; and Charles B. Hosmer, *Preservation Comes of Age: From Williamsburg to the National Trust, 1926–1949* (Charlottesville: University Press of Virginia, 1981), 625–630. On early public housing projects, see Heathcott and Murphy, "Corridors of Flight"; Heathcott, "The City Quietly Remade"; and Joseph Heathcott, "'In the Nature of a Clinic': The Design of Early Public Housing in St. Louis," *Journal of the Society of Architectural Historians* 70, no. 1 (2011): 82–103.

21. For more on the site as a source of local humiliation, see Colin Marshall, "Pruitt-Igoe: The Troubled High-Rise That Came to Define Urban America—A History of Cities in 50 Buildings, Day 21," *The Guardian* (London), April 22, 2015.

22. This has turned out to be more than a metaphor. Environmental studies have confirmed that the U.S. military sprayed toxic chemicals on Pruitt-Igoe (and its residents) in the 1950s. See Jennifer Mann, "Suit Filed over Government Test-Spraying in St. Louis during Cold War," *St. Louis Post-Dispatch,* November 21, 2014, and Megan Lynch, "Researcher: Poor St. Louis Minorities Targeted for Secret Cold War Chemical Testing," CBS St. Louis, September 24, 2016, http://stlouis.cbslocal.com. Lisa Martino-Taylor, the researcher who uncovered the evidence of the chemical testing, explores the

history and legacy of testing in St. Louis and other cities in *Behind the Fog: How the US Cold War Radiological Weapons Program Exposed Innocent Americans* (New York: Routledge, 2017).

23. McKee has been criticized for allowing the loss of important "legacy" buildings in North St. Louis—most recently, the Clemens Mansion (1858), which was owned by Samuel Clemens's second cousin and widely seen as architecturally significant, and many others with less-celebrated pedigrees. See, e.g., Doyle Murphy, "Clemens House, Owned by Mark Twain's Relative, Burns North of Downtown," *Riverfront Times* (St. Louis), July 12, 2017; Jacob Barker, "McKee Buys Pruitt-Igoe Site, a Symbol of St. Louis's Decline, and Now, a Rebirth," *St. Louis Post-Dispatch*, August 14, 2015; and the VanishingSTL blog, http://vanishingstl.blogspot.com.

24. "Proposed North St. Louis City NGA Site Has Strong Support from National, State, Local and Community Leaders," City of St. Louis, October 30, 2015, https://www.stlouis-mo.gov; Maria Altman, "City and Federal Government Soon to Sign Agreement for NGA Facility," St. Louis Public Radio, December 26, 2016, http://news.stlpublicradio.org.

25. The NGA project is being touted as the putative "hub" of a central corridor "innovation district," much of which is in in the former location of Mill Creek Valley, and as a "very elegant and very just" way for "this generation of the federal government [to undo] the injustice created many decades ago," as the former mayor's chief of staff Jeff Rainford noted in 2014. Nicholas J. C. Pistor, "National Geospatial-Intelligence Agency Names 6 Possible Sites for Move in St. Louis Area," *St. Louis Post-Dispatch*, July 9, 2014. See also arguments made in a promotional video produced by the local interest group "Let's Stay Together, NGA," St. Louis, April 1, 2016, http://letsstaytogether-nga.com.

26. "St. Louis Boarding Houses, Mansions of Yesterday: 'Rooms' and 'Board' Where the Rich of St. Louis Lived but a Few Years Ago," *St. Louis Post-Dispatch*, August 20, 1905. The phrase "slum surgery" was used in an article published in an issue of *Architectural Digest* that celebrates the CPC's logic and argues for removal of "blighted" and "obsolete" districts of a sort not seen since the campaigns that produced Carr Square Village and Clinton-Peabody. See "Slum Surgery in St. Louis," *Architectural Digest* 94 (April 1951): 128–136.

27. For more on the history of Lucas Place as a private place, see Richard Allen Rosen, "St. Louis Missouri, 1850–1865: The Rise of Lucas Place and the Transformation of the City from Public Spaces to Private Places" (M.A. thesis, University of California, Los Angeles, 1988).

28. George Lipsitz, "The Racialization of Space and the Spatialization of Race: Theorizing the Hidden Architecture of Landscape," *Landscape Journal* 26, no. 1 (2007): 10–23.

29. The most significant study of this fragmentation, and one that has profoundly influenced the public's imagination of St. Louis's urban geography, is Gordon's *Mapping Decline*. See also Paul L. Knox and Linda McCarthy, *Urbanization: An Introduction to Urban Geography* (Boston: Pearson, 2012); Douglas S. Massey, *American Apartheid: Segregation and the Making of the Underclass* (Cambridge, MA: Harvard University Press, 1993); and Kenneth T. Jackson, *Crabgrass Frontier: The Suburbanization of the United States* (New York: Oxford University Press, 1985).

30. "St. Louis Boarding Houses"; "Wrecking Mansion for Modern Hotel: Home of Gen. Harney Famous after Civil War for Social Functions," *St. Louis Globe-Democrat,* August 18, 1913.

31. The theory that the house was more intact because it had been tended by bachelors was routinely posited in the late 1930s and early 1940s. See, e.g., "Letters from the People," *St. Louis Post-Dispatch,* March 3, 1941.

32. Heathcott, "The City Quietly Remade."

33. For more on this expansionist logic, see Jay Gitlin, Barbara Berglund, and Adam Arenson, eds., *Frontier Cities: Encounters at the Crossroads of Empire* (Philadelphia: University of Pennsylvania Press, 2012), and Sandweiss, *St. Louis.*

34. This fascination found public expression in newspaper accounts and all manner of gossip, much of it focused on the brothers' reclusiveness and declining health, and the fate of their large estate. The archive associated with probate and other estate-related court proceedings is immense, spanning more than a decade (1931–1943) and encompassing multiple suits, some of them incredibly complex (Hazlett's estate having hundreds of claimants in multiple countries). See, for example, "$1,000,000 for Yale in Recluse's Will: Hugh Campbell, Indian Trader's Heir, Leaves Amount in Trust for a Brother, 75," *New York Times,* August 13, 1931; "Seeking Guardian for H. K. Campbell Aged Millionaire," *St. Louis Post-Dispatch,* September 2, 1931; "Jury Finds Invalid Millionaire Incapable of Managing Affairs," *St. Louis Globe-Democrat,* August 9, 1931; "Campbell Servants Assert Millionaire Aided Many Children: Testify for Defense in Suit of Brothers' Pleas for Adoption," *St. Louis Globe-Democrat,* June 8, 1933; and "Demented Man Target of Lawyers: Incompetent Son of Western Pioneer Holds Vast Wealth Which Is Center of Law Suit," *New York Times,* April 8, 1934. This same period is also well-documented in museum records, which include oral histories by servants and a range of print sources pertaining to the estate and court proceedings. See, e.g., Campbell Family History Photocopies, box C-4A, folders 5–9, and box C-4B, folders 7–9, CHM Collection.

35. The earliest public expression of preservationist interest in the house was made by Arthur Hoskins, future WCS president, in a 1932 op-ed. In it he argued that the residence represented a bygone era the city needed to remember, a "last link" with "the days when [Locust Street] was given over to fine mansions," and "there was no blight of dumps, industrial regions and railroad yards below to mar the picturesque view." "The Charm of Old St. Louis," *St. Louis Post-Dispatch,* April 16, 1932. These arguments would be revisited later in the decade when the newly established WCS launched the "Save the Campbell House" campaign (1938).

36. "St. Louis Tends to Move to the County," *St. Louis Post-Dispatch,* December 3, 1939.

37. Scott Herring, "Collyer Curiosa: A Brief History of Hoarding," *Criticism* 53, no. 2 (2011): 162.

38. CHM interpretations today are innovative—and at times politically progressive. But its treatment of the mythologies of white wealth, power, and domesticity is decidedly ambivalent. There is a growing literature that deconstructs these mythologies and explores their problematic hold on small museums and local preservation. See, e.g., Patricia West, *Domesticating History: The Political Origins of America's House Museums*

(Washington, DC: Smithsonian Institution, 2013); Stephanie E. Yuhl, *A Golden Gaze of Memory: The Making of Historic Charleston* (Durham: University of North Carolina Press, 2005); Richard Handler and Eric Gable, *The New History in an Old Museum: Creating the Past at Colonial Williamsburg* (Durham, NC: Duke University Press, 1997); Jessica Foy Donnelly, ed., *Interpreting Historic House Museums* (Lanham, MD: Rowman Altamira, 2002); and the special volume "Open House: Reimagining Historic House Museums," *Public Historian* 37, no. 2 (May 2015).

39. For an overview of the CHM's evolving narrative, see Mary Lynn Stevens, *From House to Museum, a Case Study: The Campbell House Museum, St. Louis, Missouri* (M.A. thesis, University of Delaware, 1982). My understanding of this narrative has also been shaped by study of docent manuals and scripts, in-house educational materials, observations made during tours, attendance at CHM board meetings, and more than a decade of conversations with interns, docents, and museum staff.

40. Several scholars of memory have theorized this kind of amnesiac or selective remembering, though not all attribute it to the same causes. See, for example, Mieke Bal's discussion in the introduction in *Acts of Memory: Cultural Recall in the Present*, ed. Mieke Bal, Jonathan V. Crewe, and Leo Spitzer (Hanover, NH: Dartmouth College, University Press of New England, 1999), vii–xvii.

41. Svetlana Boym, "Nostalgia and Its Discontents," *Hedgehog Review* 9, no. 2 (2007): 13–14; Boym, *The Future of Nostalgia* (New York: Basic Books, 2001).

42. Andrew Hurley, "Preservation in the Inner City," in *Beyond Preservation: Using Public History to Revitalize Inner Cities*, ed. Andrew Hurley (Philadelphia: Temple University Press, 2010), 22–23. There are certainly exceptions to the restorative bias of preservation, including those reflected in grassroots and archaeological projects in middle- and working-class neighborhoods around St. Louis. See, e.g., the Archaeological Research Center of St. Louis (ARC), http://arc-stl.com/, and Preservation Research Office (PRO), http://preservationresearch.com/. Andrew Hurley has documented "pockets of rejuvenation" in the broader "landscape of dereliction" in North St. Louis and argued for community-based public history that engages conflict in "An Experiment in North St. Louis," in Hurley, ed., *Beyond Preservation*, 55–94, 55 (quotations).

43. "Save Our [Gl]Ass™ Updated: A Week Later," Campbell House Museum, August 16, 2012, https://campbellhousemuseum.wordpress.com.

44. The rates of visitorship have fluctuated dramatically over the years, with the strongest numbers in the 1940s and 1950s, when the museum routinely saw a thousand visitors a month. There was an upward spike after the early 2000s restoration, and numbers have been strong recently, but traffic is still seasonal. See, e.g., Attendance Numbers, 1940s–2000, and Visitor Sign-in Guest Books, boxes CHF-30, and CHF-32A-F, CHM Collection.

45. In November 2017, the forest that had been growing at the Pruitt-Igoe site since its initial clearing more than forty years ago was bulldozed to make way for a hospital (part of Paul McKee's Northside Regeneration plan).

46. My exploration of the Campbell House as a site of memory is strongly informed by Pierre Nora's influential theory of *lieux de mémoire*. These ubiquitous byproducts of overweening "memorial consciousness," Nora argues, are a defining element of

the modern age. See, e.g., Pierre Nora, "Between Memory and History: Les Lieux de Mémoire," *Representations* 26 (April 1989): 7–24.

47. Carol Gluck, "Operations of Memory: 'Comfort Women' and the World," in *Ruptured Memories: War, Memory and the Post-Cold War in Asia,* ed. Sheila Miyosi Jager and Rana Mitter (Cambridge, MA: Harvard University Press, 2007), 47–77.

Chapter 1: The Neighborhood

1. Elizabeth Hallam and Jenny Hockey, *Death, Memory and Material Culture* (Oxford: Berg 2001), 104.

2. James Neal Primm, "The Economy of Nineteenth-Century St. Louis," in *St. Louis in the Century of Henry Shaw: A View beyond the Garden Wall,* ed. Eric Sandweiss (Columbia: University of Missouri Press, 2003), 103. For more on the city's historical role as a hub of frontier trade and business, see Adam Isaac Arenson, *City of Manifest Destiny: St. Louis and the Cultural Civil war, 1848–1877* (New Haven, CT: Yale University Press, 2008); Louis S. Gerteis, *Civil War St. Louis* (Lawrence: University Press of Kansas, 2001); Eric Sandweiss, *St. Louis: The Evolution of an American Urban Landscape* (Philadelphia: Temple University Press, 2001); and James Neal Primm, *Lion of the Valley: St. Louis, Missouri, 1764–1980* (St. Louis: Missouri History Museum, 1998).

3. This history has been influentially discussed by James Neal Primm in *Lion of the Valley* and Adam Isaac Arenson in *City of Manifest Destiny* but was first laid out in Wyatt Winton Belcher's influential book *The Economic Rivalry between St. Louis and Chicago: 1850–1880* (New York: Columbia University Press, 1947).

4. Eric Avila, *Popular Culture in the Age of White Flight: Fear and Fantasy in Suburban Los Angeles* (Berkeley: University of California Press, 2004). See also Colin Gordon, *Mapping Decline: St. Louis and the Fate of the American City* (Philadelphia: University of Pennsylvania Press, 2009), especially chapters 1 and 5; Alison Isenberg, *Downtown America* (Chicago: University of Chicago Press, 2005); and Joseph Heathcott and Máire Agnes Murphy, "Corridors of Flight, Zones of Renewal: Industry, Planning, and Policy in the Making of Metropolitan St. Louis, 1940–1980," *Journal of Urban History* 31, no. 2 (2005): 151–189.

5. Downtown retail giants are remembered with singular nostalgia, not only because they were symbolic figureheads but because they contributed to the material wealth and stability of the downtown area for so long. See, e.g., the "Stix, Baer & Fuller" and "Famous-Barr" entries in the online Department Store Museum, http://www.thedepartmentstoremuseum.org/, and Joe Huber, "The Life and Death of Great St. Louis Malls," NEXTSTL, December 5, 2012, https://nextstl.com. The charitable work of Stix, Baer & Fuller, and their involvement in the preservation and promotion of the CHM, figures prominently in chapter 5 of this book.

6. Conversations with then-candidate Donald Trump's representatives led thousands to protest outside the building in November 2016, but the project has continued with an undisclosed hotel chain partner. See "No Trump Tower at Jefferson Arms in Downtown St. Louis, Mayor Says," *St. Louis Post-Dispatch,* November 14, 2016, and "Dilapidated Downtown Jefferson Arms Makeover Could Start in January," *St. Louis*

Post-Dispatch, September 29, 2016. For more on the fashion and tech corridors, see Jackie Tucker, "Downtown St. Louis Garment District Continues to Grow with Search for New Placemaking Services," *EQ Newsletter,* July 25, 2017, https://www.notjustala bel.com, and Debra Bass, "St. Louis Fashion Fund Aims to Rival New York Garment District," *St. Louis Post-Dispatch,* November 6, 2016.

7. Designed by Cass Gilbert, architect of New York's Woolworth Building, the U.S. Supreme Court, and the St. Louis Art Museum, the library was built with $1 million from Andrew Carnegie, at the time the largest gift of its kind and evidence of St. Louis's status as a major U.S. city. A recent renovation involved stabilizing the building, restoring its more striking features, updating infrastructure, and expanding the north entrance.

8. Other buildings in the area include Confluence Preparatory Academy (a four-story brick-and-granite structure on the site that once contained the city's first public high school), a deteriorating former YWCA that for decades was occupied by the NLEC homeless shelter, a for-pay parking lot, the General American Life Insurance Corporation building (constructed in 1915 and expanded in 1923–1924), and a YMCA (1926). Between them is the Campbell House Museum, another parking lot, and a blank-looking intersection with rutted, uneven pavement.

9. Hallam and Hockey, *Death, Memory and Material Culture,* 105.

10. Larry R. Ford, *The Spaces between Buildings* (Baltimore: Johns Hopkins University Press, 2000), 31.

11. Lucas Place's founders, James H. Lucas and his sister, Anne Lucas Hunt, were children of Judge J. B. C. Lucas and siblings of Charles Hunt (a lawyer Thomas Hart Benton killed in a duel). The Lucases inherited vast railroad, banking, and real-estate holdings and were among the city's wealthiest citizens: James lived in a twenty-thousand-square-foot mansion across the street from Robert and Virginia Campbell (1515 Lucas Place) and owned five hundred acres in Normandy at the time of his death. He was the first president of the Missouri Historical Society. Anne lived at 1706 Lucas Place and gave away more than a million dollars by the end of her life in 1879. She funded the establishment of several major Catholic institutions in the area, including a local home for the Sisters of Loretto, who went on to found Webster University; the Convent of the Immaculate Heart for the Good Shepherd; St. Vincent's Orphans Home and Sanatorium; Incarnate Word Convent; and a Mother House for the Sisters of Charity. See David T. Beito and Bruce Smith, "The Private Places of St. Louis: Urban Infrastructure through Private Planning," in *The Voluntary City: Choice, Community, and Civil Society,* ed. David T. Beito, Peter Gordon, and Alexander Tabarrok (Ann Arbor: University of Michigan Press, 2002), 264–265.

12. "A Street Sketch: Some of the More Familiar Objects on Locus Street," *St. Louis Post-Dispatch,* October 18, 1880. See also "Buying in Lucas Place," *St. Louis Post-Dispatch,* January 24, 1889.

13. Positioned between 13th and 14th Streets between Olive, and St. Charles, the park was large and elaborately landscaped, featuring a sunken garden, stone benches, fountains, large shade trees, and gas lighting.

14. These and other of Lucas Place's features are described in Richard Allen Rosen,

"Rethinking the Row House: The Development of Lucas Place, 1850–1865," *Gateway Heritage* 13, no. 1 (1992): 20–27. See also Charles Van Ravenswaay, *St. Louis: An Informal History of the City and its People, 1764–1865* (St. Louis: Missouri History Museum, 1991), chapters 17–18.

15. Catherine Cocks, *Doing the Town: The Rise of Urban Tourism in the United States, 1850–1915* (Berkeley: University of California Press, 2001), 19.

16. At the height of the cholera epidemic, a thousand people were dying each week. Efforts to disinfect contaminated zones by burning tar and sulfur were futile, and it was later discovered that the disease had spread by way of contaminated water from a massive sinkhole at Biddle and 10th Streets and in Chouteau's Pond, just south of Market Street. In the decade that followed, many of the city's well-to-do settled permanently in their summer homes and plantation-style estates south and west of the city, and buried their dead in the new Bellefontaine Cemetery (where the Campbell family plot is laid). See Charles van Ravenswaay, *St. Louis: An Informal History*, 338–340, 385–390; Sandweiss, *St. Louis*, 63; Andrew Hurley, ed., *Common Fields: An Environmental History of St. Louis* (St. Louis: Missouri History Museum, 1997), 151–152; Robert Moore, "Notes upon the History of Cholera in St. Louis," *Public Health Papers and Reports* 10 (1984): 337–343; G. F. Pyle, "The Diffusion of Cholera in the United States in the Nineteenth Century," *Geographical Analysis* 1, no. 1 (1969): 59–75; and Patrick E. McLear, "The St. Louis Cholera Epidemic of 1849," *Missouri Historical Review* 63, no. 2 (1968): 171–181.

17. For more on Lucas Place's pioneering use of deed restrictions and their impact on the future of "private place" neighborhoods, see Beito and Smith, "The Private Places of St. Louis." Sandweiss provides a revealing account of the city's chronic paving and infrastructural problems in the 1850s in *St. Louis,* chapter 6.

18. "A Street Sketch."

19. Kenneth H. Winn, "Gods in Ruins: St. Louis Politicians and American Destiny, 1764–1875," in Sandweiss, ed., *St. Louis in the Century of Henry Shaw,* 20.

20. This political sensibility is fully anatomized by Adam Arenson in *The Great Heart of the Republic* (Cambridge, MA: Harvard University Press, 2011), 91. Like many elites in the "compromise" state of Missouri, the Campbells had multiple roles and split allegiances during the mid-nineteenth century. They adopted increasingly progressive views on slavery and Indian removal starting in the mid- to late 1840s, and emancipated their inherited slaves in the mid-1850s. But in the lead-up to the war they fell in line behind the city's moderate-sounding conditional unionists and continued business dealings with secessionists even as Robert's dry-goods firm outfitted Union troops. For more on the mixed political heritage of the Campbells and their peers, see Gerteis, *Civil War St. Louis*, 73–74, and "A Family Apart: The Campbells during the Civil War Years," CHM exhibition, St. Louis, May–August 2012.

21. Over the years, the Campbell family hosted Indian chiefs and white traders, Union and Confederate supporters, and Democrats and Republicans, including a high-profile dinner party for Ulysses S. Grant and other war heroes that the press treated as evidence of the city's return to the pantheon of influential western centers. See "Lucas Place at Night," *St. Louis Daily Globe*, April 22, 1873, and "General Grant:

Reception and Serenade at Colonel Robert Campbell's Last Night," *St. Louis Times*, April 22, 1873.

22. For more on St. Louis's distinctive character as a border zone city, see Arenson, *City of Manifest Destiny;* Adam Arenson, "The Double Life of St. Louis: Narratives of Origins and Maturity in Wade's Urban Frontier," *Indiana Magazine of History* 105, no. 3 (September 2009): 246–261; Jay Gitlin, Barbara Berglund, and Adam Arenson, eds., *Frontier Cities: Encounters at the Crossroads of Empire* (Philadelphia: University of Pennsylvania Press, 2012), 6–7; Gerteis, *Civil War St. Louis*, chapter 1; and Van Ravenswaay, *St. Louis: An Informal History*, chapters 17–19.

23. The Schaeffer Soap Factory made candles, soap, and lubricants (including wheel grease for countless wagon trains, riverboats, and gold mining companies that passed through St. Louis) and was routinely blamed for the stench and toxic fumes in the area. See, e.g., Tom Gronski, "Lucas Place Encyclopedia," internal research document, July 10, 2013, 53–54, and Lucas Place materials, box LP1A, folder 3, both in Campbell House Museum Collection, St. Louis.

24. "St. Louis Boarding Houses, Mansions of Yesterday: 'Rooms' and 'Board' Where the Rich of St. Louis Lived but a Few Years Ago," *St. Louis Post-Dispatch*, August 20, 1905.

25. The decision amounted to a legal and economic "divorce" from the county that has been blamed for disinvestment, fragmentation, absenteeism, shrinking revenue, and other debilitating problems ever since. See, Sandweiss, *St. Louis*, 158–165, and David T. Beito and Bruce Smith, "The Formation of Urban Infrastructure through Nongovernmental Planning: The Private Places of St. Louis, 1869–1920," *Journal of Urban History* 16, no. 3 (1990): 263–303.

26. Jerome Bibb Legg, who also designed St. Paul's Church and many other major buildings in the city, was the Exposition Hall's architect. He was known for residential architecture, including several homes of the same style and vintage (and in the same vicinity) as the Campbell House. See Carolyn Hewes Toft, "Jerome Legg (1838–1915)," Landmarks Association of St. Louis, http://www.landmarks-stl.org. For more about the history of the hall, including historic photographs of the palatial Gilbert Cass–designed public library erected on the same location in 1909, see "Construction a Century Ago," St. Louis Public Library, http://central.slpl.org.

27. Joseph Heathcott, "'The Whole City Is Our Laboratory': Harland Bartholomew and the Production of Urban Knowledge," *Journal of Planning History* 4, no. 4 (2005): 325. As other St. Louis historians have observed, local efforts to cast a more coherent planning vision, and to realize projects such as a Central Parkway (1912) and a zoning system (1919), were not especially effective or unifying, in either social-political or spatial terms. See, e.g., Sandweiss, *St. Louis*, chapter 7, and Edward C. Rafferty, "Orderly City, Orderly Lives," *Gateway Heritage: Quarterly Journal of the Missouri Historical Society* 11, no. 4 (Spring 1991): 40–62. For a discussion of these challenges in urban centers more generally, see Alison Lang, *Downtown America: A History of the Place and the People Who Made It* (Chicago: University of Chicago Press, 2004), chapter 1, and Cocks, *Doing the Town*, chapter 4.

28. See, e.g., *Gould's Blue Book for the City of St. Louis, for 1915* (St. Louis: Gould Directory, 1915).

29. The original deed contract specified that changes to zoning and other provisions would have to be authorized by a majority of the residents. The pressure to sign, especially for those who had not been original owners, must have been intense, given the high visibility of the neighborhood and all that it represented.

30. See "A Realty Sensation," *St. Louis Post-Dispatch*, December 22, 1888, and "New City Hall," *St. Louis Republic,* January 25, 1889.

31. "A Street Sketch."

32. *St. Louis Republic*, September 19, 1897, part 4. See also, "St. Louis Boarding Houses, Mansions of Yesterday."

33. As I discuss in the next chapter, Hugh Campbell generously supported Father Peter Joseph Dunne's home throughout this period, giving money for construction of a new orphanage on Washington Avenue, supporting individual orphans' education, and paying for annual holidays banquets for all the residents. For more, see "A Thanksgiving Story: Father Dunner's Boys and Hugh Campbell," Campbell House Museum, November 2013, http://www.campbellhousemuseum.org.

34. Heathcott and Murphy, "Corridors of Flight," 151–152.

35. The Campbell House has used the "City Living" slogan on stationary and other print material as well as on prominent signage and other street banners along Locust Street since the reopening of the museum after a full-scale historic restoration was completed (1999 and 2005).

36. In addition to the press about heroin overdoses by the local homeless and the closing of the NLEC shelter, there have been several high-profile protests against the September 2017 verdict in the Jason Stockley case, a white police officer who shot Anthony Lamar Smith after a high-speed chase in 2011 and was acquitted despite evidence of extraordinary force. Some of these protests (and vandalism of local businesses) happened in or near Locust and Market. See, e.g., Jeremy Kohler et al., "Undercover Cop, Air Force Officer, Med Student among Those Police Swept Up," *St. Louis Post-Dispatch,* September 25, 2017, http://www.stltoday.com.

37. At the time of this writing the banners were *at least* twelve years old, however, so their sense of "today" is admittedly dated.

38. Nelson H. H. Graburn, "Learning to Consume: What Is Heritage and When Is It Traditional?" in *Consuming Tradition, Manufacturing Heritage: Global Norms and Urban Forms in the Age of Tourism*, ed. Nezar Alsayyad (New York: Routledge, 2001), 70–71.

Chapter 2: Caretaking

1. "The Southern Hotel: A Brief Description of One of the Most Imposing and Elegant Caravaneries on This Continent," *St. Louis Post-Dispatch*, October 12, 1876.

2. Logan Reavis's speech, delivered at the Southern Hotel, was part of an 1869 convention devoted to the national-capital argument that became the basis for his book *The Future Great City of the World* (St. Louis: St. Louis Count Court, 1870). For more, see Adam Arenson, *The Great Heart of the Republic* (Cambridge, MA: Harvard University Press, 2011), 178–198.

3. As most of the Campbell children died in childhood, some in infancy, the family was in mourning for decades; Virginia had thirteen live births and "as many as 6 miscarriages and stillbirths" in twenty-two years (1842–1864). See "Campbell House History," internal research document, 2002, Campbell House Museum Collection, St. Louis.

4. Hazlett's condition would not be revealed publicly until after his brother's death, when he was ruled of "unsound mind" by the courts in 1931. In later probate court hearings, the family physician testified that Hazlett suffered from *dementia praecox,* which the doctor theorized had been triggered by grief that began decades earlier, following Robert's death in 1879. See, e.g., "Doctor Testifies Grief Upset Mind of Campbell, Heir," *St. Louis Post-Dispatch,* February 6, 1935.

5. "Demented Man Target of Lawyers," *New York Times,* April 8, 1934.

6. The precise dimensions of Hazlett's much-discussed fortune were made public several months after his brother Hugh's death. See "Rich Eccentric Dies Here in His Mystery House," *St. Louis Star-Times,* August 10, 1931, and "Aged Millionaire, H. K. Campbell, Is Held Incompetent: Declared of Unsound Mind and Probate Court Will Appoint Guardian to Manage Affairs," *St. Louis Post-Dispatch,* September 8, 1931. For more on the sensationalized case of the Collyers and their astonishing hoard in a Fifth Avenue brownstone in Harlem, New York, see Scott Herring, *The Hoarders: Material Deviance in Modern American Culture* (Chicago: University of Chicago Press, 2014), chapter 1; Gail Steketee and Randy Frost, *Stuff: Compulsive Hoarding and the Meaning of Things* (Boston: Houghton Mifflin Harcourt, 2010), prologue and chapter 1; and Franz Lidz, *Ghost Men: The Strange but True Story of the Collyer Brothers, New York's Greatest Hoarders: an Urban Historical* (New York: Bloomsbury, 2003).

7. Like his brothers, Hugh was home-schooled by his mother and then attended a private all-boys school just north of Lucas Place called Smith Academy. He graduated from Washington University in 1867, using his education primarily to draft legal documents pertaining to the family fortune. Records related to the sons' attendance at Smith Academy and Washington University are found in the "Working Research File Drawer," folder 25, and the "Campbell House History," internal research document, 2002, both CHM Collection.

8. Daddy Warbucks, a well-known character from the Broadway musical *Annie* (adapted from a print comic, *Little Orphan Annie*), is a hard-nosed New York businessman who discovers his tender heart when he takes in Annie, an orphan whom he eventually adopts. Hugh never adopted orphans, but he provided support for many, including two well-known local athletes, the Furman brothers, who were among many would-be heirs who emerged during litigation associated with Hugh's estate. The terms of his will stipulated that the income from this trust be used to educate the Furmans, and that each be given their half of the $30,000 when they turned twenty-eight (the equivalent of about $540,000 today). But they contested that award, claiming that Hugh had wanted them to "fare as if they were his sons" and inherit most if not all of his fortune. The court eventually decided "they had no more claim on the Campbell estate than did scores of other boys who were helped by Hugh Campbell," however. See "Testifies Campbell Said He Would Leave All He Had to Boys," *St. Louis*

Globe-Democrat, June 6, 1933; "Priest Testifies Campbell Aided Newsboys' Home," *St. Louis Post-Dispatch,* June 8, 1933; "Witnesses Bare Campbell's Many Acts of Charity," *St. Louis Post-Dispatch,* June 9, 1933; and "Trial of Campbell Will Suit Concluded: Lawyers to File Briefs in Fifteen Days—Two Seek to Be Declared Adopted Sons," *St. Louis Post-Dispatch,* June 10, 1933.

9. One such description is provided by Robert Campbell's grand-niece Mary Scott-Crabbs, who recollected family visits to the house when she observed Hazlett's deteriorating mental state. See "Oral History of Campbell House," box C-4B, folder 7, CHM Collection.

10. See, e.g., "He's a Princely Giver: Mr. Hugh Campbell Gave Presents to Southern Hotel Employees," *St. Louis Post-Dispatch,* December 26, 1898.

11. Although his "secrets" were sometimes blown publicly, as when the newspaper covered a large banquet that he staged for the boys at Father Dunne's. See "Benefactor of Newsboys Gives them Banquet," *St. Louis Post-Dispatch,* October 20, 1908. For more on his support of Father Dunne's orphanage, see "A Thanksgiving Story: Father Dunne's Boys and Hugh Campbell," Campbell House Museum, November 2013, http://www.campbellhousemuseum.org, and Campbell Family History Photocopies, box C-4A, folder F10, CHM Collection. For more on the posthumous disclosure of Hugh's role as benefactor, see, e.g., "Rich Eccentric Dies Here in His Mystery House," *St. Louis Star-Times,* August 10, 1931, and "Campbell Servants Assert Millionaire Aided Many Children," *St. Louis Globe-Democrat,* June 8, 1933.

12. Gail Caskey Winkler, "Furnishing Plan—LCA Associates," June 15, 1999, box CHF 20L, 17–18, CHM Collection.

13. "Campbell Home, Its Last Occupant Gone, to Be Sold," *St. Louis Post-Dispatch,* March 29, 1938.

14. The longstanding theory that Hugh took the 1880s photos is rooted in contextual and archival evidence (e.g., that he owned a high-quality camera of the sort that would have produced such photos, and the existence of similar photographs taken while Hugh and his brothers were traveling in Europe), but no definitive proof has yet been found. For more on the "systems of objects" that define domestic spaces with both "traditional" and "modern" features, as Jean Baudrillard defines them (corresponding roughly to the late Victorian and early Modernist styles), see Baudrillard, *The System of Objects,* trans. James Benedict (New York: Verso, 1996). Stephen Harold Riggins offers another useful framework for understanding domestic object "systems" in "Fieldwork in the Living Room: An Autoethnographic Essay," in *The Socialness of Things: Essays on the Socio-Semiotics of Objects,* ed. Stephen Harold Riggins (Berlin: Mouton de Gruyter, 1994), 101–147.

15. The social activities of this period, and Hugh's legendary generosity, are documented in archival records pertaining to the servants' experiences during the period. See, e.g., Rita Heller Willey, "Memories of the Campbell House" and other materials, box C-4B, folders 5–9, and Campbell Family Servant and Slave Materials, box C-12A, both CHM Collection. Such topics have also been the subject of research by museum staff and are at times mentioned on tours or in temporary exhibits.

16. Servant perspectives survive in oral histories, as well as in courtroom testimonials

about Hazlett's state of mind and regime of care during this period. See, e.g., "Aged Millionaire, H. K. Campbell."

17. The decision to care for Hazlett at home raised concerns with the extended family, who saw the toll it took on his caregivers. Scott-Crabbs, with thinly disguised revulsion, described a trip she made to the house in the 1930s when she discovered that Hazlett was all but comatose, sleeping on a "pallet" because servants could no longer keep him bed, and that the formerly "dignified and outstanding" Hugh "had changed completely" and become a "thin, stooped figure [who] shunned all contacts." Scott-Crabbs, "Oral History of Campbell House."

18. The logic of intactness and golden age mythos that emerged in the early stages of the Save the Campbell House campaign is explored more fully in subsequent chapters. See WCS arguments, for example, that the house was astonishingly well-preserved—its "luxurious" interiors having been unchanged for a half-century—and represented "the most "integral and intact display of . . . [Victorian] furnishings" found in the country." "Seek to Preserve Old Campbell Mansion for Historic Interest," *St. Louis Globe-Democrat*, February 14, 1941.

19. Virginia Campbell had been active in the MVLA until a couple of years before her death, and made donations to the organization herself, including a two hundred dollar gift in 1879, intended for construction of a greenhouse on the property, which was later repurposed for "restoration of a sun dial to the grass plot in front of the west door of the mansion." See MVLA Board, minutes, 1879, 1884–1885, Mount Vernon Ladies' Association of the Union, 1873–1899, Fred W. Smith National Library for the Study of George Washington, Mount Vernon, VA. For more on the MVLA and its influence on the work of preservation societies across the nation, see Patricia West, *Domesticating History: The Political Origins of America's House Museums* (Washington, DC: Smithsonian Institution, 2013), and Charles B. Hosmer, "Preservation Comes of Age: From Williamsburg to the National Trust, 1926–1949," *Bulletin of the Association for Preservation Technology* 12, no. 3 (1980): 20–27.

20. The sign acknowledging the Campbells' donation, which reads, "GENERAL WASHINGTON'S DEER PARK. / RESTORED, 1887. / BY THE SONS OF THE LATE MRS. ROBERT CAMPBELL, / VICE REGENT OF THE MOUNT VERNON LADIES ASSOCIATION," has not been on display for many years, and their donation is not mentioned on tours, which highlight more ambitious recent restoration projects. The original deer park can be seen in a 1792 rendering of the property in the MVLA archives that has been reproduced in Jean Butenhoff Lee, *Experiencing Mount Vernon: Eyewitness Accounts, 1784–1865* (Charlottesville: University of Virginia Press, 2006), 32. See also "Deer," George Washington's Mount Vernon online museum catalog, https://www.mountvernon.org.

21. The Campbells' donation is acknowledged in the object record (see, e.g., "Candlestand," https://www.mountvernon.org), and records exist for the donation in the Fred W. Smith National Library for the Study of George Washington and in records in the CHM Collection. See, e.g., two historical images showing the candlestands *in situ*: "Photograph of Fireplace in Banquet Room of Mount Vernon" and "Fireplace in Banquet Room of Mount Vernon" (whose caption reads: "These tripods were presented by General Washington to Dr. Thornton and his bride when visiting

Mount Vernon on their wedding trip. Recently donated by the Messeurs Campbell of St. Louis"), Album HC-2, items 178 and 191, CHM Collection.

22. Several such albums survive in the museum's collection. See, e.g., Album HC-2, CHM Collection.

23. Robert and Virginia Campbell purchased a forty-five-foot-square plot at Bellefontaine Cemetery in 1862 and had five of their dead children disinterred from Christ Church Cemetery and reburied at Bellefontaine that same year. They enclosed the plot with a low stone fence and placed at its center a thirty-foot-tall marble obelisk marked "Campbell" in raised marble lettering and the text of Luke 18:16: "Suffer little children to come unto me, and forbid them not; for of such is the Kingdom of God." See Thomas Gronski, "Campbell Family Gravesites—Bellefontaine Cemetery," undated internal research document; photographs of Campbell plot at Bellefontaine Cemetery, box C-3A, Campbell Foundation Photographs, folder 17; Thomas Gronski, "Campbell Family Gravesites," internal research document, November 15, 2010; and Robert Campbell to John Baird, Esq., October 27, 1862, internal research document, all CHM collection.

24. Bodily preservation was still of highly variable quality at this time, even in the United States, where it had been practiced since before the Civil War. It is unclear how James's body was treated or if it was embalmed at all (it might also have been submerged in a preservative liquid that was drained out before burial). For more on the emergence of preservation technologies in the late nineteenth century, including rail transit as a means of transporting bodies, see John Troyer, "Embalmed Vision," *Mortality* 12, no. 1 (February 2007): 22–47, and Robert G. Mayer, *Embalming: History, Theory, and Practice* (New York: Appleton and Lange, 1990).

25. Carol Duncan, *Civilizing Rituals: Inside Public Art Museums* (New York: Routledge, 2005), 72. Hugh's decision to donate the portrait to Yale University in 1941, where it was to be "enshrined in a memorial to James A. Campbell, Yale '82," was applauded by the local press. See "Campbell Portrait Goes to Yale: Contributions for Home Preservation Being Received," *St. Louis Globe-Democrat*, February 23, 1941, and "Yale Backs Move to Save Mansion," *St. Louis Globe-Democrat*, February 18, 1941. Yale officials built the Yale Art Gallery and Design Center in James's honor. "Yale's New Arts Gallery and Design Center," *New York Herald Tribune*, November 8, 1952. The portrait was eventually stripped of its original gilded frame and placed in storage until the 1980s, when the CHM president of the board made inquiries and was able to secure its purchase and return to the house. See, e.g., Theron Ware to Alan Shestack, director of Yale University Art Gallery, May 26, 1983, box CHF 86.6.1, CHM Collection.

26. Carol Duncan makes a similar point about donor memorials that have been given to public art and history museums, many of which share features with royal mausolea, "structures in which the dead eternally receive the living and impress upon them their greatness," and some of which include actual bodies buried in their floors or elsewhere on the grounds. Duncan, *Civilizing Rituals*, 91–92.

27. Celeste Olalquiaga, *The Artificial Kingdom* (Minneapolis: University of Minnesota Press, 1998), 282. See also Elizabeth Hallam and Jenny Hockey, *Death, Memory and Material Culture* (Oxford: Berg 2001), 141, and Katherine Grier, *Culture*

and Comfort: Parlor Making and Middle-Class Identity, 1850–1930 (Washington, DC: Smithsonian Institution, 2013), chapter 1.

28. Framed dried flower arrangement, 2009.4.1, CHM online catalog, http://campbellhouse.pastperfectonline.com.

29. For more on the nature and uses of such objects, see Lawrence Taylor, "Symbolic Death: An Anthropological View of Mourning Ritual in the Nineteenth Century," in *A Time to Mourn: Expressions of Grief in Nineteenth Century America,* ed. Martha V. Pike (Stonybrook, NY: Stonybrook Museums, 1980), 39–48, and Nelia Dias, "Looking at Objects: Memory, Knowledge in Nineteenth-Century Ethnographic Displays," in *Travellers' Tales: Narratives of Home and Displacement,* ed. John Bird and Barry Curtis (New York: Routledge, 1994), 164–176.

30. "Campbell House Opened to Outsiders for the First Time in More Than Forty Years," *St. Louis Post-Dispatch,* February 18, 1941.

31. Ben J. Selkirk & Sons Art Dispersal Galleries, *Dispersal Résumé,* St. Louis, February 1941, box CHF-33, folder 7, CHM Collection; Baudrillard, *The System of Objects,* 85.

32. For more on this category of objects, see Riggins, "Fieldwork in the Living Room."

33. Baudrillard, *The System of Objects,* 77–79.

34. We can compare the posing of the bird in this way to the practice of preparing a corpse so that it looks "as if only sleeping," as came to be the standard practice in late nineteenth-century embalming. See Troyer, "Embalmed Vision," 28–30, 41–44.

35. André Bazin and Hugh Gray, "The Ontology of the Photographic Image," *Film Quarterly* 13, no. 4 (1960): 4–8. Bazin and Gray compared photography to embalming, describing the psychology of taking photos as analogous to that of preparing relics or souvenirs, both of which "enjoy the advantages of a transfer of reality stemming from the 'mummy-complex'" (8n1).

36. Svetlana Boym's theory of "restorative nostalgia" is most fully theorized in *The Future of Nostalgia* (New York: Basic Books, 2001).

Chapter 3: The Auction

1. Ben J. Selkirk & Sons (founded 1830) is believed to be the oldest auction house west of the Mississippi. It was the city's most influential firm from long before the time of this auction, when it anchored a small antiques district in what later came to be called Gas Light Square. Its recent history has been somewhat more checkered: in 2002, businessmen Malcolm Ivey bought it from a Swiss owner and changed the name to Ivey-Selkirk's, which he ran as an art dealership in Clayton until 2014, when the 175-year-old business disintegrated following financial and legal trouble. Garth's Auctioneers and Appraisers of Delaware and Ohio bought the firm's assets and name shortly thereafter. See Landmarks Association of St. Louis, National Historic Landmark USDI-NPS NRHP application, 2005, dnr.mo.gov; "The Owners of Garth's Auctioneers and Appraisers Resurrect Historic St. Louis Action House," *St. Louis Magazine,* September

15, 2014, https://www.stlmag.com; and "The Ivey-Selkirk Saga," *St. Louis Magazine*, September 19, 2014, https://www.stlmag.com.

2. "Campbell Treasures Are Bid On by Committee as Auction Opens," *St. Louis Star-Times*, February 25, 1941.

3. "Campbell Home Furnishings Are Viewed by Public," *St. Louis Post-Dispatch*, February 23, 1941.

4. Ben J. Selkirk & Sons, *Dispersal Resumé* (St. Louis: Art Dispersal Galleries, 1941), 2.

5. Matthew 6:19–21.

6. A 2014 public history/community activism project involved an actual funeral for an old rowhouse in West Philadelphia, later repeated with other historic properties. See Patrick Grossi, "'Plan or Be Planned For': Temple Contemporary's Funeral for a Home and the Politics of Engagement," *Public Historian* 37, no. 2 (2015): 14–26. An analogous project in 2016 involved putting pink and red Valentine's Day "message" hearts on buildings slated for demolition in St. Louis. See Alex Ihnen, "Happy Valentine's Day to Clemens Mansion, St. Louis, MO," nextSTL, February 2016, https://nextstl.com.

7. "Campbell Portrait Goes to Yale: Contributions for Home Preservation Being Received," *St. Louis Post-Dispatch*, February 23, 1941.

8. "Campbell Home Furnishings Are Viewed by Public." My account of auction-goers' behaviors is informed by press accounts, the papers of the William Clark Society, and materials from the CHM collection, as well as Briann G. Greenfield's enlightening analysis of the changing dynamics of the antiques market in *Out of the Attic: Inventing Antiques in Twentieth-Century New England* (Amherst: University of Massachusetts Press, 2009).

9. "Buys Back for $52 Campbell Music Box Costing $1000," *St. Louis Post-Dispatch*, February 26, 1941.

10. "Campbell House Fund Raises Needed $5000," *St. Louis Post-Dispatch*, February 24, 1941; Selkirk & Sons, *Dispersal Resumé*, 7. Local newspapers claimed that the first session of the Campbell auction was one of the largest crowds in the city's and the firm's history (see, e.g., "Campbell Treasures Are Bid On by Committee"), and the firm's owners repeated this decades later. See Landmarks Association of St. Louis, National Historic Landmark USDI-NPS NRHP application, which maintains that it was "by far the most significant . . . from the perspective of historic preservation" to be held on the Olive Street property (15).

11. "Campbell Treasures Are Bid On by Committee"; "Buying Campbell Room as Her Gift for the Museum," *St. Louis Post-Dispatch*, February 25, 1941.

12. "Group Seeking Way to Keep Old Campbell House Intact," *St. Louis Star-Times*, February 13, 1941; Ellwood Douglass, "The Locust Street Campbell's—Indian Fighter to Fortune to the Courts," *St. Louis Post-Dispatch*, March 3, 1935.

13. William Clark Society, mission statement, quoted in a University Club invitation, March 1941, Correspondence from the William Clark Society, Missouri History Museum, St. Louis.

14. "Campbell Mansion Furnishings to Be Sold at Auction," *St. Louis Globe-Democrat*, February 18, 1941.

15. Joseph Heathcott, "'The Whole City Is Our Laboratory': Harland Bartholomew and the Production of Urban Knowledge," *Journal of Planning History* 4, no. 4 (2005): 342–344.

16. Joseph Heathcott, "Harland Bartholomew, City Engineer," in *St. Louis Plans: The Ideal and the Real St. Louis*, ed. Mark Tranel (St. Louis: Missouri History Museum, 2007), 99, and Joseph Heathcott, "The City Quietly Remade: National Programs and Local Agendas in the Movement to Clear the Slums, 1942–1952," *Journal of Urban History* 34, no. 2 (2008): 221–242. See also Eric Sandweiss, *St. Louis: The Evolution of an American Urban Landscape* (Philadelphia: Temple University Press, 2001), chapter 7.

17. The Jefferson National Expansion Memorial (officially renamed the Gateway Arch in 2018) was not completed until 1965. For more on its history and the CPC's *Plan for the Central River Front, St. Louis, Missouri* (St. Louis: City Plan Commission, 1928), see Sandweiss, *St. Louis*, 219–220; Andrew Hurley, "Narrating the Urban Waterfront: The Role of Public History in Community Revitalization," *Public Historian* 28, no. 4 (2006): 19–50; Daniel M. Bluestone, *Buildings, Landscapes, and Memory: Case Studies in Historic Preservation* (New York: Norton, 2011); Mark Tranel, introduction, in Tranel, ed., *St. Louis Plans*, 1–16; and Heathcott, "The City Quietly Remade," 221–224.

18. However, while Carr Square and Clinton-Peabody were intended to address critical low-income housing shortages in the city, they rapidly filled with middle-class workers employed by the city's munitions, aviation, and automobile industries, leaving the question of how to meet demands from the large influx of migrant workers unresolved. See Joseph Heathcott and Máire Agnes Murphy, "Corridors of Flight, Zones of Renewal: Industry, Planning, and Policy in the Making of Metropolitan St. Louis, 1940–1980," *Journal of Urban History* 31, no. 2 (2005): 221, 224, and Mark Abbott, "The 1947 *Comprehensive City Plan*," in Tranel, ed., *St. Louis Plans*, 129–130.

19. Quoted in Heathcott, "The City Quietly Remade," 224.

20. Heathcott, "'The Whole City Is Our Laboratory,'" 345–346; Abbott, "The 1947 *Comprehensive City Plan*," 111–112. The Quebecois phrase *casser maison* has been used to describe the obligatory dispersal of possessions that often occurs as a result of old age and downsizing. It is conceptually relevant to the Campbell case on a number of levels, including the fact that such divestment rituals are often pursued with the goal of "ancestralizing" the owner and his or her things. See Jean-Sébastien Marcoux, "The 'Casser Maison' Ritual: Constructing the Self by Emptying the Home," *Journal of Material Culture* 6, no. 2 (2001): 213–235.

21. For more on population and resource dispersal during this period, see Colin Gordon, *Mapping Decline: St. Louis and the Fate of the American City* (Philadelphia: University of Pennsylvania Press, 2009), and Heathcott and Murphy, "Corridors of Flight."

22. Hurley, "Narrating the Urban Waterfront," 24–25.

23. Jesse P. Henry was a successful St. Louis businessman who got involved with preservation of historic buildings during the Depression and came to be known for his work saving the childhood home of poet Eugene Field at 600 South Broadway. The "children's poet," Field was also a son of Roswell Martin Field, the St. Louis attorney who represented Dred and Harriet Scott in federal court in 1853; Eugene Field's house was long owned and operated by the St. Louis Public Schools as a museum of children's

toys, books, and artifacts related to the Field family. See F. A. Beyhmer, "Saver of Landmarks," *St. Louis Post-Dispatch,* March 9, 1941; "Move to Preserve Campbell House Gaining Headway," *St. Louis Star-Times,* February 16, 1941; and "Group Seeks to Preserve Civil War Campbell Home before Contents Are Sold," *St. Louis Post-Dispatch,* February 18, 1941.

24. "Preservation Committee Gets More Campbell Home Furnishings," *St. Louis Globe-Democrat,* February 26; 1941.

25. Ibid. See also "Buyers Urged to Give Up Campbell Objects," *St. Louis Star-Times,* February 25, 1941.

26. "Campbell Auction Goes On; Museum Group Still Chief Buyer; Who Would Own Campbell House as Museum Still Unsettled," *St. Louis Star-Times,* February 26, 1941.

27. "Campbell Home Furnishings Are Viewed by Public."

28. "Club Moves to Preserve Campbell Home as Downtown Museum," *Advertising Club Weekly,* March 9, 1941.

29. "Preservation Committee Gets More Campbell Home Furnishings"; "Campbell Dinner Set Brings $750: Service Said to Have Been Imported for Visit by U. S. Grant," *St. Louis Post-Dispatch,* February 27, 1941.

30. A dozen sterling goblets were bought by a local family at the Selkirk's auction for $2.25 each, for example; they were recently returned to the museum. "Campbell Goblets Are on Their Way Home!" Campbell House Museum, January 5, 2015, https:// campbellhousemuseum.wordpress.com.

31. "Campbell Dinner Set Brings $750: Service Said to Have Been Imported for Visit by U. S. Grant," *St. Louis Post-Dispatch,* February 27, 1941.

32. Jean-Sébastien Marcoux notes that the breaking apart of the household can be experienced by individuals as a literal and symbolic end to family patrimony—a traumatic event that he compares to "the dispossession process concomitant to the institutionalization . . . by which a person is stripped of the belongings that help define him or herself [and] are at the heart of the constitution of a sense of place." These possessions include "inalienable things," dear "inherited objects . . . family heirlooms," and the like by which one knows and represents him- or herself in the world. Marcoux, "The 'Casser Maisson' Ritual," 215–216.

33. "Campbell Dinner Set Brings $750."

34. "Old Campbell Residence, Reopened after Fifty Years, Relic of a Vanished Past," *St. Louis Post-Dispatch,* February 18, 1941; "Yale Backs Move to Save Mansion: Promises Cooperation in Obtaining of Campbell Home," *St. Louis Globe-Democrat,* February 18, 1941.

35. "Symbolic ecology" describes the spatial-structural order of one's possessions and their social-cultural meanings. See, for example, Mihaly Csikszentmihalyi and Eugene Rochberg-Halton, *The Meaning of Things: Domestic Symbols and the Self* (New York: Cambridge University Press, 1981), and Stephen Harold Riggins, "Fieldwork in the Living Room: An Autoethnographic Essay," in *The Socialness of Things: Essays on the Socio-Semiotics of Objects,* ed. Stephen Harold Riggins (New York: Walter de Gruyter, 1994), 101–147.

36. "Old Campbell Residence, Reopened after Fifty Years."

37. For a discussion of the varying perspectives and practices of private, elite collectors and museum curator-experts during this period, see Greenfield, *Out of the Attic,* chapter 3. The specific views held by these individuals can be perceived in press accounts about the opening of the house (e.g., "Old Campbell Residence, Reopened after Fifty Years") and the WCS's activities (especially "Seek to Preserve Old Campbell Mansion for Its Historic Interest," *St. Louis Globe-Democrat,* February 14, 1941, and "Group Seeking Way to Keep Old Campbell House Intact"), and Selkirk invoices and early inventories (box CHF-33, folders 7–10, CHM Collection) as well as documents related to the opening of the museum (e.g., Arthur C. Hoskins, "The Story of the Campbell House," radio address, February 6. 1943, box CHF-11A, CHM Collection).

38. This contradiction and the implications that it would have for future museum display are explored more fully in chapter 4.

39. "Group Seeking Way to Keep Old Campbell House Intact."

40. The figure would go up to $15,000 in the weeks following the auction, when the WCS registered just how much more it would need to open the museum. See "Group Seeks to Preserve Civil War Campbell Home" and "Old Campbell Residence, Reopened after Fifty Years."

41. "$1200 Donated to Buy Campbell Furniture," *St. Louis Post-Dispatch,* February 21, 1941.

42. "$2000 Needed by Museum Backers: Fund for Purchasing Campbell Furnishings Now at $3000," *St. Louis Globe-Democrat,* February 23, 1941.

43. "2500 Raised to Acquire Campbell House Furnishings," *St. Louis Post-Dispatch,* February 22, 1941; "Preservation Committee Gets More Campbell Home Furnishings."

44. "Seek to Preserve Old Campbell Mansion for Its Historic Interest." The opinion expressed here might be that of architect and future Campbell House Foundation president John Bryan, who is quoted extensively in the preceding paragraph, and reflects the WCS's position as stated throughout the period.

45. "Yale Backs Move to Save Mansion."

46. These perspectives are captured in press accounts of the WCS's early visits to the house. See, e.g., "Campbell Mansion Furnishings to Be Sold at Auction"; "Campbell Residence, Reopened after 50 Years"; "A Visit to Old Campbell House," *St. Louis Star-Times,* February 18, 1941; and Selkirk invoices and auction-related material, box CHF-33, folders 7–9, CHM Collection.

47. "$2500 Is Raised to Buy Campbell Furnishings: Committee Head Says Fund Probably Will Be Completed for Monday's Auction," *St. Louis Globe-Democrat,* February 22, 1941.

48. This sense of urgency is expressed in the WCS's founding documents, including their bylaws and establishment papers, box CHF-1, folders 1–3, CHM Collection, as well as public statements of mission and purpose, including views of their members quoted by the press. See, e.g., "Move to Preserve Campbell House Gaining Headway: Jesse P. Henry to Be Chairman of Committee Set Up to Push Effort," *St. Louis Post-Dispatch,* February 14, 1941; "New Committee Formed to Save Campbell House," *St. Louis Star-Times,* February 19, 1941; "Campbell House Foundation Launches $15,000 Campaign," *St. Louis Globe-Democrat,* May 3, 1941; "Club Moves to Preserve Historic

Campbell Home as Downtown Museum"; and Campbell House Foundation and Publications, 1940s–50s, CHF 11-A, folder 1, CHM Collection.

49. A distinct subfield has emerged in European cultural studies known as "valuation studies," which has much to say about such subjects. See, for example, Fabian Muniesa and Claes-Fredrik Helgessen, "Valuation Studies and the Spectacle of Valuation," *Valuation Studies* 1, no. 2 (2013): 119–123.

50. Cynthia Wall, "The English Auction: Narratives of Dismantlings," *Eighteenth-Century Studies* 31, no. 1 (1997): 1–25. See also Charles Smith, *Auctions: The Social Construction of Value* (London: Harvester Wheatsheaf, 1989).

51. Gordon addresses these trends on a very broad scale in *Mapping Decline,* chapter 3, as does Sandweiss, *St. Louis,* chapter 7. For a spatial-material analysis of these shifts in wealth and social capital, see J. Rosie Tighe and Joanna P. Ganning, "The Divergent City: Unequal and Uneven Development in St. Louis," *Urban Geography* 36, no. 5 (2015): 654–673, and Robert A. Beauregard, "Urban Population Loss in Historical Perspective: United States, 1820–2000," *Environment and Planning A* 41, no. 3 (2009): 514–528.

52. Baudrillard describes the "mythological status" of antiques, which enjoy a special psychological standing as signifiers of "reverse birth"—the idea of "that which is founded on itself, that which is 'authentic.'" Antique objects acquire "moral grandeur" through systems of possession (for example, through collecting). See Jean Baudrillard, *The System of Objects* (London: Verso, 2005), 77–81, 97–98.

53. This ideal has been persuasively discussed by Rachel P. Maines and James J. Glynn in "Numinous Objects," *Public Historian* 15, no. 1 (1993): 9–25.

54. Baudrillard, *The System of Objects,* 84. Baudrillard notes that "since blood, birth and titles . . . have lost their ideological force, the task of signifying transcendence has fallen to material signs—to pieces of furniture, objects, jewellery, and works of art" that can be claimed as embodiments of an "inherited nobility" or even as "symbolic ancestors" (89, 85).

55. Selkirk & Sons, *Dispersal Resumé,* 2.

56. The tour is mentioned in press accounts of the opening, e.g., "Old Campbell Residence, Reopened after Fifty Years," and in later recollections of Gus Meyer's involvement with the house in the years following the creation of the museum. See, e.g., a tour of the house given by curator Theron Ware, box CHF-37A, folder 18, CHM Collection.

57. "Preservation Committee Gets More Campbell Home Furnishings."

58. "Buys Campbell Music Box He Installed 26 Years Ago: Theodore Harris Exultant When He Bids In for $52.50 Ornate Device That Cost about $1000," *St. Louis Post-Dispatch,* February 26, 1941.

59. Ibid. Horatio Alger's best-known rags-to-riches tale, *Ragged Dick; or, Street Life in New York with the Boot Blacks* (1868), features plucky street children of the sort Harris seems to have been when he was a boy living in Father Dunne's orphanage.

60. "Preservation Committee Gets More Campbell Home Furnishings."

61. "Campbell Dinner Set Brings $750."

62. "Campbell Auction Goes On with Museum Group Still Chief Buyer," *St. Louis Star-Times,* February 26, 1941.

63. "Woman Gets $1800 Start on Entire Plan to Buy Entire Campbell Room for Museum Gift," *St. Louis Post-Dispatch*, February 25, 1941.

64. Ashley spent $2,662 on the parlor furnishings alone. Her other purchases are documented in the Selkirk invoices in the CHM Collection. See also "Campbell Dinner Set Brings $750."

65. The plan to create a costume room was not mentioned in the initial press accounts of her purchase (see, e.g. "Buying Campbell Room As Her Gift to the Museum"), but work to develop it began shortly after the museum's creation, and the official opening happened in 1946. For more on its history, see Gordon Hertslet to Leonard Hall, June 6, 1949; Hertslet to Otey McClelland, March 17, 1950, box CHF 9A, folder 3, and costume room signage and promotional material, box CHF-36A, folders 1–3, both CHM Collection.

66. F. A. Behymer, "Saver of Landmarks," *St. Louis Post-Dispatch*, March 9, 1941.

67. Landmarks Association of St. Louis, National Historic Landmark USDI-NPS NRHP application, 16.

68. "Campbell Auction Ends; Committee Successful," *St. Louis Post-Dispatch*, February 27, 1941. This request was actually honored by many at the time, and repatriation of Campbell objects continues to this day.

Chapter 4: The Opening

1. "Robert Campbell's Historic Home," *St. Louis Globe-Democrat*, February 22, 1941.

2. "Groups Join to Seek Old Campbell Home: Will Meet Tomorrow to Consider Making It Museum of Period," *St. Louis Post-Dispatch*, February 28, 1941.

3. "Campbell Auction Ends; Committee Successful," *St. Louis Post-Dispatch*, February 27, 1941.

4. At the end of the probate hearings, Yale officials suggested they would sell for less than the appraised value of the house ($57,000) if the house was opened as a public museum. See "Campbell Foundation to Confer with Yale on Acquiring House," *St. Louis Globe-Democrat*, April 11, 1942; "Robert Campbell's Historic Home"; "Yale Wants $10,000 for Campbell House," *St. Louis Post-Dispatch*, April 14, 1941; and "Campbell Museum Plan May Be Dropped," *St. Louis Post-Dispatch*, May 16, 1941.

5. "Social Activities" and "$15,000 Sought to Buy, Restore Campbell Home," *St. Louis Post-Dispatch*, May 2, 1941.

6. The WCS continued to pursue activities unrelated to the Campbell House, but several of their affiliates would serve as early CHF promoters, and a few were elected officers, including Arthur C. Hoskins, the CHF's first president.

7. "Campbell House Appeal Renewed: Sponsors of Drive Bewildered by Lack of Public Response," *St. Louis Globe-Democrat*, May 21, 1941; "Campbell Museum Plan May Be Dropped."

8. "Becker Urges New Efforts for Campbell House Funds: Mayor Declares He Is 'Greatly Concerned' about Possibility Drive May Fail," *St. Louis Post-Dispatch*, May 23, 1941.

9. Morris Anderson, "The Campbell House," *St. Louis Post-Dispatch*, May 16, 1941; N. Dickson, "To the Editor of the Post-Dispatch," *St. Louis Post-Dispatch*, June 7, 1941; Morris Anderson, "For Preserving the Campbell House," *St. Louis Post-Dispatch*, June 6, 1941. Jesse Henry appeared before St. Louis's Board of Education in early March to request permission to invite schoolchildren to donate to the campaign. See "Gifts from School Children to Campbell Fund Requested," *St. Louis Globe-Democrat*, March 5, 1941.

10. For more on the history of the preservation movement and its patrons during the interwar years, see Charles B. Hosmer, "Preservation Comes of Age: From Williamsburg to the National Trust, 1926–1949," *Bulletin of the Association for Preservation Technology* 12, no. 3 (1980): 20–27; Michael Kammen, *Mystic Chords of Memory: The Transformation of Tradition in American Culture* (New York: Vintage, 2011); and Fitzhugh W. Brundage, "White Women and the Politics of Historical Memory in the New South, 1880–1920," in *Jumpin' Jim Crow: Southern Politics from Civil War to Civil Rights*, ed. Jane Elizabeth Daley et al. (Princeton, NJ: Princeton University Press, 2000), 115–139.

11. "Women Authors Donate to Campbell House," *St. Louis Globe-Democrat*, June 12, 1941.

12. The "trust estate" in question was Hazlett's portion of the family fortune, which was valued at over $2 million. His brother's portion had been willed to Yale; its disbursement would take additional time. See "Campbell Estate Worth $2,057,641," *St. Louis Globe-Democrat*, July 1, 1941; "Court Approves Nangle Report in Campbell Estate: Denies Claims to Shares by Yale University and Former Public Administrator Madden" and "Charles Hamilton Clarke, Patient in City Charity Hospital Ward, Says He Will Continue to Fight," *St. Louis Post-Dispatch*, June 20, 1941; "Two Campbell Heirs Off Aid-Rolls, Face 2-Month Wait for Inheritance," *St. Louis Post-Dispatch*, July 14, 1941; and "Heirs to $20,000 Apiece—But Broke," *St. Louis Post-Dispatch*, July 17, 1941.

13. "Gay Nineties Roller Skating Party Planned," *St. Louis Post-Dispatch*, November 23, 1941; "Skating Party," *St. Louis Post-Dispatch*, December 14, 1941.

14. The properties were listed for sale by a St. Louis realtor in April 1942, which alarmed the CHF. See "Properties Deeded to Yale University," *St. Louis Star-Times*, March 22, 1942, and "Historic Campbell House Listed for Sale at $25,000," *St. Louis Post-Dispatch*, April 10, 1942.

15. "It Now Depends on Yale," *St. Louis Post-Dispatch*, March 1, 1942; "Campbell Foundation to Confer with Yale."

16. "Save the Campbell House," subscription form, *St. Louis Globe-Democrat*, May 30, 1941.

17. "Seek to Preserve Old Campbell Mansion for Its Historic Interest," *St. Louis Globe-Democrat*, February 14, 1941.

18. "Campbell Museum Proposal Rejected," *St. Louis Globe-Democrat*, May 5, 1942. The board rejected the proposal on the grounds that it would violate the terms of Shaw's will.

19. Also referred to colloquially as the "Grand Leader," Stix, Baer & Fuller was a publicly traded company and the dominant player in the city's large upscale retail

market, helmed by four well-known dry goods entrepreneurs: Charles Stix, Julius and Sigmund Baer, and Aaron Fuller (later joined by his son Leo C. Fuller). The downtown store was eight stories tall and 700,000 square feet, and would grow still larger in later years. See "Landmark Saved: Old Campbell House Bought for Museum," *St. Louis Star-Times,* September 24, 1942, and "Store Buys Campbell House, Gives It to Foundation for Museum," *St. Louis Post-Dispatch,* February 24, 1942.

20. "Thank You, St. Louis, for Granting Us 50 Rich Years," *St. Louis Daily Globe-Democrat,* September 24, 1942; "Grand Leader Buys Home, Gives It to City as Museum," *St. Louis Globe-Democrat,* September 24, 1942.

21. "Thank You, St. Louis."

22. Clarence Lang explains that African Americans had not benefited from the new jobs in St. Louis created by the booming war industry (20% of the city's black laborers were unemployed, and "another 11 percent were on WPA projects"), but "wartime tumult created new opportunities for black working-class struggle" and increased "racial-class consciousness." Clarence Lang, *Grassroots at the Gateway: Class Politics and Black Freedom Struggle in St. Louis, 1936–75* (Ann Arbor: University of Michigan Press, 2009), 45–46, 51–52.

23. "Save the Campbell House," subscription form; "Have You Visited the Campbell House? Special Rates for SBF-ites," *The Flying Horse* (SBF company newsletter), April 14, 1944, M-231: Stix, Baer & Fuller Collection, box 2, Mercantile Library Collection, University of Missouri–St. Louis.

24. "Thank You, St. Louis"; "Have You Visited the Campbell House?"

25. "'Lucas Place 1944' Victorian Wonderland," *The Flying Horse,* September 22, 1944, M-231: Stix, Baer & Fuller Collection, box 2, Mercantile Library Collection.

26. Stix, Baer & Fuller advertisement, *St. Louis Post-Dispatch,* February 21, 1946.

27. "Gracious Living—Yester-Year and Today," *St. Louis Post-Dispatch,* May 18, 1948.

28. Mark H. Leff, "The Politics of Sacrifice on the American Home Front in World War II," *Journal of American History* 77, no. 4 (1991): 1296–1318.

29. For more on the role of women in the early preservation movement and their marginalization from the field as it professionalized in the twentieth century, see Barbara J. Howe, "Women in Historic Preservation: The Legacy of Ann Pamela Cunningham," *Public Historian* 12, no. 1 (1990): 31–61, and Gail Lee Dubrow and Jennifer B. Goodman, *Restoring Women's History through Historic Preservation* (Baltimore: Johns Hopkins University Press, 2003).

30. George Lipsitz, "The Racialization of Space and the Spatialization of Race: Theorizing the Hidden Architecture of Landscape," *Landscape Journal* 26, no. 1 (2007): 16–17.

31. Charles van Ravenswaay, "Three Missouri Houses: In the American Tradition," *Antiques* 43 (March 1944): 137. Van Ravenswaay, an architectural historian and author of the WPA-sponsored *Missouri: A Guide to the Show-Me State* (1938), seems to have been an occasional member of the WCS; his account of the Campbell House in the *Antiques* article represented an early acknowledgment by national preservation circles.

32. Arthur C. Hoskins, "The Story of the Campbell House," radio broadcast

delivered on opening day, February 7, 1943, portions of which were used later; see promotional materials, box CHF-12A, folder 14, CHM Collection.

33. Josephine Walter, "Where Door Swings Open into the Past," *St. Louis Post-Dispatch*, February 7, 1943. The low fee made it possible for St. Louisans of many classes to see the house when it first opened. After the war, the entry fee was raised to forty cents, but public school groups, who visited in large numbers throughout the late 1940s and 1950s, continued to be given a reduced group rate. See, e.g., "Old Campbell House Open to Public Now," *St. Louis Star-Times*, February 8, 1943.

34. This estimate is based on a count of names in a museum register by "Boo," a society columnist. Museum guest books confirm that hundreds of museumgoers per week came during the first several months, although no exact tally exists. See "'Boo' Dropped by the Old Campbell House . . . for the Second Time Last Week," *St. Louis Censor*, May 13, 1943.

35. The phrase was used by CHF president Arthur G. Hoskins and quoted often by the press. See "The Charm of Old St. Louis," *St. Louis Post-Dispatch*, April 16, 1932.

36. F. A. Behymer, "Rise and Fall of Lucas Place: 'Quality Street' of Another Generation Is Only a Phantom Now, but Its Dignified Elegance Is Recalled by Move to Preserve Campbell Home, Last of Its Mansions," *St. Louis Post-Dispatch*, May 15, 1941.

37. "Campbell House, of Golden Age, Dedicated," *St. Louis Globe-Democrat*, February 7, 1943.

38. Walter, "Where Door Swings Open into the Past."

39. Untitled promotional copy, n.d. (ca. 1943), box CHF-12A, folder 9, CHM Collection. Similar ideas were expressed in the pamphlet *The Campbell House: A Romantic Survival of Early St. Louis* (St. Louis: Campbell House Museum, 1943, 1944, 1960).

40. *The Campbell House* (1944 edition), 4.

41. Richard L. Bushman, *The Refinement of America: Persons, Houses, Cities* (New York: Vintage, 1993); Katherine Grier, *Culture and Comfort: Parlor Making and Middle-Class Identity, 1850–1930* (Washington, DC: Smithsonian Institute Press, 1989).

42. Jesse Henry's speech was reprinted in *The Campbell House* (1944 edition), 6–7.

43. *The Campbell House* (1943 edition), 2; Behymer, "Rise and Fall of Lucas Place."

44. "The Color Camera at the Campbell House," *St. Louis Post-Dispatch*, February 28, 1943.

45. "Old Campbell Residence, Reopened after Fifty Years, Relic of a Vanished Past," *St. Louis Post-Dispatch*, February 18, 1941.

46. Jean Baudrillard, *The System of Objects*, 2nd edition (London: Verso, 2005), 79.

47. Arthur C. Hoskins, "The Story of Robert Campbell," reprinted in *The Campbell House* (1944 edition), 5–6.

48. "Old Campbell House Bought for Museum," *St. Louis Post-Dispatch*, February 15, 1943.

49. "Campbell House Opened to Outsiders First Time in More Than 40 Years," *St. Louis Post-Dispatch*, February 18, 1941.

50. "Group Seeks to Preserve Civil War Campbell Home before Contents Are Sold," *St. Louis Post-Dispatch*, February 24, 1941.

51. "Group Seeking Way to Keep Old Campbell House Intact," *St. Louis Star-Times*, February 13, 1941; "Store Buys Campbell Home."

52. Many popular home decor magazines advocated for the simplification and updating of the modern parlor, responding not only to new styles of furniture but new emphases on practicality and frugality that emerged during the Depression and World War II. Emily Post's treatise *The Personality of a House: The Blue Book of Home Design and Decoration* (1930), which was especially popular and influential, is typical. For more on trends in periodicals, see Jean Gordon and Jan McArthur, "Popular Culture, Magazines, and Domestic Interiors, 1898–1940," *Pop Culture* 22, no. 4 (Spring 1989): 35–59.

53. Both the china service and the "bog oak" furniture are mentioned in early publications. See, e.g., "The Color Camera at the Campbell House" and *The Campbell House* (1943 edition).

54. Ned Kaufman describes the distinctive "associational aesthetics" of house museum displays in *Race, Place and Story: Essays on the Past and Future of Historic Preservation* (New York: Routledge: 2009), 210–217. See also Carol Duncan, *Civilizing Rituals: Inside Public Art Museums* (New York: Routledge, 2005), 90–10; Patricia West, *Domesticating History: The Political Origins of America's House Museums* (Washington, DC: Smithsonian Institution Press, 1999), 87–91; Penny Sparke et al., eds., *The Modern Period Room: The Construction of the Exhibited Interior, 1870–1950* (New York: Routledge, 2006); and Amelia Peck, *Period Rooms in the Metropolitan Museum of Art* (New York: Metropolitan Museum of Art, 1996).

55. These period room logics found expression in internal CHF documents, including photographs, inventories, and records about placement and restoration of furnishings, as well as tour narratives and public statements made by CHF members during this period. See, in particular, John A. Bryan, "The Campbell House Museum—How It Came into Being" (St. Louis: Campbell House Museum, 1943), box CHF-11A, CHM Collection.

56. One could certainly argue the opposite—that the assemblage of possessions in question *very much* reveals a regional sensibility or cultural style of the sort explored by Adam Arenson in *City of Manifest Destiny: St. Louis and the Cultural Civil War, 1848–1877* (New Haven, CT: Yale University Press, 2008).

57. Van Ravenswaay, "Three Missouri Houses" 138.

58. Eric Hobsbawm, "Introduction: Inventing Traditions," in *The Invention of Tradition*, ed. Eric Hobsbawm and Terrence Ranger (Cambridge: Cambridge University Press, 1983), 1–14.

59. See, e.g., Harland Bartholomew, "The Neighborhood: Key to Urban Redemption," *Planners Journal* 7 (1941): 212–214. For more on Bartholomew's vision-casting work in the city, see Joseph Heathcott, "'The Whole City Is Our Laboratory': Harland Bartholomew and the Production of Urban Knowledge," *Journal of Planning History* 4, no. 4 (2005): 342–344; Mark Abbott, "The 1947 *Comprehensive City Plan*," in *St. Louis Plans: The Ideal and the Real St. Louis*, ed. Mark Tranel (St. Louis: Missouri History Museum, 2007), 129–130; and Christopher Silver, "Neighborhood Planning in Historical Perspective," *Journal of the American Planning Association* 51, no. 2 (1985): 161–174.

60. City Plan Commission, *St. Louis after World War II* (St. Louis: City Plan Commission, 1942).

61. Joseph Heathcott and Máire Agnes Murphy, "Corridors of Flight, Zones of Renewal: Industry, Planning, and Policy in the Making of Metropolitan St. Louis, 1940–1980," *Journal of Urban History* 31, no. 2 (2005): 157.

62. Joseph Heathcott, "The City Quietly Remade: National Programs and Local Agendas in the Movement to Clear the Slums, 1942–1952," *Journal of Urban History* 34, no. 2 (2008): 221–242.

63. Jesse P. Henry, "The Campbell House Museum and the Spirit of American Democracy," February 6, 1943, reprinted in *The Campbell House* (1944 edition).

64. "How America Lived: Six Old Houses Give a Realistic Record of the Past," *Life*, May 7, 1945, 33–38, 51–56.

65. Ibid., 51–56.

66. For more on *Life's* style of journalism during this period, see James Guimond, *American Photography and the American Dream* (Chapel Hill: University of North Carolina Press, 1991), 154–162.

67. "How America Lived," 57.

68. Patricia West emphasizes the important role that house museums of the early twentieth century played by presenting a domestic universe that bridged more primitive but dignified "golden ages" past with the world of modern progress. See West, *Domesticating History*, 87.

69. "How America Lived," 52.

70. Hobsbawm and Ranger, eds., *The Invention of Tradition*. My understanding of how to read these photographs is also informed by the literature on reenactment, including Iain McCalman and Paul Pickering, eds., *Historical Reenactment: From Realism to the Affective Turn* (New York: Palgrave McMillan, 2010); Vanessa Agnew, "History's Affective Turn: Historical Reenactment and Its Work in the Present," *Rethinking History* 11, no. 3 (2007): 299–312; and Stephen Gapps, "Mobile Monuments: A View of Historical Reenactment and Authenticity from Inside the Costume Cupboard of History," *Rethinking History* 13, no. 3 (2009): 395–409.

71. For more on Sarah Yorke Jackson's involvement in the preservation of the Nashville house now known as Andrew Jackson's Hermitage, see Heather A. Huyck and Peg Strobel, eds., *Revealing Women's History: Best Practices at Historic Sites, Featuring Five Case Studies* (Ukiah, CA: National Collaborative for Women's Historic Sites, 2001), and Mary C. Dorris, *Preservation of the Hermitage, 1889–1915: Annals, History, and Stories: The Acquisition, Restoration, and Care of the Home of General Andrew Jackson by the Ladies' Hermitage Association for Over a Quarter of a Century* (Nashville: Smith and Lamar, 1915).

72. "Preservation," The Hermitage, http://www.thehermitage.com.

73. The federal-style homestead was built and decorated between 1819 and 1821. According to Chris Young, the Hermitage's paper conservator, the scenic wallpaper visitors see on the walls now is in fact the third version of the print chosen by Rachel Jackson in 1819. It was installed in the 1990s during a major restoration of the house and was salvaged from a house in France. See "Wallpaper Restoration at the Home of

Andrew Jackson," The Hermitage, https://www.youtube.com. The wallpaper that can be seen in the *Life* photo is likely the prior, or second, of three installations.

74. West, *Domesticating History,* 94–96.

75. Jesse P. Henry, fundraising letter, May 5, 1941, box CHF 13A, F5, CHM Collection.

76. *Life* cover image, caption appearing on page 5.

77. John A. Bryan, CHF president, 1945–1947, to editors of *Life,* May 21, 1945, box CHF 2B, CHM Collection.

78. "How America Lived," 56.

Chapter 5: The Receipt Book

1. The columnist used her *nom de plume* in quotation marks, always with a touch of sarcasm that made it seem like a spoof (perhaps mocking the lingo of socialites) or some other running joke.

2. "'Boo' Dropped by the Old Campbell House," *St. Louis Censor,* May 13, 1943.

3. Ibid.

4. Tim Edensor, "The Ghosts of Industrial Ruins: Ordering and Disordering Memory in Excessive Space," *Environment and Planning D: Society and Space* 23 (2005): 836.

5. Karl Marx, "The Commodity," in *Capital: A Critique of Political Economy,* trans. Ernest Mandel (London: Penguin, 2004), 1:163, 165–167.

6. "'Boo' Dropped by the Old Campbell House."

7. *The Campbell House: A Romantic Survival of Early St. Louis* (St. Louis: Campbell House Museum, 1944), 1.

8. "Book," 1992.898, Campbell House Museum, http://campbellhouse.pastper fectonline.com. Judging by the surviving records, the "receipt book," as it was called by those seeking to emphasize its quaintness, never garnered much if any attention from the WCS or Selkirk's auction officials, who focused almost exclusively on fine furnishings and a few ancestral objects of the kind discussed in chapter 3. It seems to have survived accidentally, perhaps included among personal effects (letters, photo albums, etc.) that were set aside or stashed in drawers and rediscovered during the restoration of the house.

9. "Recipes of a Famous Hostess," *St. Louis Post-Dispatch,* June 6, 1943.

10. "Last Week, You Remember, 'Boo' Raved about the Old Campbell House," *St. Louis Censor,* May 20, 1943.

11. Gaile Dugas, "Century House," *South,* November 1945, 17–18.

12. Josephine Walter, "Where Door Swings Open into the Past," *St. Louis Post-Dispatch,* February 7, 1943.

13. John Drury, *Historic Midwest Houses* (Minneapolis: University of Minnesota Press, 1947), 95.

14. Ibid., 57. For more on the history of homespun, see Laurel Thatcher Ulrich, *The Age of Homespun: Objects and Stories in the Creation of an American Myth* (New York: Vintage, 2009).

15. Drury, *Historic Midwest Houses,* 94.

16. "Last Week, You Remember." Boo assumed that Virginia brought these recipes to St. Louis as part of her trousseau, but there are no references to them in the museum archive. Such an interpretation may well have been part of early museum narrative, however; Theron Ware, who curated the CHM collection for three decades starting in 1967, called frequent attention to "trousseau" items such as "evening costumes" in promotional material, including his *Guidebook for Volunteers,* box CHF-12A, folder 8, CHM Collection.

17. "Campbell Jewels," Famous Barr advertisement, *St. Louis Globe-Democrat,* November 21, 1943.

18. Virginia's dresses have always been a major draw. Local theater companies have worn reproductions for a variety of onsite productions (dramatizing aspects of the Campbell history), and the (now very fragile) originals, some of which have been professionally conserved, are still sometimes pulled out for temporary exhibitions such as one in August 2013 called "Glorious Gowns." See "'Glorious Gowns' on Display," Campbell House Museum, August 5, 2013, http://www.campbellhousemuseum.org.

19. *The Campbell House: A Romantic Survival of Early St. Louis* (St. Louis: Campbell House Museum, 1953).

20. Boo's count of visitors may have been inflated, but minutes from early CHF meetings indicate that thousands of visitors passed through (they also record a few concerns over petty theft). The display of the receipt book is referenced in several internal documents from the period, but I have not been able to find photographs of it on display in this fashion.

21. Walter, "Where Door Swings Open into the Past."

22. The myth of Washington's wooden teeth emerged in the early decades of the nineteenth century and was reinforced by the reliquary-style displays favored by the Mount Vernon Ladies' Association. See, e.g., Edward G. Lengel, *Inventing George Washington: America's Founder in Myth and Memory* (New York: Harpers, 2011).

23. Rachel P. Maines and James J. Glynn, "Numinous Objects," *Public Historian* 15, no. 1 (Winter 1993): 9–25.

24. "Recipes of a Famous Hostess."

25. Gordon Hertslet, "Living Was Luxurious in the Good Old Days at the Campbell House," *Advertising Club Weekly,* 1943, box CHF11-A, folder F1, CHM Collection.

26. *Virginia Campbell's Cook Book* (St. Louis: Campbell House Foundation, 1953), 32.

27. Hertslet, "Living Was Luxurious."

28. The *American Woman's Cook Book* and General Foods' widely circulated *Recipes for Today* (1943) and *Your Share: How to Prepare Appetizing, Healthful Meals with Foods Made Available Today* (1943) presented traditional recipes revised to conform to rationing protocols. For more on the wartime political and social messages of these and other cookbooks from Missouri during the period, see Carol Fisher, *Pot Roast, Politics, and Ants in the Pantry: Missouri's Cookbook Heritage* (Columbia: University of Missouri Press, 2008), 153–163, and Emily Yellin, *Our Mothers' War: American Women at Home and at the Front during World War II* (New York: Simon and Schuster, 2004).

29. Hertslet, "Living Was Luxurious."

30. See, e.g., Katherine Fisher, "Rationing Has Brought a New Cookery," *Good Housekeeping*, July 1943, 90–93.

31. Ibid.

32. "'Boo' Dropped by the Old Campbell House"; "Task Force," *Good Housekeeping*, January 1943, 45. As the example quoted from *Good Housekeeping* suggests, these new housekeeping protocols often destabilized sacred ideals of white middle- and upper-class domesticity, which frequently relied on the presence of African American or immigrant labor. For more on these developments, see Phyllis Palmer, *Domesticity and Dirt: Housewives and Domestic Servants in the United States, 1920–1945* (Philadelphia: Temple University Press, 2010), and Amy Bentley, *Eating for Victory: Food Rationing and the Politics of Domesticity* (Champaign: University of Illinois Press, 1998), especially chapter 2.

33. Popular magazines literalized this idea in the trope of the housewife-as-soldier. In the aforementioned *Good Housekeeping* example, fashions were promoted to "Kitchen Commandos"—women who wanted to look "fresh and crisp" as they joined the ironing, mopping, and laundry brigades in fighting the "Battle on the Home Front," while "looking pretty all day." See "Task Force," 43–46.

34. Harry Burke, "Recipes of Mrs. Robert Campbell as Served in 1850s Listed in Cook Book," *St. Louis Globe-Democrat*, May 13, 1943.

35. CHF Board of Directors, minutes, October 10, 1946, box CHF-2A, CHM Collection.

36. Celeste Olalquiaga, *The Artificial Kingdom* (Minneapolis: University of Minnesota Press, 1998), 77.

37. The CHF published a miniature, folded version of *Virginia Campbell's Cook Book* entitled "My Favorite Recipes: Virginia Campbell: A Celebrated Cookbook Featuring Recipes for the Dishes Served at the Campbell's Famous Table in the 1850's" in the late 1940s. See Campbell House Foundation, In-House Publications and Printed Material, 1940–1979, box CHF-12A, folders 5–6, CHM Collection. The popularity of both souvenir items motivated a proposal for a full-length, "updated" version of the book, which would include photographs of the house, photostat images of pages from the original receipt book, adapted versions of her recipes, and "a description of cooking methods and their development during the Campbell's' lifetime, and of the family and its home." See "A Cookbook by Virginia Campbell, circa 1860," Working Research File Drawer, box 71, file 1, CHM Collection. While the proposal was not pursued for cost reasons, the idea was compelling enough that CHM officials revisited it every decade or so. It was finally realized with the publication of a coffee-table-style publication (authored by local food historian Suzanne Corbett with CHM staff) called *The Gilded Table: Recipes and Table History from the Campbell House* (Virginia Beach, VA: Donning Company, 2015). And in the decades between the museum has hosted all manner of events—annual "Victorian high teas," Easter garden parties, harvest festivals (with costumes), multi-course "Victorian Thanksgiving" feasts, and so on—that partook of the mythologies of Virginia the "cook-hostess." The largest scale and most significant was the Grant dinner reenactment discussed in the next chapter. At every stage too aspects of the receipt book's

heritage mystique could be made to speak to the sensibilities of the museum patrons. For more on these events, see Special Events, box CHF-9A, folders 7–8, and Newspaper Clippings, 1940s–1950s, box CHF-13A, folder 23, both CHM Collection.

Chapter 6: The Dinner Party

1. The title and epigraph of this section are taken from the opening line of Selma Robinson's "The Magnificent Campbell House, Our Living Heritage," *McCall's,* July 1957, 46–48, 88–92. Details from the fictionalized account that serves as the opening to the chapter are also drawn from this and other newspaper accounts, including especially "Lucas Place at Night," *St. Louis Daily Globe,* April 22, 1873, and "General Grant: Reception and Serenade at Colonel Robert Campbell's Last Night," *St. Louis Times,* April 22, 1873.

2. Another dinner for Grant, perhaps the more famous one, was held at the Campbell House in late September 1875; see, e.g., "Presidential Visit—Dinner at Campbell House," *St. Louis Republican,* September 28, 1875. Robert's grand-niece Mary Scott-Crabbs claimed many years later that this dinner "cause[d] the greatest social and political acclaim" in the family's history. See Mary Scott-Crabbs, "Oral History of Campbell House," box C-4B, folder 7, CHM Collection.

3. Robinson, "The Magnificent Campbell House," 88.

4. Details related to planning the reenactment appear in correspondence and records from box CHF 10A, CHM Collection.

5. Robinson, "The Magnificent Campbell House," 88.

6. For more on *McCall's* and other influential lifestyle magazines in this period, see Margaret Walsh, "The Democratization of Fashion: The Emergence of the Women's Dress Pattern Industry," *Journal of American History* 66, no. 2 (1979): 299–313; Nancy A. Walker, "Introduction: Women's Magazines and Women's Roles," in *Women's Magazines, 1940–1960,* ed. Nancy A. Walker (New York: Palgrave Macmillan, 1998), 1–20; and Daniel Delis Hill, preface, in *As Seen in Vogue: A Century of American Fashion in Advertising,* ed. Daniel Delis Hill (Lubbock: Texas Tech University Press, 2007), ix–xiii.

7. The ads described here were published in household and style magazines between 1931 and 1955, and can be found, along with many others, in the Douglas D. Dowd Modern Graphic History Library, Washington University Library Special Collections, St. Louis.

8. Charles van Ravenswaay, "Three Missouri Houses: In the American Tradition," *Antiques* 43 (1945): 134–139.

9. G. Gordon Hertslet, "Campbell House after Five Years," *Advertising Club Weekly,* 1946, box CHF11-A, folder F1, CHM Collection.

10. Harland Bartholomew, *Expressway Plan for the Saint Louis and Adjacent Missouri Area* (St. Louis: Urban Area Expressway Report Project, 1951). See also Bartholomew's *Comprehensive City Plan* (St. Louis: City Plan Commission, 1947).

11. "Heritage Styles: St. Louis Designers Get 1949 Fashion Ideas in New Campbell House Exhibit," *St. Louis Post-Dispatch,* January 23, 1949.

12. See, e.g., "Campbell House Room to Be Opened," *St. Louis Post-Dispatch,* April 17, 1950, and "Campbell House Children's Room Opened; Furnished in 1850 Period," *St. Louis Post-Dispatch*, April 23, 1950.

13. For more on the increasing visibility of toys and mass marketing to children during this period, see Gary Cross, *Kids' Stuff: Toys and the Changing World of American Childhood* (Cambridge, MA: Harvard University Press, 2009), and Stephen Kline, *Out of the Garden: Toys, TV, and Children's Culture in the Age of Marketing* (New York: Verso, 1995).

14. "Repairs to Home," CHF Board, minutes, box CHF 2A, folders 2–3, CHM Collection.

15. "Symbol of an Era: Campbell House: Charming 1851 House Contains Priceless Examples of Home Furnishings," *Advertising Club Weekly,* December 12, 1955.

16. Mary Scott-Crabbs, "Oral History of Campbell House."

17. "Some Dinner Givers: A View of the Notable Private Entertainments," *St. Louis Post-Dispatch,* November 11, 1888.

18. F. A. Behymer, "Rise and Fall of Lucas Place: 'Quality Street' of Another Generation Is Only a Phantom Now, but Its Dignified Elegance Is Recalled by Move to Preserve Campbell Home, Last of Its Mansions," *St. Louis Post-Dispatch,* May 15, 1941. Grant sold his property and disavowed his Missouri attachments following the humiliations of the Whiskey Rebellion in 1875. In retirement, he found a new purpose as an historian of the Civil War but never regained his reputation or his fortune, or reclaimed his ties to St. Louis. See Adam Arenson, *The Great Heart of the Republic* (Cambridge, MA: Harvard University Press, 2011), and Joan Waugh, "Ulysses S. Grant, Historian," in *Memory of the Civil War in American Culture*, ed. Alice Fahs and Joan Waugh (Chapel Hill: University of North Carolina Press, 2005), 5–38.

19. Richard H. Stewart, "Missouri Mirrors of 1946," *National Geographic,* March 1946, 287, color plate iii; Campbell House Advertising Poster, ca. 1950, box CHF 10-A, CHM Collection. A 1946 pamphlet titled "St. Louis: City of a Thousand Sights," claimed Robert Campbell "entertained many notables in his home, including President Grant." Box CHF 10-A, CHM Collection.

20. See, e.g., "Fashions from History," *Advertising Club Weekly,* December 1949, and copy in *St. Louis Hotel Greeters Guide,* November 1949, box CHF-10A, CHM Collection.

21. John A. Bryan to Helen McCully, December 27, 1956, box CHF-10A, CHM Collection. For more on the distorting logics of reenactment, see Vanessa Agnew, "Introduction: What Is Reenactment?" *Criticism* 46, no. 3 (2004): 327–339.

22. Agnew, "Introduction"; Stephen Gapps, "Mobile Monuments: A View of Historical Reenactment and Authenticity from Inside the Costume Cupboard of History," *Rethinking History* 13, no. 3 (2009): 395–409; Bill Nichols, "Documentary Reenactment and the Fantasmatic Subject," *Critical Inquiry* 35, no. 1 (2008): 72–89.

23. John A. Bryan to Helen McCully, December 27, 1956, box CHF-10A, CHM Collection.

24. Helen McCully to John A. Bryan, February 1, 1957, box CHF-10A, CHM Collection, emphasis added.

25. Robinson, "The Magnificent Campbell House," 45.

26. Ibid., 45–46. The caption of the dinner scene notes that the "source of many of the recipes was Mrs. Campbell's own handwritten cookbook, still preserved in her kitchen."

27. Ibid., 48.

28. Ibid., 46

29. Ibid., 48.

30. Ibid., 46.

31. Richard G. Baumhauf, "Progress or Decay? St. Louis Must Choose," *St. Louis Post-Dispatch,* March 5, 1950. The title of this section is taken from Behymer's "Rise and Fall of Lucas Place."

32. Ron Fagerstrom has collected stories about the thriving MCV community in *Mill Creek Valley: A Soul of St. Louis* (St. Louis: R. Fagerstrom, 2000). For maps and descriptions, see "Virtual City," University of Missouri–St. Louis, http://www.umsl.edu.

33. The evidence in the CHM archives suggests that Augustus (Gus) Meyers, who served as a personal attendant and driver for the Campbells for half a century, was the closest they had to a butler, but the family did not call him by that title.

34. Robinson, "The Magnificent Campbell House," 46.

35. See census data for 1860, 1880, and 1900 in "Mercantile Library Materials Concerning Campbell Family," box C-4A F10, and the oral history of Louis Horowitz, box C-4B F8, both in CHM Collection.

Chapter 7: Two Buckskin Suits

1. Adam Arenson describes how St. Louis's vision of itself as a center of the expanding national empire came to be compromised by economic, political, and social realities in *The Great Heart of the Republic* (Cambridge, MA: Harvard University Press, 2011), chapter 10 and epilogue.

2. The debate about whether buckskin suits such as Robert's were made by the Canadian Métis (or other "mixed bloods" living in frontier contexts) continues, although most scholars agree that there was a robust production of such goods by many Indian peoples during the period in question (and, for that matter, by white trappers with advanced tailoring skills who learned from them). See James Hanson, "Laced Coats and Leather Jackets: The Great Plains Intercultural Clothing Exchange," in *Plains Indian Studies: A Collection of Essays in Honor of John C. Ewers and Waldo R. Wedel,* ed. Douglas H. Ubelaker and Viola J. Herman (Washington, DC: Smithsonian Institution Press, 1982), 105–117. For more on the Métis, see Mohan B. Kumar and Teresa Janz, "An Exploration of Cultural Activities of Métis in Canada," *Canadian Social Trends* 89 (2010): 63–69, and Daniel Francis, *The Imaginary Indian: The Image of the Indian in Canadian Culture* (Vancouver: Arsenal Pulp Press, 2012).

3. Hanson, "Laced Coats and Leather Jackets," 116. See also Ronald P. Koch, *Dress Clothing of the Plains Indians* (Norman: University of Oklahoma Press, 1990); John Canfield Ewers, "Folk Art in the Fur Trade," in *Plains Indian History and Culture: Essays*

on Continuity and Change, ed. John Canfield Ewers (Norman: University of Oklahoma Press, 1997), 150–168; and Marcia G. Anderson, "Every Object Tells a Story," *Minnesota History* 56, no. 4 (Winter 1998–1999): 1–2.

4. Hanson, "Laced Coats and Leather Jackets," 111–112.

5. "Museum Buys Indian Costumes: Committee to Save Campbell Furnishings Backed by Crowd," *St. Louis Globe-Democrat,* February 26, 1941; "Campbell Auction Goes On with Museum Group as Chief Buyer," *St. Louis Star-Times,* February 26, 1941.

6. F. A. Behymer, "The Rise and Fall of Lucas Place: 'Quality Street' of Another Generation Is Only a Phantom Now, But Its Dignified Elegance Is Recalled by Move to Preserve Campbell Home, Last of Its Mansions," *St. Louis Post-Dispatch,* March 4, 1941.

7. "Museum Buys Indian Costumes."

8. The album included photographic portraits of Red Cloud (Oglala Sioux), Lone Wolf (Kiowa), and White Ghost (Dakota).

9. The lack of interest in historical or biographical significance, or linkages between these objects, is clear in auction catalogue entries. See Ben J. Selkirk & Sons, *Dispersal Resumé* (St. Louis: Art Dispersal Galleries, 1941). But it is also visible in the views the WCS shared with the press about their acquisitions and subsequent descriptions provided of the collection in early editions of *The Campbell House: A Romantic Survival of Early St. Louis* (St. Louis: Campbell House Museum, 1943, 1944, 1960) and other museum promotions.

10. "The Last Haven of a Frontiersman" as it was described, the Daniel Boone House was built around 1822 just outside Defiance, Missouri. In the early 1940s, it became a public museum, although its provenance was still in dispute. For more on the historic homes of Missouri and Illinois that would have been known in 1943, see John Drury, *Historic Midwest Houses* (Minneapolis: University of Minnesota Press, 1947), 85.

11. "Letters from the People: Our 'Memorial to National Expansion,'" *St. Louis Post-Dispatch,* February 17, 1941.

12. "The Old Campbell House," *St. Louis Post-Dispatch,* February 14, 1941.

13. "Fund to Preserve Campbell Home Furniture Is Sought," *St. Louis Post-Dispatch,* February 19, 1941.

14. Pierre Chouteau was the grandson of St. Louis founder Auguste Chouteau and John Jacob Astor's highly successful local trade partner. Most of the famous trappers and fur agents were either from the St. Louis region or developed ties in the city, which was the launching point for trade expeditions.

15. For an example of the persistence of a general mythology of the mountain man, see Arthur Chapman, "Jim Bridger, Master Trapper and Trailmaker," *Outing: An Illustrated Monthly,* January 1906, 431–433.

16. Hiram Martin Chittenden, *The American Fur Trade of the Far West* (New York: Harper, 1902), 1:x–xi.

17. William H. Goetzmann, "The Mountain Man as Jacksonian Man," *American Quarterly* 15, no. 3 (1963): 402. Bernard DeVoto's *Course of Empire* (1952) and the Lewis and Clark journals (1953) were the first major twentieth-century histories of that expedition. DeVoto's Pulitzer Prize–winning book *Across the Wide Missouri* (1947), discussed

below, followed two works by others (Robert Glass Cleland's *This Reckless Breed of Men* [1952] and Ray Billington's *The Far Western Frontier* [1956]) that brought new analytical perspective to the heavily mythologized history of the fur trade and influenced later studies such as Goetzmann's *Army Exploration in the American West, 1803–1863* (1959).

18. For more on Robert's early years, see Jay H. Buckley, "Rocky Mountain Entrepreneur: Robert Campbell as a Fur Trade Capitalist," *Annals of Wyoming* 75, no. 3 (2003): 8–23, and Marilyn Irvin Holt, "Joined Forces: Robert Campbell and John Dougherty as Military Entrepreneurs," *Western Historical Quarterly* 30, no. 2 (1999): 183–202.

19. "Robert Campbell's Historic Home," *St. Louis Globe-Democrat,* February 22, 1941.

20. Ibid.

21. This "fire-water" story, while it sounds apocryphal, has been told repeatedly at the CHM and is mentioned in written accounts by Campbell relatives. See, e.g., Mary Scott-Crabbs, "Campbell House," Original Letters and Documents Pertaining to the Campbell Family, box C2-A, CHM Collection.

22. Joseph Desloge, "Robert Campbell, Fur Trader," lecture given at the Missouri Historical Society, May 28, 1941, box CHF 11A, CHM Collection.

23. Ellwood Douglass, "'The Locust Street Campbells.'—Indian Fighter to Fortune to the Courts," *St. Louis Post-Dispatch,* March 3, 1935.

24. Stories about Robert and his weakly son Hazlett echoed those made about the "neurasthenic" effects of life in modern cities by physician Silas Weir Mitchell, whose masculinist theories about the value of vigorous outdoor activity for powerful male city dwellers influenced Theodore Roosevelt and Owen Wister, author of *The Virginian* (1901).

25. Douglass, "'The Locust Street Campbells.'" Robert's friendships with figures like Sherman had once been known locally (especially in relationship to recollections of the Grant dinner parties discussed in chapter 7), but they reemerged in the mid-1930s and early 1940s in the context of court hearings about the Campbell estate. See, e.g. "Hazlett Campbell When 24, Described," *St. Louis Post-Dispatch,* March 11, 1935.

26. "Robert Campbell's Historic Home."

27. Compare to Pekka Hämäläinen's "Reconstructing the Great Plains: The Long Struggle for Sovereignty and Dominance in the Heart of the Continent," *Journal of the Civil War Era* 6, no. 4 (2016): 481–509.

28. See, e.g., Arenson, *The Great Heart of the Republic,* chapter 2.

29. Chittenden postulated that the fur trade was not just "the leading branch of commerce in the western world" but the lynchpin of the region's economy and the basis for St. Louis's midcentury dominance as a frontier "emporium." See Chittenden, *The American Fur Trade,* 1:1–2, 97. See also Isaac Lippincott, "A Century and a Half of Fur Trade at St. Louis," *Washington University Studies* 3, no. 14 (1916): 205–242. The RMFC embodied the city's core contributions to frontier expansion in the mid-1830s, as when Campbell and Sublette introduced a new model of distribution that made it possible for hundreds of trapping partnerships to form and hundreds of subsidiary businesses (hubbed in St. Louis) to flourish. For more on the Opposition, see David

J. Wishart, *The Fur Trade of the American West, 1807–1840: A Geographical Synthesis* (Lincoln: University of Nebraska Press, 1992), 144–146.

30. The AFC withdrawal from Rocky Mountain territory—a mostly symbolic coup, since the RMFC eventually sold some of their properties back to the AFC—is also explored by Wishart, *The Fur Trade of the American West*, 144–146, and Chittenden, *The American Fur Trade of the Far West*, 1:chapters 18–22.

31. Arthur C. Hoskins, "The Story of the Campbell House," radio address, February 6, 1943, box CHF-12 A, folder 14, CHM Collection.

32. Charles van Ravenswaay claimed Robert was chosen for "Indian commissions [because] the red men knew and trusted him." See Van Ravenswaay, "Three Missouri Houses: In the American Tradition," *Antiques*, March 1945, 134–139.

33. Philip Joseph Deloria, *Playing Indian* (New Haven, CT: Yale University Press, 1998), 184–186.

34. Ken and Alice Jones, "Partners in Adventure," *The Land We Live In*, part 1, Union Electric Studio, St. Louis, January 18, 1948 18–19, transcripts, box CHF-12A, CHM Collection. The punctuation (including ellipses) is original.

35. The highly successful *Land We Live In* program ran from 1935 to 1957 during which time St. Louis met hundreds of local historical figures: physicians, sports figures, musicians, artists, and so on. See "The Top St. Louis Radio Drama," St. Louis Media History, http://stlmediahistory.org.

36. Jones, "Partners in Adventure," 3–4.

37. Ibid., 8–9. The new way of fighting involved building fortifications.

38. Ibid., 19, 5–6. Washington Irving's *A Tour of the Prairies* (1835) recounts some of the adventures of Campbell, Sublette, and their partners.

39. Ken and Alice Jones, "Robert Campbell's Romance," *The Land We Live In*, part 2, January 18, 25, 1948, 1–2, 4, CHF-12A, CHM Collection.

40. "He Rejected Pleas to Return to 'Security,' Wrote That He Liked Adventure and Money-Making" and "Old Letters Show Campbell Family's Worry Over Fur Trader Robert's Safety," *St. Louis Post-Dispatch*, March 5, 1941.

41. *The Land We Live In*, part 2, 4. See also "Letters Tell of Courtship of the Robert Campbells," *St. Louis Post-Dispatch*, March 7, 1941.

42. *The Land We Live In*, part 2, 9–10.

43. Ibid., 15.

44. Ibid.

45. William R. Nester, *From Mountain Man to Millionaire: The "Bold and Dashing Life" of Robert Campbell* (St. Louis: University of Missouri Press, 2011), 1:101–102.

46. *The Land We Live In*, part 2, 16–17.

47. Gordon Hertslet to Walter Heren, Union Electric Company president, March 3, 1948, box CHF 12A, CHM Collection.

48. Van Ravenswaay, "Three Missouri Houses," 137.

49. Gordon Hertslet to Leonard Hall, June 6, 1949; Hertslet to Otey McClelland, March 17, 1950, box CHF-9A, CHM Collection; Arthur C. Hoskins, "New Children's Museum Dedicated at the Campbell House," *Advertising Club Weekly*, April 22, 1950, 48–49, CHF11-A, folder 1, CHM Collection; "Children's Room of 100 Years Ago in

Campbell House" and "Campbell House Room to Be Opened," *St. Louis Post-Dispatch*, April 17, 1950.

50. "Campbell House Children's Room Opened; Furnished in 1850 Period," *St. Louis Post-Dispatch*, April 23, 1950; "A Children's Room in the Campbell House," CHM promotional copy, March 17, 1950, box CHF 9-A, CHM Collection.

51. "Cow on Wheels," *St. Louis Post-Dispatch*, May 23, 1950.

52. "Famous American Homes," advertisement, Home Insurance Company, *Time*, June 26, 1950, 73.

53. "The House across the Street—The Campbell House," *Universal Tips Newsletter*, June 1947, 1, box CHM 13-A, CHM Collection; "Lonely Relic of a Gracious Past," *St. Louis Post-Dispatch*, February 20, 1953.

54. Gordon Hertslet to CHF members, April 20, 1948, box CHF 9A F1, CHM Collection.

55. Bernard DeVoto's book was illustrated with color reproductions of works by George Catlin, Charles Bodmer, and Alfred Jacob Miller, an artist who accompanied Scottish adventurer Sir William Drummond Stewart on an expedition between 1832 and 1838 and was "discovered" by a Kansas City collector in the early 1940s. See, e.g., DeVoto, *Across the Wide Missouri* (Boston: Houghton Mifflin, 1947), xi–xiii.

56. The "cast of thousands" claim appeared on several of MGM's movie posters. The supporting cast included Ricardo Montalbán (as a vengeful Blackfoot chief named Iron Shirt), John Hodiak (as a Scottish nobleman, Brecan, who "turns Indian" and tries to make peace), Adolphe Menjou (as a kind-hearted French trapper), and María Elena Marqués (as Kamiah). The quotations are from the *Across the Wide Missouri* press book and official trailer, 1951. See, e.g., http://www.imdb.com.

57. Gordon Hertslet to Bernard DeVoto, March 4, 1949; DeVoto to Hertslet, April 16, 1948, box CHF 9A F1, CHM Collection.

58. Gordon Hertslet to CHF members, April 20, 1948; Bernard DeVoto to Hertslet, February 15, 1950, box CHF 9A F1, CHM Collection.

59. Gordon Hertslet to CHF members, April 20, 1948; Hertslet to Bernard DeVoto, May 1948; DeVoto to Hertslet, February 15, 1950, box CHF 9A folder 1, CHM Collection.

60. Gordon Hertslet to Howard Strickling, MGM publicity director, December 26, 1950; Hertslet to Strickling, January 17, 1951, box CHF 9A F1, CHM Collection.

61. Howard Strickling to Gordon Hertslet, February 3, 1951, box CHF 9A F1, CHM Collection.

62. Gordon Hertslet to W. S. Rodgers, Loew's, January 30, 1951, box CHF 9A F1, CHM Collection.

63. Charles M. Reagan for W.S. Rodgers to Gordon Hertslet, February 13, 1951; Hertslet to Bernie Evens, February 19, 1951, box CHF 9A F1, CHM Collection.

64. *Across the Wide Missouri*, directed by William A. Wellman, MGM, 1951.

65. Ibid., minutes 75–77.

66. For example, Sir John Archibald Stewart, a Scotsman who traveled west after serving in the Napoleonic wars and joined Campbell and Sublette on their way to the 1833 rendezvous, appears in the film as Captain Humberstone Lyon (Alan Napier). He

has his historical counterpart's penchant for danger and flamboyant display of heritage (he performs a Scottish reel in kilts during a rendezvous scene early in the film) but serves no plot purpose. Ibid., minutes 18–19.

67. John Francis McDermott, review of DeVoto, *Across the Wide Missouri, Minnesota History* 29, no. 1 (March 1948): 58–61. Other reviewers agreed that the narrative was overly ambitious (especially when it came to representations of Native peoples) and fragmented. See Levette J. Davidson, review of DeVoto, *Across the Wide Missouri, Western Folklore* 7, no. 2 (April 1948): 208–209, and Stanley Vestal, review of DeVoto, *Across the Wide Missouri, Pacific Historical Review* 17, no. 2 (May 1948): 207–209.

68. Vestal, review of DeVoto, *Across the Wide Missouri,* 207.

69. Goetzmann, "The Mountain Man as Jacksonian Man," 402–415. See also William H. Goetzmann and William N. Goetzmann, *The West of the Imagination* (Norman: University of Oklahoma Press, 2009).

70. See, e.g., Holt, "Joined Forces"; Chris Smallbone, "How the West Was Lost," *History Today* 56, no. 4 (2006): 42; W. N. Davis, "The Sutler at Fort Bridger," *Western Historical Quarterly* 2, no. 1 (1971): 37–54; and Buckley, "Rocky Mountain Entrepreneur."

71. Chapman, "Jim Bridger, Master Trapper and Trailmaker," 433.

72. Goetzmann analyzed the biographies of 446 mountain men active between 1804 and 1845 and found that 182 were killed in the line of work, some 200 sought other occupations (especially farming, ranching, and mining), and very few—just 5—remained trappers for most or all of their lives. Goetzmann, "The Mountain Man," 409–410.

73. "Miller Water Color at Campbell House: Painting Executed in 1830s Is Considered Representative of Time," *St. Louis Post-Dispatch,* November 21, 1951; Visitor's Register, nos. 6 and 7, box CHF-32D, folders 4–5, CHM Collection.

74. CHF records from this period reflect efforts to build on this publicity momentum with events keyed to themes and fur trade subjects. See, e.g. *Across the Wide Missouri*—Bernard DeVoto's Visit, 1948–51 and Event Ideas, box CHF-9A, folders 1, 12, CHM Collection.

75. Among these local elites were Stix, Baer & Fuller executives, members of the Advertising Club, and the CHF's own leadership, including Grace Ashley.

Chapter 8: Restoration

1. Ernest Kirschten et al., "St. Louis: The Harmonies That Time Makes," *St. Louis Post-Dispatch,* December 12, 1965.

2. James E. Sprehe, "Slum Houses Disappearing Piece by Piece: Scavengers Strike at Vacant Flats—City Takes a Hand," *St. Louis Post-Dispatch,* December 12, 1965. For more on the clearance controversies that continued into the next year, see Robert A. Dunlap, "Slums Cleared on 600 Acres in City 12 Years," *St. Louis Post-Dispatch,* May 8, 1966.

3. Theodore C. Link, "Renewal Delay by U.S. and City Found to Help Create Slums; Condition of Buildings Deteriorate While Rehabilitation Work Lags," *St. Louis Post-Dispatch,* December 12, 1965.

4. Kirschten et al., "St. Louis." The house's status as a certified local landmark is suggested by its inclusion, starting with Charles van Ravenswaay, "Three Missouri Houses: In the American Tradition," *Antiques* 43 (1945): 134–139, in all manner of historic site and guidebooks, including those produced for the hospitality and tourist industries. See, e.g., *St. Louis Hotel Greeters Guide,* November 1949, and St. Louis Junior Chamber of Commerce's 1944 "Historic Site Markers" list (showing metal and wood markers placed around the city at various landmarks including the Campbell House), both in box CHF-11A, folder 5, CHM Collection.

5. Kirschten et al., "St. Louis," 2.

6. Ibid.

7. I discuss the regimes of place that have taken hold in the area just west of downtown in the introduction and chapter 1. For more on the politics of place memory and how regimes of place take hold in the city and impact issues of public memory, see Niamh Moore and Yvonne Whelan, eds., *Heritage, Memory and the Politics of Identity: New Perspectives on the Cultural Landscape* (New York: Routledge, 2007); Lucy R. Lippard, *The Lure of the Local: Senses of Place in a Multicentered Society* (New York: New Press, 1997); Victor Burgin, *In/Different Spaces: Place and Memory in Visual Culture* (Berkeley: University of California Press, 1996), chapter 7; and Delores Hayden, *The Power of Place: Urban Landscapes as Public History* (Cambridge, MA: MIT University Press, 1995), especially chapters 1 and 2.

8. The charter and bylaws for the Campbell House Foundation, which were drafted in 1941 and authorized in 1942, characterize the mission of the Campbell House Foundation as follows: "To restore the Campbell property at 1508 Locust Street, in the City of St. Louis, Missouri, and other places of historical interest; to operate such places as historical and educational museums." Incorporation Papers of the CHF, box CHF-1, folder 2, CHM Collection. As of 2002, when the bylaws were revised, the mission of the museum was conceived not in terms of "restoration" but of "preservation"— namely, preservation "of one of the most historically significant nineteenth century buildings in St. Louis" and its contents—and ongoing "reinterpret[ation of] its collections for exploring issues such as: the development of the fur trade, exploration and development of the west, the growth of urban economies, emigration, historic preservation, principles of Victorian interior design, and the urban issues that continue to shape our region today." CHF Bylaws, Bylaw Revision, November 2002, box CHF-1, folder 1, CHM Collection.

9. Richard J. Compton and Camille N. Dry, *Pictorial St. Louis, the Great Metropolis of the Mississippi Valley: A Topographical Survey Drawn in Perspective, A.D. 1875* (St. Louis: Compton, 1876).

10. "Seek to Preserve Old Campbell Mansion for Its Historic Interest," *St. Louis Globe-Democrat,* February 14, 1941.

11. The official donation of the album was recorded in the minutes of the May 21, 1973, CHF board meeting, where it was declared "one of the most valuable [gifts] ever received." See CHF Board Meeting, minutes, box CHF 2C, CHM Collection. The story of its discovery has been told repeatedly—and in more places than can be named; the version offered here represents an assemblage of many sources, including two relatively recent accounts: "Campbell House, a City Landmark, Needs a Face

Lift," *St. Louis Post-Dispatch*, April 13, 1999, and "1885 Campbell House Photographs," Campbell House Museum, November 8, 2013, http://www.campbellhousemuseum .org.

12. Suzanne Corbett, *The Gilded Table: Recipes and Table History from the Campbell House* (Virginia Beach, VA: Donning Company, 2015). See also chapter 5, note 37.

13. Alan Trachtenberg, "Through a Glass, Darkly: Photography and Cultural Memory," *Social Research* 75, no. 1 (Spring 2008): 116, 121–122.

14. Charlotte Rumbold, *Housing Conditions in St. Louis: A Report of the Housing Committee of the Civic Planning League* (St. Louis: Civic Planning League, 1908).

15. Didier Aubert, "The Doorstep Portrait: Intrusion and Performance in Mainstream American Documentary Photography," *Visual Studies* 24, no. 1 (2009): 4–5.

16. Ibid., 13.

17. For more on Hugh's patronage of Father Dunne's Newsboys' Home and support of other local children, see chapter 2.

18. Roland Barthes, *Camera Lucida: Reflections on Photography* (New York: Hill and Wang, 1981), 27–28, 76–77.

19. The vocabulary of "authenticity" dominates the museum's print and online material, and as in earlier stages of the institution's history, is reinforced by local media and boosters invested in claiming St. Louis as a unique, historically significant, and well-preserved city.

20. See, for example, CHF Board, minutes, May 21, 1973, box CHF 2C, CHM Collection.

21. Mary Lynn Stevens, *From House to Museum, a Case Study: The Campbell House Museum, St. Louis, Missouri* (M.A. thesis, University of Delaware, 1982), 80–81.

22. CHF Board, minutes, April 17, 1978; December 12, 1977, box CHF 2A F5, CHM Collection.

23. Ann Morris, interview of Theron Ware, 1992, 21–22, box CHF-37A, folder 18, CHM Collection.

24. "Campbell House Museum Notes on Seminar Given by Theron R. Ware, Curator," February 26, 1984, box CHF 2D, folder 2; CHF Board, minutes, February 15, 1998, box CHF 2D, folder 6, all in CHM Collection; Morris, interview of Theron Ware, 13. For more on restoration work based on photographic and other evidence in the mid- to late 1970s, see CHF Board, minutes, June 19, 1978; May 14, 1979, box CHF 2A, folder 5, CHM Collection.

25. The 1988 fire and its aftermath are discussed in CHF Board, minutes, July 27, 1988, box CHF 2D F6, CHM Collection.

26. Some of Ware's archival findings from the late 1970s are captured in "Lucas Place: A Brief History," October 23, 1977, box CHF 12A F9, and *Guidebook for Volunteers*, 1967, box CHF 12A, folder 8, both CHM Collection. His onsite research was pretty much continuous from the date of his hire until his retirement in 1993 (see, e.g., Morris, interview of Theron Ware) and informed his famously detailed tours of the house (see, e.g., recordings of his tour in boxes CHF 37A, folders 15, 18, CHM Collection). However, the formal cataloguing of the collection did not begin in earnest until his successors arrived.

27. Henry Ames, "Robert Campbell House, 1508 Locust Street, Saint Louis, Independent City, Missouri," n.d. (post-1933), Historic American Buildings Survey, Library of Congress, http://www.loc.gov; Theodore LaVack, "North Elevation—Robert Campbell House, 1508 Locust Street, Saint Louis, Independent City, MO," June 23, 1936, Historic American Buildings Survey, Library of Congress, http://www.loc.gov; Lester Jones, "Summer House and Trellis—Robert Campbell House, 1508 Locust Street, Saint Louis, Independent City, Missouri" and "Front, Showing Fence and Summer House—Robert Campbell House, 1508 Locust Street, Saint Louis, Independent City, MO," April 3, 1940, Historic American Buildings Survey, Library of Congress, http://www.loc.gov.

28. "Robert G. Campbell House," National Register of Historic Places, nomination form, April 12, 1976, https://dnr.mo.gov.

29. In addition, new stained glass windows were installed, their designs based on a surviving window sash and evidence from the photographs. The colors used in each room were identified through analysis of traces of old paint. See Gail Caskey Winkler, "Furnishing Plan—LCA Associates," June 15, 1999, box CHF 20L, 17–19, CHM Collection.

30. Mimi Kerth, statement of resignation, in CHF Board, minutes, October 21, 1991, box CHF 2E, folder 2, CHM Collection.

31. CHF Board, minutes, February 4, 1992, box CHF 2E, folder 2, CHM Collection.

32. The scope of work for this report included requests for guidance on everything from historical colors and finishes to HVAC improvements to the vexing structural issues (such as ADA compliance) that would need to be addressed in the context of thoroughgoing restoration. See "Request for Proposals for a Historic Structures Report/Architectural Assessment of the Campbell House Museum," August 15, 1995, and "Historic Structure Report and Architectural Assessment of the Campbell House Museum," August 1996, box CHF 20B, folders 1, 4, CHM Collection.

33. "Request for Proposals," 2.

34. See CHF Board, minutes, June 19, November 20, December 11, 1995; January 15, 1997; February 19, May 15, 1996, box CHF 2E, folder 5, CHM Collection.

35. Morris, interview of Theron Ware.

36. "Restoration Policy," adopted by CHF Board, November 20, 1999, box CHF 20L, CHM Collection.

37. Gail Winkler to Jeffrey Huntington, May 13, 1997, January 19, 1998, box CHF 20K, CHM Collection. Winkler studied the historic structure report, the HABS floor plans, and other archival documents, including photographs and inventories, before offering her assessment.

38. Winkler objected especially to the desire for quick results and easy assignment of dates, finishes, and contractors, which were "incompatible" with her methods and philosophy of "authentic recreation." Gail Winkler to Jeffrey Huntington, January 19, 1998, box CHF 20K, CHM Collection.

39. Gail Caskey Winkler, "What Makes an Interior Victorian?" public lecture, Stupp Center in Tower Grove Park, August 6, 1998. For more on Winkler's view of the CHM project and Victorian houses, see Katie Rasp, "History Restored," *Ladue News*

(Missouri), July 24, 1998. At the time of their hire, Winkler and Moss were known for their comprehensive historical study of Victorian styles of decor aimed at mainstream audiences, and were full of advice on how one might recreate them at home. See Gail Caskey Winkler and Roger W. Moss, *Victorian Interior Decoration: American Interiors, 1830–1900* (New York: Henry Holt, 1986).

40. CHF Board, minutes July 19, 1999, box CHF 2E, folder 7, CHM Collection. See also CHF Board, minutes, June 21, September 20, October 18, November 15, 1999, box CHF 2E, folder 7, CHM Collection. Winkler, "Furnishing Plan," summarized by Jeffrey L. Huntington at the request of the CHF on September 20, 1999, box CHG 20K Interior Restoration, CHM Collection.

41. Winkler, "Furnishing Plan," 2.

42. The approach Winkler advocated shared the basic premises of period-oriented restoration pursued by numerous museums of the late 1990s and early 2000s, many of which showed interest in household-level authenticity of a single domestic environment but had to reconstruct it out of remnants from different households. For a discussion of how archaeological and archival research has informed these efforts at reconstruction, see, e.g., John D. Krugler, "Behind the Public Presentations: Research and Scholarship at Living History Museums of Early America," *William and Mary Quarterly*, 3rd series, 48, no. 3 (1991): 347–338, and Marla R. Miller, *Reclaiming the Past: Women's History in Deerfield: An Interpretive Sourcebook* (Deerfield, MA: Historic Deerfield, 1999), http://www.historic-deerfield.org.

43. Winkler and Moss acknowledged that such a narrow target restoration date is rare, because "most domestic interiors encompass a variety of furnishings that a family has amassed throughout a lifetime," and few survive in this "natural" complex state. The Campbell home survived with this variety intact because the family had "lavished attention on it, [and] one generation recorded it with photographs and other day book entries . . . [and also because] interested citizens saved both the house and the majority of its contents for present day visitors to enjoy." Winkler, "Furnishing Plan," 3.

44. "From the Archives: 1941—The First Restoration of the Campbell House," *Campbell House Courier*, Winter 2001, box CHF 12C, CHM Collection. The official start of the restoration was 1995, when the historic structure report was commissioned. In 1999, the museum received a major donation from Jack Taylor and the Enterprise Rent-a-Car Foundation and physical restoration of the Carriage House began. The exterior renovation began in 2000 and ended in 2001, when several phases of interior renovation began (and continued through early 2005). These procedures are documented in the Architecture, Development, and Interior Committees' reports and CHF Board minutes from these years; see boxes CHF 2E, 2F, and 2G, CHM Collection. See also the *Campbell House Courier*, box CHF 12C, CHM Collection.

45. As public relations documents emphasize, the restoration of the interiors was an ongoing process. But in the end, about $3 million was successfully raised in three years, and support for smaller projects continued after the official end of the restoration. See the *Campbell House Courier*, Spring/Summer 2004, box CHF-12C, CHM Collection; "Campbell House Museum Launches Fund-Raising Drive for Renovation," *St. Louis Post-Dispatch*, March 26, 1999; and CHF Board, minutes, November 15 2004, box CHF 2F F5, CHM Collection.

46. Wollenberg Architectural Conservation, "Report on the Finishes Investigation and Analysis in the Parlor and First Floor Hall of the Campbell House Museum," September 22, 1998, box CHF 20L, CHM Collection.

47. *Campbell House Courier,* Spring/Summer 2004, box CHF 12C, CHM Collection; "Campbell House Museum 2000–2001 Restoration: Parlor Room #102," box CHF 20F Interior Notes, CHM Collection.

48. "Campbell House Museum 2000–2001 Restoration: Entry Hall #101 and #104," box CHF 20F Interior Notes, CHM Collection.

49. Campbell House Museum Interior Restoration Project Lists, phases I and II, box CHF 20K, CHM Collection.

50. Tim Woodcock, "Restoring a Classic: Campbell House Is Stepping Back in Time, One Layer of Paint at a Time," *West End Word* (St. Louis), July 10–16, 2002.

51. Erin Piel, "Campbell House Interior Renovation a Step Back in Time," *St. Louis Daily Record,* August 2003, box CHF-11C, folder 15, CHM Collection.

52. The methods included studying property-related records in nearby archives such as the deed, city and county maps, and photographs; creating a scrapbook of relevant documents; and writing a timeline or even a narrative history. Barbara Hertenstein, "These Walls *Can* Talk," *St. Louis Post-Dispatch,* August 8, 2001.

53. Svetlana Boym, *The Future of Nostalgia* (New York: Basic Books, 2001), 49–50.

54. Compare to the Aiken-Rhett House in Charleston, which was damaged when a hurricane blew part of the roof away. Expecting intact interiors like those seen in the Campbell House, visitors are surprised to see that the layers of the past have been dramatically exposed: both decay and a century's worth of redecoration schemes can be seen throughout the house, whose walls have been stabilized but not restored. This state of incomplete restoration (or arrested decay?) has a distinct pathos we associate with ruins. See by contrast Anthony Vidler, *The Architectural Uncanny: Essays in the Modern Unhomely* (Cambridge, MA: MIT Press, 1992).

55. Barthes, *Camera Lucida,* 28.

56. These discoveries are often announced on the blog and cross-promoted on other social media platforms as well as in the *Campbell House Courier* and then usually mentioned on tours.

57. A December 2016 display was typical of *in situ* interpretations drawing on recently repatriated objects. Virginia's shawl was shown on a mannequin in the parlor, which had been decorated with the usual elaborate Victorian Christmas display. See "All Wrapped Up in Finery," Campbell House Museum, December 14, 2016, https://campbellhousemuseum.wordpress.com.

Conclusion: No Place Like Home

1. "Groups Join to Seek Old Campbell Home: Will Meet Tomorrow to Consider Making It Museum of Period," *St. Louis Post-Dispatch,* February 28, 1941.

2. The terms are fully discussed in my introduction, but see Svetlana Boym, *The Future of Nostalgia* (New York: Basic Books, 2001).

3. The Freudian theory of the uncanny—a familiar place or thing made strange (un-homelike) by ineffable fears of death or loss—has been influentially discussed by

Boym and Jean Baudrillard, but see also Anthony Vidler, *The Architectural Uncanny: Essays in the Modern Unhomely* (Cambridge, MA: MIT Press, 1992).

4. Elizabeth Hallam and Jenny Hockey, *Death, Memory and Material Culture* (Oxford: Berg 2001), 104.

5. The police chant, which was staged on an empty street a few blocks from the Campbell House (after protestors had dispersed), was widely seen as problematic. See, e.g., Osita Nwanevu, "St. Louis Police Chant 'Whose Streets? Our Streets!' as Protests against Stockley Verdict Continue," *Slate*, September 18, 2017, http://www.slate.com.

6. "Save Our [Gl]Ass, Continued: A Daunting Task," Campbell House, October 29, 2012, https://campbellhousemuseum.wordpress.com. See also "Save Our [Gl]Ass ™ Updated: A Week Later," Campbell House, August 16, 2012, https://campbellhouse museum.wordpress.com.

7. "Save Our [Gl]Ass, Continued."

8. Fort Knox is the epitome of a fortified historic site and has long served as a repository for the nation's gold stores. After 9/11, some of the nation's most valuable artifacts (including paper documents like the Declaration of Independence) were temporarily relocated from Washington, DC, to the site for safe-keeping. While generally seen as inviolable, the fort has been a target of gun violence several times in recent years.

9. The announcement about the relocation of the Rams represented a moment of humiliation for the city but also of compensatory bravado, as I explain in the introduction to this book.

INDEX